CHAKRA & KUNDALINI
WORKBOOK

The Best of East and West

- Experience total release from everyday stress and worries with a drugless inner relaxation
- Learn techniques to use for burn-out, mild to moderate depression, insomnia, general anxiety and panic attacks, reduction of mild to moderate hypertension
- Rejuvenate the nervous system and sharpen sensory perception
- Develop your psychic potential: telepathy, clairvoyance, psychometry
- Enter states of ecstasy, realization, and cosmic consciousness
- Unleash supernatural powers such as photographic memory, self-anesthesia, and mental calculations
- Stimulate latent memory tracts of the subconscious and recall forgotten material
- Experience sex for consciousness expansion, ESP development, positive thinking

This book is unique because it truly does capture the best of East and West in a modern synthesis of purely efficient, concise, and powerful "psychic" techniques combined with breath and posture—thus enabling you to use the Mind-Body interface constructively for health, long life, and psychic and spiritual development.

This is, in every sense, a "workbook." Dr. Mumford provides exact, step-by-step guidance to the progressive Mind-Body exercises. Yet, as concise as it is, there is humor in this text. And there is inspiration. In the final section you will discover a beautiful Tantric Ritual that demonstrates how there are "levers" with which you can transform the everyday moment into one of transcendence.

When you spend only a few minutes each day on these exercises, you will build a solid experience of psycho-physiological techniques that promote better health and greater control over your personal destiny. At the same time, you will lay a solid foundation for the subsequent chapters in which you can look forward to the attainment of supernormal powers, an enriched Inner Life, and ultimate enlightenment.

This book is nether a quick fix nor a panacea. The exercises are grounded in classical technique, with contemporary innovations, and developed over a lifetime of learning, experimenting, and teaching. The text has been augmented with illustrations and tables to help bridge the gap between instruction and understanding.

CHAKRA & KUNDALINI
WORKBOOK

Psycho-Spiritual Techniques for Health, Rejuvenation, Psychic Powers and Spiritual Realization

Dr. Jonn Mumford
(Swami Anandakapila Saraswati)

PUSTAK MAHAL®
Delhi • Bangalore • Mumbai • Patna • Hyderabad

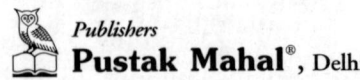

Publishers
Pustak Mahal®, Delhi
J-3/16 , Daryaganj, New Delhi-110002
☎ 23276539, 23272783, 23272784 • *Fax:* 011-23260518
E-mail: info@pustakmahal.com • *Website:* www.pustakmahal.com

Sales Centre
10-B, Netaji Subhash Marg, Daryaganj, New Delhi-110002
☎ 23268292, 23268293, 23279900 • *Fax:* 011-23280567
E-mail: rapidexdelhi@indiatimes.com

Branch Offices
Bangalore: ☎ 22234025
E-mail: pmblr@sancharnet.in • pustak@sancharnet.in
Mumbai: ☎ 22010941
E-mail: rapidex@bom5.vsnl.net.in
Patna: ☎ 3294193 • *Telefax:* 0612-2302719
E-mail: rapidexptn@rediffmail.com
Hyderabad: *Telefax:* 040-24737290
E-mail: pustakmahalhyd@yahoo.co.in

Reprinted from:
A CHAKRA & KUNDALINI WORKBOOK
By: **Dr. John Mumford**

Published in India by: **Pustak Mahal,** in arrangement with
Llewellyn Publications, Str. Paul, Minnesota 55164 0383, USA

The Copyright of this book, as well as all matter contained herein (including illustrations) rests with the Publishers. No person shall copy the name of the book, its title design, matter and illustrations in any form and in any language, totally or partially or in any distorted form. Anybody doing so shall face legal action and will be responsible for damages.

ISBN 81-223-0003-0

Printed at : Unique Colour Carton, Mayapuri, Delhi-110064

Contents

Preface vii
Introduction xi

Part 1: Hatha Yoga for the Body

Chapter One: Mind Over Matter: Sukhasana 14
Chapter Two: Shavasana: The Mind-Body Relaxer 24
Chapter Three: Yoni Mudra: The Voice of Silence 47

Part 2: Raja Yoga for the Mind

Chapter Four: Polarization 58
Chapter Five: Concentration 65
Chapter Six: Pranic Rejuvenation: The Key to Psychic Healing ... 73

Part 3: Laya Yoga for the Super-Sensible Body

Chapter Seven: Laya Yoga: The Psychic Centers 80
Chapter Eight: Chakra Dharana: Focusing Psychic Power 97
Chapter Nine: Solar Plexus Charging 124

Part 4: Siddha Yoga and Supernormal Powers

Chapter Ten: Yogic Power Flows 134
Chapter Eleven: Yoga and the West 147

Part 5: Gnana Yoga for the Inner Life

Chapter Twelve: Meditation and Inner Being 156
Chapter Thirteen: Advanced Techniques 172

Part 6: Tangible Transcendental Yoga for the Higher Life

Prologue: Magical Sexuality 202
Chapter Fourteen: Tantra Yoga for the Shared Life 203
Epilogue: The Ultimate Ritual 220
Appendix 1:   Twelve Week Practice Schedule 233
Appendix 2:   Loss of Consciousness During the Yoga Class:
                         A Guide for Yoga Teachers 235
Appendix 3:   A Note Regarding Indian Yoga Schools 240
Sanskrit Glossary 243
Bibliography 257

Dedicated to

Carl Llewellyn Weschcke
"Father of the New Age"

without whose support, guidance, and encouragement, this book would never have been written.

Preface

"I've come half way 'round the world to meet you," were the first words spoken by Jonn Mumford when we first met twenty years ago in the lobby of the Minneapolis Holiday Inn.

Of course, that was literally true since he then, as now, resided in Australia. But it was as if there were another "truth" involved with those words, as if we were meeting "at long last, once again." This meeting was the beginning of a friendship that is as deep and meaningful as few relationships can be, and "Uncle Jonn" is as close to my wife and son as he is to me.

He came to the Twin Cities to give a week-long series of seminars on Kriya and Tantra Yoga as part of the fifth of the annual Gnostic-Aquarian Festivals (nicknamed "Gnosticons") that Llewellyn sponsored back in the 1970s when the "New Age" was still new. Earlier that day of our first meeting, my wife Sandra had met Jonn at the airport and brought him to the Holiday Inn where she briefed him on the schedule of events and gave him the various items and equipment he had requested for his workshops. Suddenly, with a lemon in one hand and a twelve-inch long sterilized hat pin in the other, Jonn shouted a mantra and Sandra found that the hat pin was now in one side of her lower lip and out the other!

No pain, no bleeding—Jonn had effectively demonstrated "mantra anesthesia" when, for a second, her consciousness was focused outside the body on the mantra he had suddenly shouted. Instead, as realization came flooding in, she experienced a euphoria in the new awareness that indeed she was more than the body, and that mind was not confined to the brain.

The workshops with Jonn were filled with practical work and demonstrations building on this same theme. Among them was "Yoga Nidra: The Sleep of the Yogis" during which we were guided into a deep state of relaxation followed by the movement of consciousness throughout the body and into the brain itself. Another practice involved Tratak—fixed gazing on the projected image of one of a series of Tattwas, by means of which we experienced the "mind outside of the body," while also stimulating various chakras in turn. Yet another practice guided our imaginations through a series of colorful and often incongruous images, often projecting consciousness right out of the physical body.

These were exciting, mind-expanding experiences for all of us. But all of them were solidly based on Jonn's primary training in Yoga and meditation techniques that started when he, at fourteen years of age, visited India. During his many extended stays in India he studied with such prestigious people as Yogendra of Bombay, Shatananda of Delhi, Gitananda of Pondicherry, and Satyananda of Monghyr. These "Eastern" studies were supplemented over the years by his "Western" studies during which he qualified as a psychotherapist and as a chiropractor. In addition, he studied in London, and later in Sydney, with several occult lodges, and studied hypnosis, autogenics, and other techniques all related to the mind-body interface and the acceleration of "normal" evolution.

Jonn Mumford is a "global" person, bringing East and West together in a new synthesis. He has been initiated as a Swami in three different ashrams and is recognized and honored in India for his knowledge and teaching. And he is a Doctor of chiropractic therapy and a lecturer of international repute on psycho-physiological disorders. Several years ago he retired from active chiropractic practice and opened an esoteric school in a Sydney (Australia) suburb under the name of "The Scientific Samkhya Yoga Association."

In addition to his deep knowledge and amazing ability to condense esoteric practices to their essence, Jonn is a charismatic person. He radiates love, vitality, and—above all—joy. He infects you with his presence, but unlike all too many charismatic teachers and leaders, he gives his knowledge and withholds nothing. He knows that the wisdom necessary to properly use knowledge is something that comes only with experience, and it is experience as well as knowledge that he works to give his students, whether they study with him in person or through his books.

As a "Westerner" studying in India, Jonn was not merely a theoretician. He has many times given proof of his own self-mastery in public demonstrations of cardiac cessation (voluntary stopping of the heart), obliteration of individual pulsebeat at will, sensory withdrawal (tolerance of pain), voluntary breath retention over the five-minute range, peristalsis control using ground glass as media, start and stop bleeding on command, ability to handle white hot steel rods, etc.

Even more importantly, just as he demonstrated on his first meeting with Sandra, he leads his students to experience this same kind of control. As he writes in this book, "Theory without practice is sterile!" Many students have experienced that "hat pin," while others—with only hours of training—have been able to experience much greater control over the normal physiological responses as you will see pictured in this book when two students at another Gnosticon likewise were able to handle, and even lick, white hot steel bars in public demonstration.

That "first" meeting in Minneapolis was neither the first or the last. Aside from any esoteric considerations, Llewellyn had already published Jonn's second pioneering book, *Sexual Occultism* (since revised and enlarged as *Ecstasy Through Tantra*), and he came to other Gnosticons. One year we put on a full week "mini-ashram" entirely of his teaching on Kriya Yoga. Since the last of these teaching visits, he has joined us nearly every year around the time of my wife's and son's birthday (yes, they have the same birthday), July 1.

Every visit has been both a learning experience for me and an inspiration. I've learned more from this one person than I have from anyone else, and in some ways he has fulfilled my own youthful ambition to study in India through his powerful, effective, and efficiently condensed teaching. And it is that—powerful, effective, and efficiently condensed, experiential instruction—that you will find in this book.

The book itself is a vastly expanded and augmented edition of Jonn's first book, *Psychosomatic Yoga*, that was first published in English in 1962 and later in eight additional languages. I need to emphasize that this not merely a revised version of that early very successful book; rather, it is totally rewritten and expanded beyond the original concept based on the thirty years of experience during which that first edition was used as a textbook and manual by tens of thousands of students and teachers around the world.

In addition, I have used my own experience as one of Jonn's students and as an editor and publisher to make many suggestions that he has incorporated into this book to add to its power and effectiveness in hopes that it can serve the reader/student not only as a practical text and personal manual, but also, as nearly as is possible, as a direct and real contact with the charisma of this master teacher!

The text is supplemented with tables and illustrations to bridge the distance from information to personal understanding. In addition, the author has added a simple outline of a twelve-week practice schedule referenced directly back to the first nine chapters. Only a relatively few minutes each day—no more time than you might otherwise spend in less efficient physical workouts—will quickly build a solid experience of psycho-physiological techniques that will lead toward better health, a longer life, greater control over your personal destiny, and lay a firm foundation for the subsequent chapters leading to the attainment of supernormal powers, an enriched Inner Life, and ultimate transcendence.

And, unlike too many teachers, Jonn does not advocate a life of celibacy and seclusion, but teaches ways that you can use the experiences and opportunities of everyday life, and most particularly of the shared life, as levers toward spiritual attainment.

This is a truly global kind of Yoga, a practical system of personal training most suited for anyone in today's active and complex world. Indeed, as Jonn writes, you—each of us—are destined for the stars, to be a star. We are "gods in the making," but god realization is totally your choice, and your responsibility.

—**Carl Llewellyn Weschcke**
Marine-on-St.Croix, MN, USA

Introduction

I wrote my first book, *Psychosomatic Yoga*, in Hardwar, Uttar Pradesh State, India, in 1961. This was a concise training manual in Mind-Body disciplines, and some of the techniques had never been published before. This book was to become a classic, translated into over a dozen languages over the next thirty years.

In the interim since that beginning of my public teaching career, I have continually polished and refined the methodology expounded in that first manual, and this present volume is flesh and muscle built upon the intact skeletal structure of the earlier writings.

I have been fortunate to experience something that is difficult for Westerners to comprehend: the Guru-Chela relationship, devoid of the "cult" trappings associated with the popular movements of more recent times—some more notorious and sensational than others—creating an image of dependency and abuse that is far from the reality of the genuine experience.

There is always one special Guru, and that is the one to whom you give your heart. When I was seventeen years of age I met Dr. Rishi Swami Gitananda of Pondicherry, Tamil Nadu, South India, and that meeting began a discipleship of many years. Words could not and can not ever express my gratitude to him, and I don't know what would have become of me had I not met him at that time and benefited so greatly from his teaching and wise guidance. Such techniques as Chakra Dharana, Polarization, and Solar Plexus Charging came from him, for me to release in writing.

Much later, another major influence was to come into my life, Swami Paramhansa Satyananda Saraswati. I took initiation from him in Monghyr, Bihar State, India, in 1973. By example he taught me, among other things, humility, something I will struggle with to the end of my life. He was a great Tantric technologist; the exposition of Yoga Nidra in Chapter 13 is a sample of his insight.

These men gave me the most precious gift humans can grant one another: *unconditional regard*. For this I owe a debt that can only be paid by honoring all sentient beings.

This book, although entitled *A Chakra and Kundalini Workbook*, is neither a quick fix or a panacea. The exercises are grounded in classical technique, with contemporary innovations, and developed over a lifetime of learning, experimenting, and teaching.

I write in the same way that I teach: Information is added incrementally and we take various stances or viewpoints according to necessity and convenience. My Western education has enamored me of the hypothesis, and my Indian training has made more than willing to sacrifice understanding for experience and logic for being.

By lifestyle I am Western and by disposition Hindu. Philosophically, I adhere to the classical school of Samkhya. Samkhya was developed by a contemporary of Buddha, Kapila, around 500 BC, and, like Buddhism, is non-theistic. Samkhya provides the theoretical constructs for the practice of Yoga, and, again like Buddhism, is perfectly reconcilable with the new religion of the West—Science.

The theory of Samkhya and the practice of Yoga are so compatible with certain Western positions that I, without paradox, support sociobiology and favor biochemical reductionism. Sociobiology is the belief that human behavior is deeply cemented in biological necessity, while biochemical reductionism is the doctrine that sees changes in neurotransmitter brain levels as responsible for brain function variations and, hence, psychiatric states and mood.

Both sociobiology and reductionism seem quite probable and reasonable—they present no problem for the Samkhya philosopher, as Samkhya views mind and body as merely different manifestations of the energy-matter dance of creation and neither affect the core essence of being, the transcendental self, or Purusha.

We are at the end of a millennium and the close of a century. Such periods are always marked by tremendous social upheavals and radical political changes. Dr. Swami Gitananda stated, in the 1950s, that "it used to be the problems of man, now it is man, the problem!" Sigmund Freud, Carl Jung, and Herman Hesse were just a few of the great European minds that saw the forthcoming social and psychological chaos, inherent in the transition to the twenty-first century. The great Indologists, Heinrich Zimmer and Mircea Eliade, and their compatriot, mythologist Joseph Campbell, have all passed away, leaving us a heritage of understanding and a pointer for the future.

English-speaking countries have rabidly espoused the new Maoism, "political correctness," a vitriol that corrodes creativity and art, accompanied by social engineering, both conspiring to reduce everyone to a common denominator. And what is the outcome of such communism? The pursuit of mediocrity! It will be a sad, colorless, effete, twenty-first century if individualism, eccentricity, mysticism, and the pursuit of the contemplative life are no longer permitted or even merely accepted. Is humanity only social creatures, herd animals, or are we—potentially and individually—destined for the stars?

I would like to believe that my efforts with this workbook will contribute, as a small part with many others, of a great tidal outpouring of authentic esoteric technology to ensure survival of, as Aldous Huxley so elegantly phrased it, the "Perennial Philosophy."

May the Perennial Philosophy find a bridge into the brave new world order!

—Jonn Mumford
St. Paul-Minneapolis, MN, USA

Part One

Hatha Yoga for the Body

*Let this mortal clay (self)
be the immortal God.*

— Rig Veda viii, 19

Chapter One

Mind Over Matter: Sukhasana

He who practices Sukhasana becomes an immobile, frozen, transcendent sculpture of living flesh—dwelling in freedom beyond space and time.

— Anon

*H*atha is perhaps the aspect of Yoga best known to Westerners. To most students it is simply a difficult system of physical control involving the use of static poses *(asanas)* and the learning of specialized breathing techniques *(pranayama)*.

The introduction of dynamic, calisthenic-like movements for the performance of the poses, as seen in the last twenty-five years, is strictly a modern innovation, for the original Sanskrit meaning of *asana* is simply "a firm seat."

Few realize that the base upon which Hatha Yoga rests is an implicit axiom stating that if the mind can influence the body (psychosomatics), then the converse is equally true. The body influences the mind (somatopsychics).

When we are nervous, depressed, or suffer from chronic anxiety, our mental state is reflected in the function, control, and appearance of our physical being. At a later stage (in chronic anxiety, for instance), our mental state and the concomitant arousal of the sympathetic nervous system may encourage organic changes in the body resulting in such disabilities as (depending upon our genetic predispositions) ulcers, colitis, heart disease, immune system impairment, and a host of other manifestations.

Hatha Yoga reestablishes the mental stability of the individual and thus reverses the process which results in psychosomatic diseases. This is accomplished by first teaching the student to acquire control of his or her body. Control of the body, in turn, requires effort at controlling the mind, since no muscle is flexed, no nerve activated, and no blood circulated unless under the control (voluntary or involuntary) of the mind.

The Sanskrit roots of Hatha break down into *Ha* and *Tha*. *Ha* refers to the sun, a positive masculine symbol, while *Tha* refers to the moon, a receptive feminine symbol. Generally Hatha is understood as indicating the union of the positive, sun-drenched inhalation *(Ha)* with the cleansing, cooling exhalation *(Tha)*. Given a deeper interpretation, we see that Ha esoterically symbolizes the positive mind uniting with its polar opposite, the material vehicle of Tha, the body. Herein lies the clue to the true esoteric teaching of Adam (the mind) and Eve (the body) as depicted in Genesis.

Hatha Yoga may be defined as the "science of uniting and coordinating the physical and mental aspects of one's being through consciously attempted discipline of the body."

We may also note that the original Sanskrit root from which Hatha derives is HATH, meaning "to strike a blow against" (by implication, working to overcome the inherent inertia of the mind-body complex).

It was during this century that the Russian scientist Pavlov rediscovered the principle of conditioning and the conditioned reflex known for several thousand years by the Hatha Yogis. It is with this idea of being able to condition the body and consequently the mind that we begin our study of the first exercise, Sukhasana.

> *The mind has great influence over the body and maladies often have their origin there.*
> —Moliere (1622-1673)

THE "EASY POSE"

Sukhasana literally means "Easy Pose" (Sukha = Easy; Asana = Pose). It is one of a number of meditative poses. It has several characteristics in common with other meditation forms.

Specific Advantages

1. A solid, triangular base for trunk and head.
2. The spine is kept straight and thus the nerve flow along spine and between vertebrae is uninhibited.
3. The lungs are free for exercises in deep breathing as taught in *Pranayama*.
4. Said to aid awakening of *kundalini* (latent nervous energy locked within the central nervous system).

Sukhasana has specific physiological and psychological advantages. Physiologically, the internal viscera are relaxed because of the crossed legs, while psychologically the mind and body are brought into a harmonious state of stability through the consciously willed attempt to remain motionless.

Sukhasana is the ideal technique for those who wish to condition themselves for shutting the door upon everyday worries, and thus prepare themselves for the meditative peace to be found within the recesses of their own minds. This technique is also valuable for nervous disorders involving poor neuromuscular coordination, twitches, nervous movements, and "tics."

For those who cannot bend their legs or sit upon the floor, similar mental advantages may be cultivated by sitting in the "Egyptian Pose," or "Egyptian God Posture," on a chair. We will discuss this variant after the floor method.

Technique

1. Place a cushion or folded blanket on the floor. Sit upon the blanket or cushion using only the front edge, or first third of the support—this assists by tilting the hips forward. Have your legs stretched out in front of you in preparation for bending.

2. Bend your right leg under your left thigh and the left leg under the right thigh, assuming the cross-legged "tailor pose." Check that your kneecaps are roughly level with each other. If they are not, your trunk will lean slightly to the lower side, disturbing body symmetry and balance.

3. Keep your spine erect and your head nicely poised upon your shoulders.

4. Place your hands, palms down, upon your knees in such a fashion that they will not slip off. Be certain that your elbows relax naturally against your body.

5. Firmly close your eyes as if you were drawing down shutters. Continue to keep your eyelids under control for the duration of the session.

6. You are now introverted within yourself. Concentrate your mind upon the natural rhythm of your breath, control yourself from dreaming, reasoning, or otherwise becoming mentally active, and keep your body erect, motionless, and as relaxed as possible. Concentrate upon just "being." Meditate upon the movement of Life Force by attentively observing the natural, spontaneous breath cycle as it goes through four phases: i.e., inhalation, momentary pause, exhalation, momentary pause. Each time your mind wanders, return to this breath awareness, simultaneously cultivating a sensation of total frozen immobility in your body—utter motionlessness.

> *The mind is a dangerous weapon, even to the possessor, if he knows not discreetly how to use it.*
> —Michel de Montaigne (1533-1592)

SUKHASANA: CLASSICAL FLOOR POSTURE

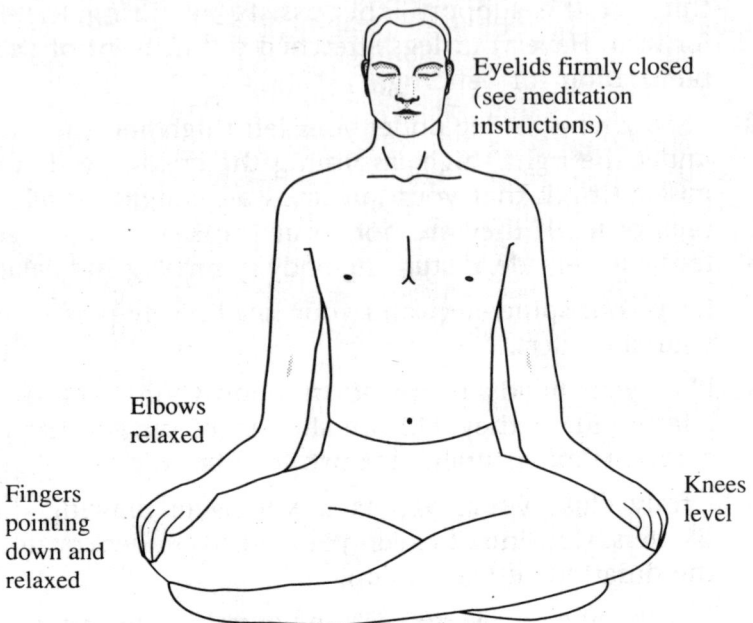

EGYPTIAN CHAIR POSE

This pose for those who cannot sit upon the floor or bend their knees is also known as "The Egyptian God Posture," and is often seen as the Western equivalent of an asana for meditation.

Technique

1. Sit upon the forward half of the chair with your spine away from the chair back.
2. Let your feet turn slightly out and check that the lower legs are at a 90-degree angle with your thighs. Place books or cushions under your feet to ensure this. Your thighs may be open and comfortably separated.

3. Your kneecaps should now be level and you may place your hands, palms down, upon your knees, in such a fashion that the four fingers are pointing downward (earthward) and they will not slip off. Allow your elbows to relax naturally against your body.
4. Keep your spine erect and your head nicely poised upon your shoulders. Vertically align your nose with your navel.
5. Firmly close your eyes as if you were drawing down shutters; continue to keep your eyelids under control for the duration of the session.
6. You are now introverted within yourself. Concentrate your mind upon the natural rhythm of your breath, control yourself from dreaming, reasoning, or otherwise becoming mentally active, and keep your body erect, motionless, and as relaxed as possible. Concentrate upon just "being." Meditate upon the movement of Life Force by attentively observing the natural, spontaneous breath cycle as it goes through four phases: i.e., inhalation, momentary pause, exhalation, momentary pause. Each time your mind wanders, return again to this breath awareness, simultaneously cultivating a sensation of total frozen immobility in your body—utter motionlessness.

> *You are now in a position to experience yoga (union) by sacrificing thinking for "being."*

At some stage you may wish to add a simple visualization to the exercise, such as imagining an object in your mind's eye: a geometric pattern, a flower, a color, or an image.

Performance Time

Perform this exercise for a minimum of five minutes in the first week, rapidly building to twenty minutes by the third week. Using a timing device (pocket alarm, watch, kitchen timer, etc.) is helpful.

EGYPTIAN CHAIR POSE

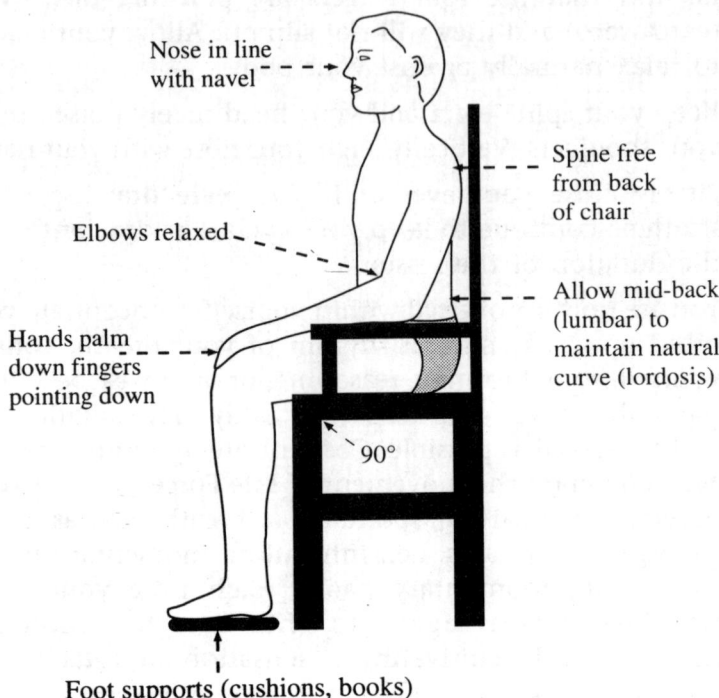

Check Points

1. After commencement of the exercise, check your elbows to see that they are relaxed and swing freely.
2. Check your eyelids to see that they are steady and controlled. Any flickering of the lashes indicates mental agitation and lack of absorption in the exercise.
3. Make certain that you do not unconsciously slip into a slouch and thus bend the upper (dorsal) spine.

As with any of the classical Hatha asanas, very distinct performance problems arise. Let us list them along with appropriate remedies.

1. The pressure of the floor upon your feet may cause pain and thus distract attention. This is overcome by practice in which the feet are gradually conditioned.
2. The spine may tend to slouch. The remedy lies in sustained, disciplined effort.
3. The mind may become agitated and refuse to become calm. We follow the same principle of quieting a bored or upset child: We provide something suitable in the way of distraction, such as concentration upon simple objects. This particular problem is the crux of the exercise. Eventually, you train yourself to relax mentally upon beginning the exercise, and this conditioning becomes stronger with repetition.

Sukhasana should be practiced consistently for a week before starting practice of the next exercise. All the exercise routines that follow in this book should be commenced with Sukhasana and the minimum time of five minutes lengthened to twenty minutes maximum.

In review, remember that Sukhasana, as practiced in the described manner, is a specific therapy for nervous disorders arising from lack of neuromuscular control. In this exercise, control over the body is increased and willpower is strengthened. Above all, the mind is trained to achieve a quiet state, and this conditioning prepares the student for advanced exercises.

Traditionally, admission to certain Eastern occult schools depended upon the *chela's* (a disciple, or dedicated student) ability to remain motionless for a three-hour test period. The average individual, in our tension-fraught age, cannot remain mentally absorbed and physically motionless for three minutes or even ten minutes (not to suggest three hours), as you are expected to accomplish through Sukhasana.

A Note About Eyelid Flutter

Eyelid flutter denotes extroversion and agitation. For people of certain temperaments, abstracting themselves from the environment may represent an initial difficulty. In a personal communication, my publisher and friend of many years Carl Weschcke suggested the making of a meditation hood, and this would definitely have manifold benefits. I might say that in the Indian ashram we would pull our robes over our head to replicate a similar effect; the hood of a traditional "monk's robe" as seen in medieval illustrations would serve the same purpose. In Carl's own words:

> For those who have problems with eyelid flutter, I have discovered a very simple and effective remedy. A functional "meditation hood" can be easily made from a piece of spandex material, roughly 18" x 14", folded over to 9" x 14" and sewn together on one short side and the remaining long sides, leaving the other short side open so as to pull it over the entire head and face like a ski mask. If desired, the top portion (the first short side) can be rounded before sewing. The advantage of the spandex is that it exerts just enough pressure against the eyelids to hold them firmly but comfortably shut—hence no flutter—but the material is thin and porous enough for easy breathing. The further advantage of such a "meditation hood" is that it does give a feeling of isolation, as would a cave or a magical ritual, from the everyday world. Even though the spandex material is too thin to block out sound, the feeling of isolation given by the hood makes it a kind of portable meditation chamber.

We include a simple drawing to explain the home sewing. Obviously, the concept can be modified if materials other than spandex, such as thin kidskin, are preferred. Then it would be necessary to fit the hood more carefully to actual shape and measurements of the head, and to provide a shaped form for the nose with an opening at the nostrils for breathing as well as an opening from the crown down to the neck that can be laced or zippered shut. To accomplish the effect of a minimal amount of pressure against the closed eyelids, the hood (or head-mask) must be firm-fitting, but not uncomfortably tight. For persons who suffer a degree of nasal congestion, this shaped form of hood may be preferred to the spandex.

MEDITATION HOOD CONSTRUCTION

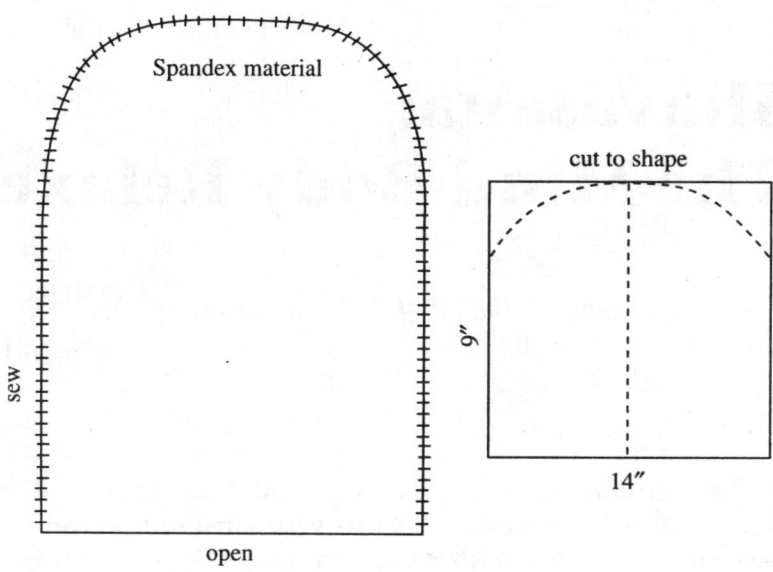

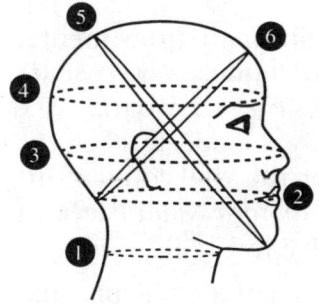

1	TOP NECK
2	AROUND MOUTH
3	AROUND NOSE
4	AROUND FOREHEAD
5	AROUND CHIN AND CROWN
6	AROUND HAIRLINE AND BASE OF SKULL

★★

Chapter Two

Shavasana: The Mind-Body Relaxer

The tranquil, the blissful, the undivided ...
— Mandukya Upanishad

Unfortunate as it may be, you and I are immersed in a tension-filled world. It is this very tension that forms the basis for psychosomatic disturbances. We are left asking ourselves what we can do about our individual tensions and what we may do about world tension, which, after all, is only the result of accumulated individual tension. Psychiatry offers tranquilizers, but Hatha Yoga offers drugless inner relaxation through the ancient practice of Shavasana.

Seldom do you find physical tension apart from mental tension; curiously enough, mental tension almost always arises first and is the cause of physical tension. Shavasana, like Sukhasana, reverses the usual mind-body arc and teaches the individual to gain conscious control over the vital zones of his or her body and thus relax the mind into *Yoga Nidra* (sleep of the Yogis) through first relaxing the physical body.

This again confirms our elementary Hatha principle that the mind and the body are linked, and whatever happens to one will affect the other as surely as goading one of two yoked oxen will force the other to move along with it. Knowing this, we may confidently proceed to use Shavasana as an adjunctive therapy for such diverse conditions as old-fashioned neurasthenia (not unlike "burn-out"), early stages of mild to moderate depression, sleep-onset insomnia, general anxiety and panic attacks (between attacks, not during), and reduction of mild to moderate hypertension (high blood pressure), particularly the systolic or "high reading."

Shavasana means "corpse pose" (Shava = corpse, asana = pose) and it has also been called Mritasana, or "dead pose" (Mrit = dead).*

The student will discover that the classical names given to this exercise rather dramatically emphasize the relaxation accruing from its practice.

Specific Advantages

1. A deep state of muscular relaxation is brought about.
2. The blood pressure is lowered (individuals with unusually low blood-pressure may suffer discomfort from practice of Shavasana), while at the same time heartbeat and respiration are considerably slowed.
3. A transfer of *prana* (nervous energy) to the internal organs takes place.
4. The nervous system is rested and rejuvenated.
5. The mind is brought to the point of complete relaxation from which it may go into a deep, dreamless sleep. (This is optional, depending on the student's desire.)

Elementary Technique

The practice of Shavasana is conveniently divided into two steps or stages.

In the first stage, you learn to relax the body as a unit and give in completely to the force of gravity. If you observe an animal or a baby sleeping, you will see that upon awakening they leave a deep impression in the cushion or mat slept upon. Animals and babies instinctively "let go" completely and allow gravity to do the work.

---

*Sanskrit *Mrit* is the etymological antecedent to such English words as mortal, post-mortem, and moribund.

TECHNIQUE ONE

1. Lie supine (face up) on the floor upon a suitable folded blanket or mat. Loose clothing should be worn, and the room temperature ought to be comfortably warm.
2. Place your feet about twenty inches apart and allow your ankles and toes to relax to the outside.
3. Place your hands palms up (or comfortably on the little finger edge of the hands) as we are trying to avoid stimulus to the sensitive tactile receptors underneath the fingertips, thus dampening the alerting responses in the brain.
4. Check that your shoulders are flat and that the small of your back is relaxed into the floor.
5. Adjust your head to a comfortable position.
6. Completely surrender your body weight to the floor.

Note: In steps 4 and 5 you may place small cushions under your knees, neck, and shoulders to increase comfort. Anyone with low back trouble must be certain to place several pillows under each knee. Also be aware that Shavasana may be practiced upon a bed or couch, but training on a floor teaches you to overcome discomfort by melting into the floor.

7. Preliminary Rotation Sequence: Tighten-Lift-Release-Drop

    The following sequence commences on the right side of the body and progresses to the left, for both arms and legs, and finishes with awareness of the whole trunk of the body. If necessary, you may repeat the routine several times before progressing to the more classical Step 8.

    Right arm: On inhalation (breathing naturally), make a firm fist, extending the contraction up the arm to the shoulder, while simultaneously stretching your arm and raising your whole arm a few inches from the floor. Upon exhalation, release the tension in your arm and let it "flop" (drop) to the floor.

    Left arm: Switch the searchlight of your mind to your left arm, mentally scanning from shoulders to fingertips;

on inhalation, make a fist, stretch your arm from the shoulder, and lift it several inches from the floor. Upon exhalation, allow your arm to relax and collapse to the floor.

Right leg: Focus your attention down your right leg (from groin to toes). On inhalation, bend your foot back (dorsiflexing), pointing your toes toward your kneecap (stretching the calf muscle), and raising your leg several inches from the floor. With the exhalation, relax your leg and let it drop to the floor.

Left leg: Turning your concentration to your left leg, sense and feel it, repeating the inhalation-contraction-elevation sequence, as with the right leg, and following with the exhalation-relaxation-releasing sequence, letting it drop to the floor.

Whole body awareness: In this inhalation-exhalation cycle, direct your awareness to your spine and trunk, mentally traveling from your pelvis to the back of your head, cultivating a "melting" sensation on exhalation.

ADVANTAGES OF STEP 7

This step begins elementary Shavasana proper, and basically is intended as a five-part routine to commence the practice at each session.

The specific advantages of Step 7 are:

1. Encourages release of physical tension in the limbs by muscular contraction followed by flaccidity.
2. The contraction-release phases increase proprioceptive, kinesthetic, and circulatory consciousness of the limbs.
3. Both hemispheres of the brain, alternatively, become involved with the sequential firing of motor strips (contractive phase) and sensory strips (relaxation phase) within each cerebral cortex. This becomes an automatic psychophysiological attention fixer for centering consciousness.

Summary of Step 7

1. **Right arm:**
   Inhalation while sensing, contracting, and lifting.
   Exhalation while relaxing, dropping, and melting.

2. **Left arm:**
   Inhalation while sensing, contracting, and lifting.
   Exhalation while relaxing, dropping, and melting.

3. **Right leg:**
   Inhalation while sensing, contracting, and raising.
   Exhalation while relaxing, dropping, and melting.

4. **Left leg:**
   Inhalation while sensing, contracting, and raising.
   Exhalation while relaxing, dropping, and melting.

5. **Whole trunk:**
   Mentally scan from the pelvis, up the spine, to the back of the head while "surrendering" the trunk of the body to gravity.

8. Commence concentrating upon your upper and lower extremities (the arms and legs), and with each exhalation feel your arms and legs becoming heavier and heavier. Imagine yourself melting or sinking into the floor.

It should be noted that the placing of the extremities permits the individual to take maximum advantage of the natural pull of gravity. Hatha Yoga teaches, as a fundamental tenet, the use of natural forces such as gravity.

This exercise should be practiced for a minimum of ten to fifteen minutes and should be performed for a week before starting the second phase of Shavasana.

Focus upon a feeling of total sagging, going with gravity, and simultaneously cultivate the imagined sensation that the ground or floor is moving up to meet you, rather like an elevator going up.

Advanced Technique

In the advanced step we learn to localize each part of the body and systematically relax and inhibit afferent and efferent (sensory and motor) nervous impulses. This is accomplished through commencing concentration at the feet and slowly working up to the head.

The Yogis (whose knowledge of neuroanatomy was gained by introspection) long ago discovered the secret nerve zones of the human body and divided them into sixteen major areas called Marmasthanani. These positions are as follows:

1. Feet
2. Shins
3. Kneecaps
4. Thighs
5. Abdomen
6. Solar plexus
7. Upper chest
8. Spine
9. Hands
10. Forearms
11. Upper arms
12. Throat
13. Back of head
14. Jaw
15. Eyes
16. Scalp or Bramapura

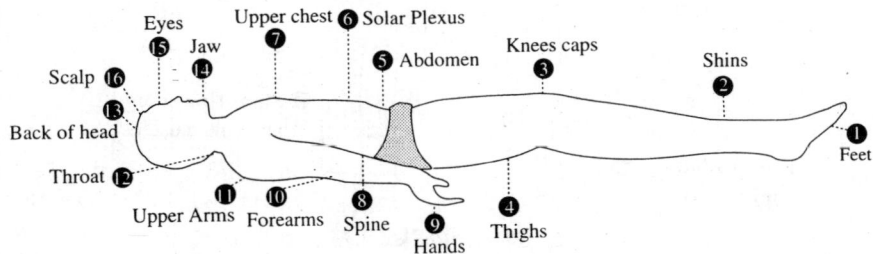

> Our worst misfortunes never happen,
> and most miseries lie in anticipation.
> —H. de Balzac (1799-1850)

CLASSICAL MARMASTHANANI CHART I

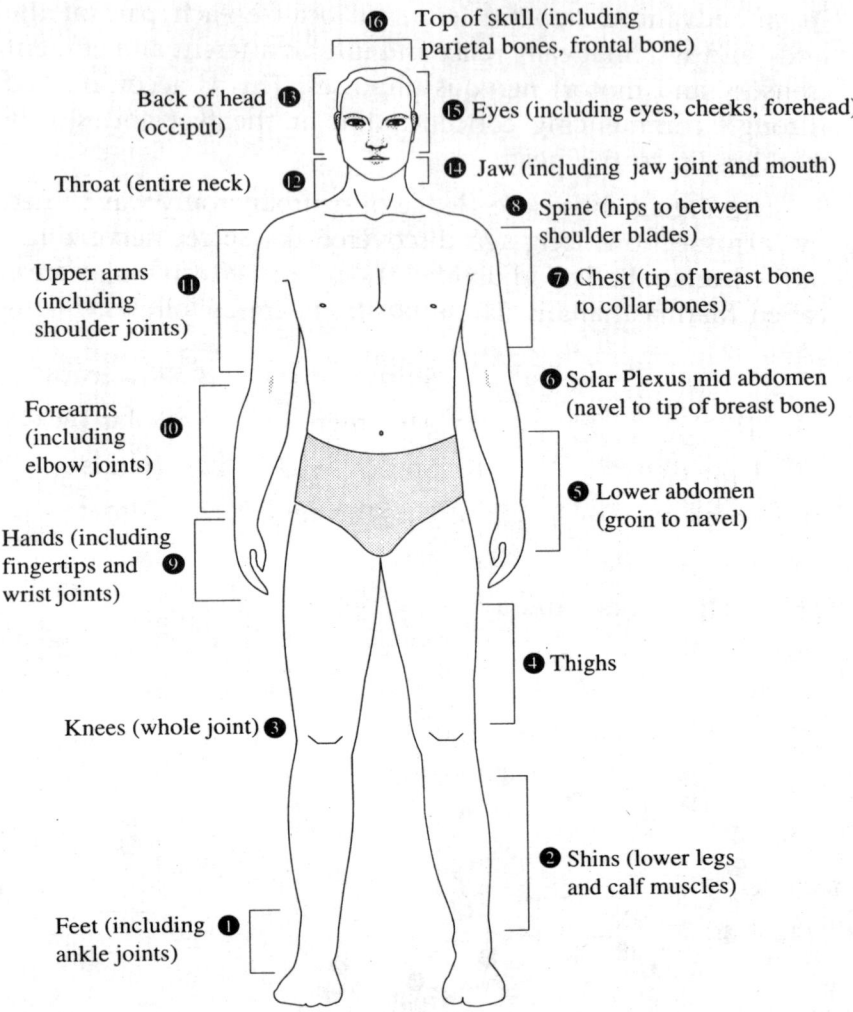

CLASSICAL MARMASTHANANI CHART II

In fact, there are 108 of these zones listed in the Ayurvedic (Hindu) medical texts; the above list is just one classical selection used for concentration. They divide the body up conveniently, from major joint to joint, cavities, and partitions.

The word "Marma" is usually translated "joint," but is better rendered "joint complex." The Hindu surgeons maintained that a person would die or be permanently maimed if struck in these areas. In fact, they were correct because any injury to a joint by an non-sterile, penetrating weapon, from arrow to bullet, guarantees septic arthritis, barely treatable with modern antibiotics. When these joints and inclusive areas are reduced to heaviness, relaxation, and motionlessness through Yoga concentration, we disconnect major nerve receptors called proprioceptors (from the same Latin root that gives us the word "property," meaning "one's own"), thus blurring body-mind boundaries and escaping physical confines.

The first stage is to experientially fix the order of the sixteen places in memory. This is done by a combination of visualization and physical contraction of each Marma. Lie supine as per instructions for the Elementary Technique.

Visualization-Contraction Exercise

1. **Feet:** *Visualize-Sense-See* your feet, including the ankle joints. Simultaneously curl the toes of both feet, then relax suddenly and be aware of any tingling sensations. Mentally repeat: "Feet, First Zone."
2. **Shins:** *Visualize-Sense-See* your lower legs and calf muscles. Increase awareness of your calf muscles by turning your toes up toward your knee-caps (dorsiflexion), then suddenly relaxing while consciously scanning your shins and calves. Mentally repeat: "Shins, Second Zone."
3. **Knees:** *Visualize-Sense-See* both knee joints and become aware of the area in a 360° area. Push the hollows (popliteal spaces) behind each knee against the floor, release, access any sensations, and repeat silently: "Knees, Third Zone."
4. **Thighs:** *Visualize-Sense-See* the thighs, tense them by inverting the toes (turning them in toward each other, causing the adductor muscles to contract), relax, and let go, allowing your legs to flop back outward (eversion).

Note the sensations and verbalize to yourself: "Thighs, Fourth Zone."

5. **Abdomen** (navel to pubic bone): *Visualize-Sense-See* the pelvic basin from groin to navel, expel your breath while simultaneously squeezing your buttocks together, and suck in your abdomen in as if trying to pull your navel and anus together. Release, letting air rush into your lungs, note the sensations, and mentally state: "Lower abdomen, Fifth Zone."

6. **Solar plexus** (navel to tip of breastbone): *Visualize-Sense-See* your midriff, expelling your breath while contracting the navel, as if your were pulling it back and up to touch your spine. Release abdominal tension while letting air reflexively flood back into your lungs, and with an awareness of midriff sensations, affirm silently: "Solar plexus, Sixth Zone."

MNEMONIC TIP: "S" is common to the words solar plexus and sixth, so later, when mentally going over these zones, you will know you are at the sixth Marma when you reach the solar plexus.

7. **Chest** (thoracic cavity/rib margins to collar bones): *Visualize-Sense-See* and inhale, deliberately expanding your ribs to obtain the maximum volume. Relax, and allow the ribs to drop with a natural exhalation. Note the sensations. Silently say: "Chest, Seventh Zone."

8. **Spine** (from the tailbone to the point where the neck joins the thoracic vertebrae): *Visualize-Sense-See* and flatten the small of your back against the floor, release, then push the rest of your spine against the floor. Relax, and perceive all the feelings you receive from your spinal column while silently echoing: "Spine, Eighth Zone."

9. **Hands** (fingertips to wrists—multiple joints): *Visualize-Sense-See* while slowly making tight fists of your hands

(put your thumb in your palm before curling the fingers to increase sensations). Relax, letting go suddenly, and note your feelings while silently saying: "Hands, Ninth Zone."

10. **Forearms** (including elbow joints): *Visualize-Sense-See* your forearms; press back your wrists isometrically against the floor to build tension sensations up to the elbows. Release, note your feelings, and silently say: "Forearms, Tenth Zone."

11. **Upper arms** (including shoulder joints): *Visualize-Sense-See*. Focus on pressing your elbows isometrically against the floor, allowing the sensation to spread into the shoulder joints. Relax, note any sensations, and silently say: "Upper arms, Eleventh Zone."

12. **Neck** (cervical vertebrae): *Visualize-Sense-See*. Keeping the back of your skull in contact with the floor while flexing, pull your chin as close to the jugular notch (top of breastbone) as possible. Feel the neck flexing for a few moments, then release, silently saying: "Neck, Twelfth Zone."

13. **Back of the head** (occiput): *Visualize-Sense-See*. Push the back of your head against the floor for a few seconds, then relax, silently saying: "Back of the head, Thirteenth Zone."

14. **Jaw** (from the tip of the chin to the hinge joint of the jaw): *Visualize-Sense-See*. Keeping your lips together, push your tongue strongly against the roof of your mouth. Relax, silently saying: "Jaw, Fourteenth Zone."

15. **Eyes** (including cheeks and forehead): *Visualize-Sense-See*. Squeeze your eyelids together, becoming aware of your cheeks and forehead. Let go, relax, sense, and silently say: "Eyes, Fifteenth Zone."

16. **Top of skull** (scalp): *Visualize-Sense-See*. Sense the weight of the brain inside your skull while cultivating a "letting go" sensation in the scalp. Silently say: "Scalp-brain, Sixteenth Zone."

TECHNIQUE TWO: ADVANCED SHAVASANA USING THE SIXTEEN MARMASTHANANI

Work through the entire visualization-contraction sequence of the Marmas before completing Step 1, below.

1. Begin with the first Marmasthanani, the feet, and:
    (a) Create a mental picture of your toes and ankles.
    (b) Increase your awareness of the area by concentrating upon feeling internally the bone, muscle, sinew, and blood.
    (c) Having increased your consciousness of the area, mentally develop a state of relaxation, heaviness, and sinking into that particular spot.
2. Switch your attention to the next zone and repeat parts a, b, and c of Step 1. Work your way up over the whole body in this fashion. Allow at least half a minute for each zone and go over the body repeatedly until you relax so completely that you fall into Yoga Nidra.

Shavasana is the ancient and natural contribution of Yoga to this very modern problem of tension and insomnia. Because of the effect Shavasana has in slowing the metabolic processes, while at the same time conserving nervous energy, it is one of the hidden keys to the many medically authenticated cases of hibernation involving the burying alive of Yogis for weeks at a time.

A mastery of Shavasana will enable the student to gain conscious control over his or her muscular and nervous system. A good test of mastery of this technique is the ability to fall asleep within three minutes.

Shavasana represents a first step towards alteration of brainwave patterns from active, alert Beta right down to dreamless Delta. Advanced techniques can involve guided imagery with affirmations (sometimes called psychic energizers), through to a profound state of altered consciousness known as Yoga Nidra. Yoga Nidra is also best done through voice or audiotape guidance, or placing your own script on audio cassette.*

PSYCHIC SHAVASANA

This exercise can produce out-of-body experiences and profound altered states of consciousness. The method is dependent upon prior mastery of the elementary and advanced Shavasana techniques.

The essence of the exercise involves two keys:

1. The amalgamation of the Marmasthanani zones into ten areas by verbal cue.
2. Preliminary conditioning through performing Tratak (open-eyed fixation) upon a rotating spiral disk, followed by gazing at a picture or the wall and experiencing apparent expansion of the environment.

STAGE ONE: Preparation of Ten-Zone Marmasthanani Chart

Spend at least twenty minutes attempting to fill in the following chart as per these instructions: Starting at the feet, list ten body parts spelled with three letters only, in ascending order, and when you reach the face go from the surface to deeper structures. Example: TOE. Slang expressions (gut, bum) are not permitted. Many permitted words are not necessarily anatomical terms, but common words.

---

*See Chapter 14.

Ten-Zone Chart for Completion
1. TOE
2.
3.
4.
5.
6.
7.
8.
9.
10.

Below we present the complete list with associated, inclusive body parts. The exercise of attempting to fill in the chart helps integrate these zones into memory and bridges the area with the classical Marmasthanani you have already learned.

Ten-Zone Chart

Body part	Anatomical area inclusive of
1. TOE	Entire foot
2. LEG	Ankle to knee, knee, thigh to groin
3. HIP	Buttocks, abdomen, solar plexus region, midriff
4. RIB	Entire chest
5. ARM	Hands, forearm, elbow, upper arms, shoulder
6. JAW	Neck, jaw (lower mandible) from tip of chin back to TMJ (jaw joint)

> **SSS Rule:**
> *Sense it!*
> *See it!*
> *Say it!*

7.	LIP	Upper and lower lips in relationship to upper and lower jaws and teeth
8.	GUM	Space between lips and teeth, teeth sockets embedded in gums, tongue and mouth cavity
9.	EYE	Eyeball, eye socket, cheek bones, forehead
10.	EAR	Ear, entire side and back of skull, brain

We are now ready to rotate the consciousness through the established ten regions. This is done bilaterally—i.e., going from the toes up the left half of the body to the left ear and down the right half of the body from the right ear and ending at the right toe.

Sweeping the attention up the left side Marmas and down the right side may be practiced sitting in a chair, although for the full Yoga Nidra it is better to recline on a couch or the floor. Your eyes are to be closed and you may even use a sleeping mask or meditation hood.

Focusing involves simultaneously feeling the part, visualizing the anatomy, and mentally repeating the name of the zone. This will produce intense monoideism, or a single-pointedness of consciousness with an ensuing trance(scendant) state.

Become aware of your left foot and sense circulation pressure, tingles, and any other sensations from toes to ankles. See (visualize) a picture of your left foot, and silently say "Toe." Next, encompass your entire left leg with your attention and repeat the procedure. Continue to work up the left side in this manner, and then down the right side. Repeat three times. (See the diagram on the following page.)

> ***The point at which reentry occurs confers spontaneous harmony according to your psychic needs at the time of the exercise.***

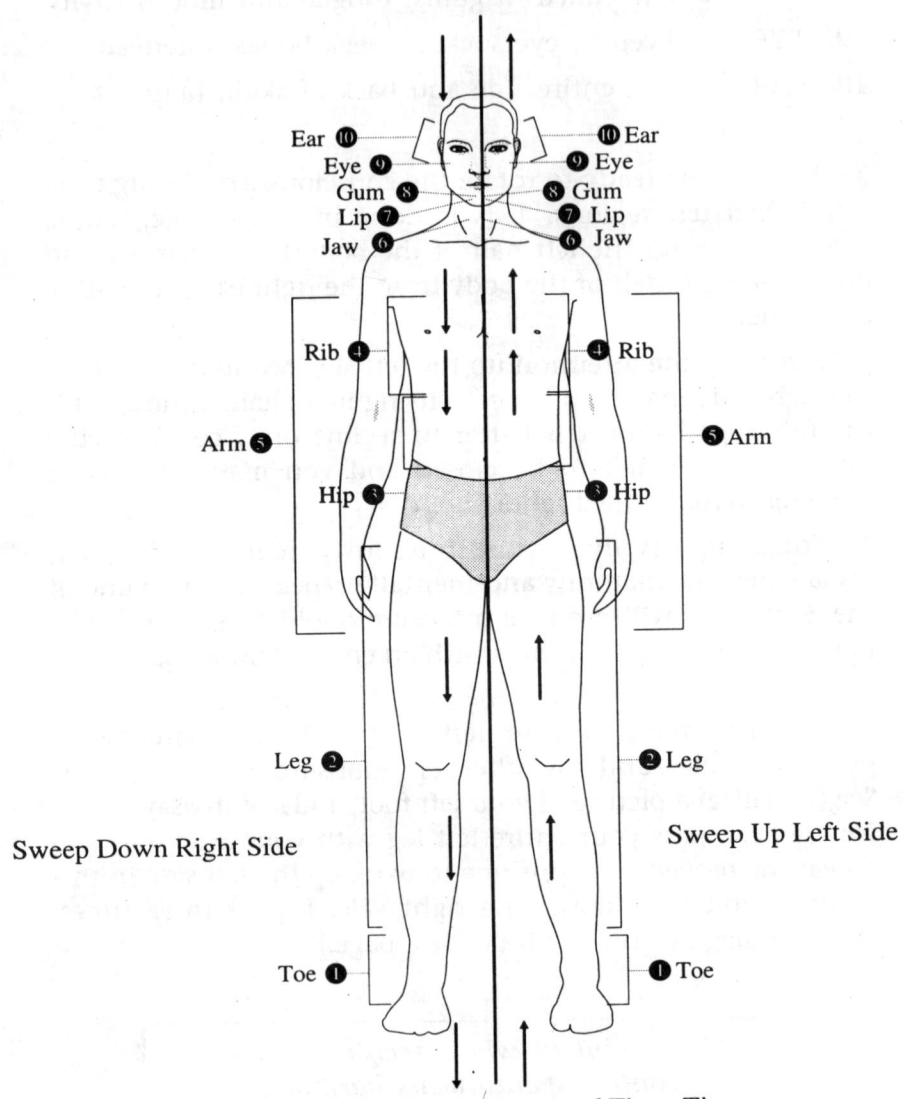

STAGE TWO: Preliminary Consideration of Spiral Visualization

In the second phase of Shavasana, we are going to extrude our consciousness from the body by visualizing a commencing spiral, perhaps of white mist, centered at the navel, rotating counterclockwise in ever expanding circles, slowly lifting up out of the body, and slowly exceeding the circumference of the physical body.

PSYCHIC SHAVASANA COUNTER-CLOCKWISE EXTRUSION SPIRAL

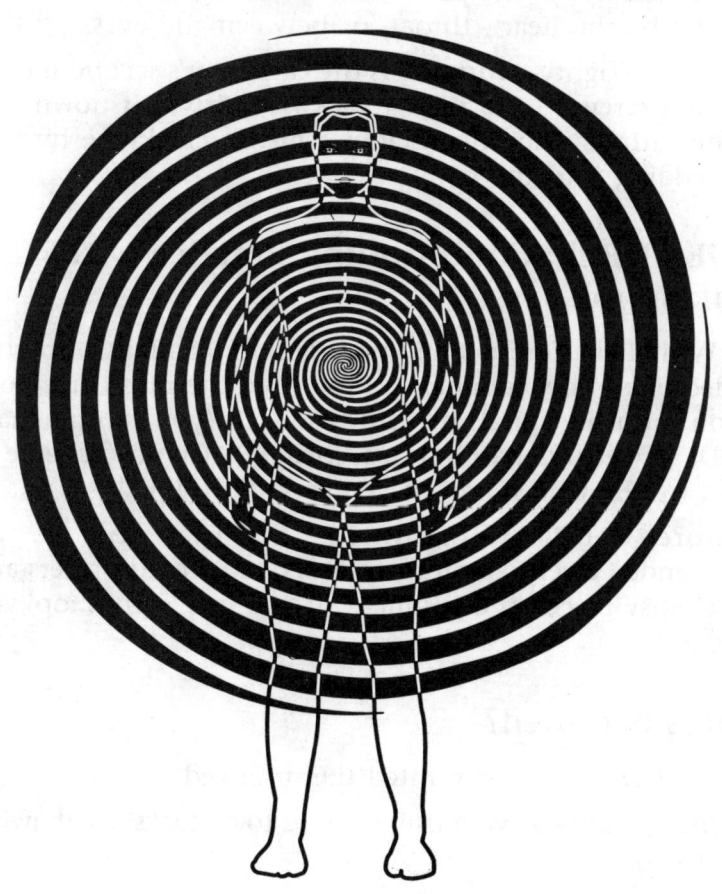

Remember "Lefty—Loosey—Lifty," the carpenter's motto. Undoing a screw involves twisting with a screwdriver to the left (counterclockwise), and the screw lifts up and out as you do so. Consequently, it follows that at a deep, archetypal, unconscious level, counterclockwise movement of the attention equals extrusion from the physical body.

This mental creation of a spiral will lead you, figuratively and literally, into a "spaced" area and level of consciousness. If you do not drop into a dreaming or dreamless state (in which case you will drop back into the body and awaken deeply rejuvenated), the process is reversed for re-entry by imagining a clockwise spiral which, vortex-like, draws you back into the body. The point of entry may not be the navel, but could be the heart, throat, or between the eyes.

"Righty—Tighty—Turn In" is the carpenter's second motto Twisting a screw to the right (clockwise) drives it down and into the surface. The unconscious registers clockwise turning as embedding into the body.

STAGE THREE: Conditioning Practice with Tratak Spiral

Geoff Whitefield, founder and president of "Spiral Concepts," attended one of my seminars and devised the most ingenious solution for using spirals by using old CDs (you can purchase old CDs at second hand shops cheaply). Geoff's scheme is marked by the true stamp of genius—it's SIMPLE!

Before Geoff brainstormed this idea for us, we recommended electric motors, rotators, old record players and other clumsy pieces of equipment. If you can 'spin a top' you can do this!

What is Required?

A) One CD no longer wanted (i.e. unloved)

B) One thumbtack (variously referred to as 'tacks' or 'drawing pins')

PSYCHIC SHAVASANA CLOCKWISE REENTRY SPIRAL WITH ALTERNATIVE CHAKRA ENTRANCE POINTS

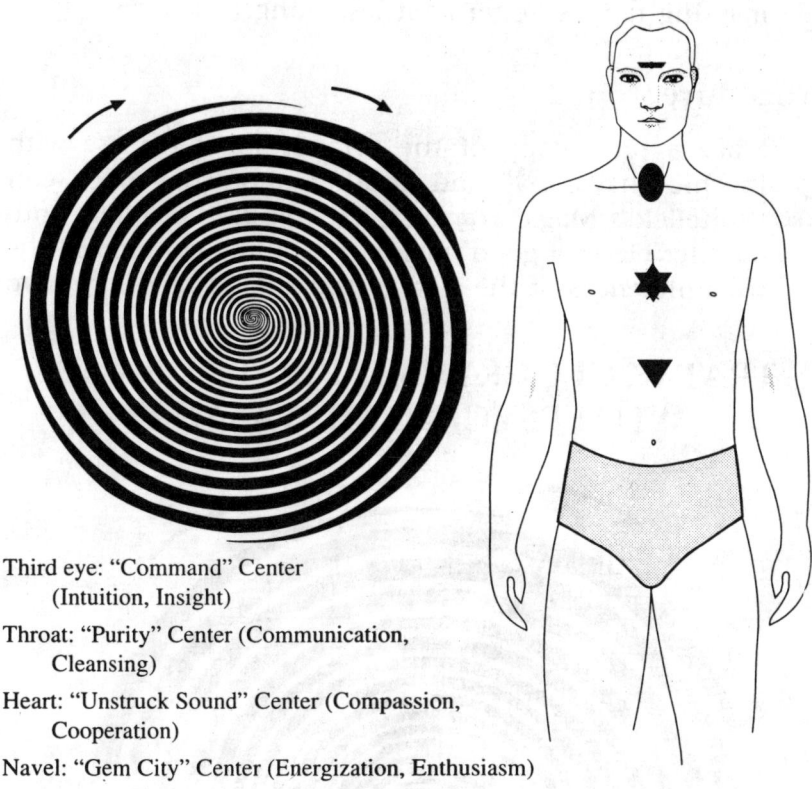

Third eye: "Command" Center (Intuition, Insight)

Throat: "Purity" Center (Communication, Cleansing)

Heart: "Unstruck Sound" Center (Compassion, Cooperation)

Navel: "Gem City" Center (Energization, Enthusiasm)

*All of the body is in the mind,
but not all the mind is in the body.*
— *Swami Rama*

C) Blu-tack or freshly chewed wad of gum (Plastercine could also be used)

D) Some masking tape (the kind used to seal up packing cartons) or Scotch tape (Geoff tells me the adhesive on masking tape is better as it lasts longer!)

Procedure

1. Make a photocopy of the "Tratak Spiral for use with Psychic Shavasana" and another photocopy of "Geoff Whitefield's Magic Trance Spiral". Paste the spirals onto another piece of good quality paper and cut around the circumferences of the spirals. You should now have two

TRATAK CLOCKWISE SPIRAL FOR USE WITH PSYCHIC SHAVASANA

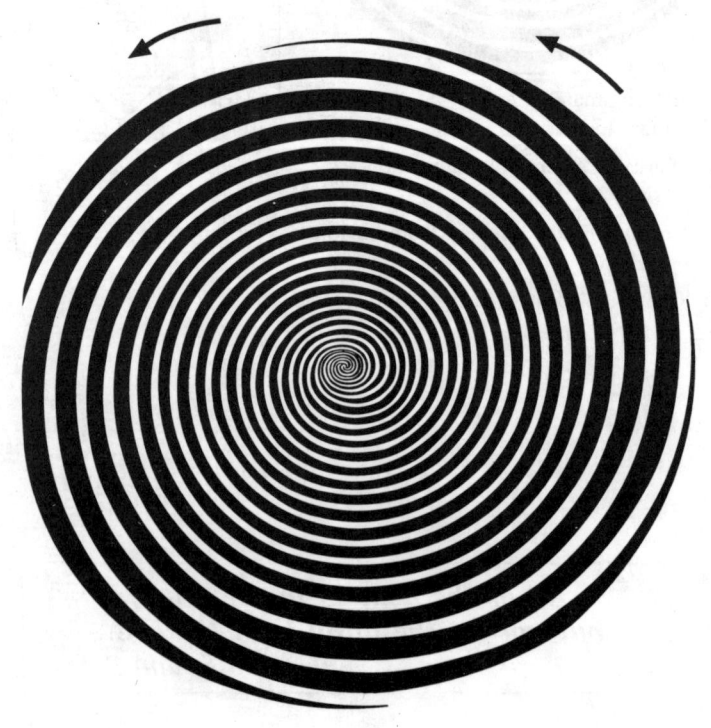

spirals, exactly the size of a CD. They both will attach to a CD, as we shall see, which allows them to be spun on a smooth surface.

2 . Take the CD and put two pieces of masking tape over the central aperture, in an 'x' pattern. Do this on both sides of the CD (As per diagram page 45).

3. Put a small blob of blu-tack on the playing (grooved) side of the CD and flatten it out so a circle is made over the masking tape covering the aperture.

4. Take the thumbtack and push it through the masking tape (on the label side) and at the very center, so the point projects through both the masking tape and blu-tack on the grooved side.

We now have a perfect spinning device as the convex surface on the head of the brass thumbtack provides a perfect pivot for the CD to spin around on any smooth surface.

5. Now it becomes a simple matter to carefully align the center of one of the spirals with the point of the thumbtack and then settle it onto the CD surface; the blu-tack will firmly mount the spiral onto the CD.

Geoff recommends cutting the tip of the thumbtack back by a third with pliers. The point of the tack sometimes protrudes enough above the spiral to throw a shadow and distract the attention. A smooth-surface clipboard provides a good portable surface for spinning the CD and spiral.

Geoff emphasizes two additional points:

1. Best effects are produced under a bright fluorescent white light. You could also experiment with colored light bulbs.

2. Resist the tendency to "smooth out" the jagged lines and serrations along the vanes of the spiral. These serrations are a design feature incorporated into the spiral design to produce a light diffraction of white light into the component colors of the visible spectrum.

Using The Spirals For Accelerating 'Out of the Body' Experiences with "Psychic Shavasana"

i. Place one of the CD mounted spirals on a smooth table surface (i.e. plastic CD case) and give it a vigorous spin, either clockwise or counterclockwise.

ii. Gaze without blinking (Tratak) into the center of the spiral (where the tip of the thumbtack comes through). Gaze as long as the spiral is spinning. The spiral should turn into a visual 'whirlpool' or emerging 'vortex' (depending on the direction of the rotation) and your impression will be of going down into it—or alternatively—that it is coming up to meet you in an endless unraveling.

iii. When the spiral stops spinning quickly shift your gaze to:

   a. An adjacent wall (preferably with patterned wallpaper or several pictures).

   b. A picture in a book (preferably of a Hindu Deity or a symbolic religious depiction); try gazing at Albrecht Durer's "The Crucifixion" on page 84 of this book.

   c. Your hand, your reflection in a mirror, or into a friend's eyes (many students have their first impression of an aura doing this).

iv. Be prepared for an initial shock as the environment scintillates and retreats. Relax totally into the visual experience of the vibrating surroundings and try to feel yourself, or a subtle part of you, expand or contract with the experience.

This exercise should be done for a week. Special receptors in the visual cortex (back of your brain) called feature detectors, are being stimulated to the point of fatigue. As an example, (depending on which spiral and the direction of 'spin') feature detectors that are responsive to clockwise rotation will tire, and when you look away the adjacent feature detectors sensitive to counterclockwise movement are activated, producing the illusion of an "expanding universe." We are using this

CD   Thumbtack   Tape

1. Apply tape in 'X' pattern on both sides

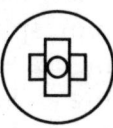

2. Flatten blob of blu-tack over tape covering aperture on grooved side

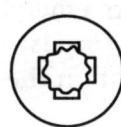

3. Push thumbtack through center of masking tape on label side so point penetrates masking tape and blu-tack on the grooved side

4. Use point of thumbtack to guide cut-out photocopy of "Magic Trance Spiral" onto the center of the CD and push firmly onto blu-tack

GEOFF WHITEFIELD'S MAGIC TRANCE SPIRAL

phenomena to encourage the consciousness to release, with awareness, beyond the physical body (sometimes, in this context, referred to as the "shell").

A Special Note about Geoff Whitefield's Magic Trance Spiral:

Geoff showed me a number of different spirals and I particularly liked one basic design used in America as a Hypno-disk. Geoff promptly went to work, modifying and improving the design radically. One of the special features of his 'Magic Trance Spiral' is the serrated edges which act as a diffraction pattern for light waves. The consequence of this is that, like a Benham's disk, you will start to see colors emerging as the spiral spins. The colors vary at different speeds and Geoff comments that the colors "are also dependent on the clockwise or counterclockwise rotation of the spiral."

Chapter Three

Yoni Mudra: The Voice of Silence

As salt dissolves in water and camphor in fire, so the self dissolves in the Eternal.

— Hindu Proverb

The eternal, age-old path of Yoga has techniques which permit a person not just to escape the illusion *(Maya)* we term life, but to escape within him or herself to a true inner reality wherein may be found the flaming lamp of transcendental consciousness. As we use Yoga to probe deeper within the grottoes of our own minds, we approach the core of our own beings until we experience self-reintegration physically, mentally, and emotionally.

One such technique of turning within is Yoni Mudra. "Yoni" means "womb or source." This reference is to the Absolute, or Brahman, as the source of all existence. The word "Mudra," in this case, denotes a physical practice which has effect on the mind. Yoni Mudra has also been called *Shatmukhi* ("Shat" means "six" and "mukhi" means "orifice or mouth") indicating that the six body orifices (namely eyes, ears, nose, mouth, anus, and genital opening) are closed. Another classical name is Parang Mukhi. "Parang" suggests a turning away from the outside world and a closing of the senses, resulting in *Pratyahara* (sense withdrawal).

Specific Advantages

1. The five senses are shut off mechanically, leading to a semiautomatic state of Pratyahara.
2. The nervous system is rejuvenated, particularly in terms of diminished gross sensory input through blocking the eyes and ears by the forefingers and thumbs respectively. The remaining three fingers produce partial sensory blocking (tactile) via pressure on branches of the trigeminal cranial nerve. (See "Neurological Basis for Psychosomatic Action of Yoni Mudra" on page 53.)
3. Psycho-physiological homeostasis, or balance, is induced through pressure on the Nadis (psychic channels in Yoga). This is most easily understood in terms of acupuncture points and meridians. (See "Acupuncture Points Stimulated During Yoni Mudra" on page 56.)
4. Cooperation is brought about between the mind and the body as a result of the disciplined conditioning required to maintain the pose.
5. The mind is given an opportunity to introvert and experience a complete withdrawal from what may be a disturbing environment.
6. In the advanced phase, the student uses a powerful procedure that ends in Self-realization or an intense U3 experience ("Ultimate Universal Unity").

Yoni Mudra, like Shavasana, is divided into an elementary technique and an advanced technique. Western students need to note that, although tradition uses Sukhasana, a chair may be substituted. I would also point out that those with osteoarthritis of the arms and shoulders may compensate by concentrating upon the mantra in the advanced technique.

> *This means that every performance of Yoni Mudra is an acupressure rejuvenation treatment.*

Carl Weschcke has drawn my attention to this, and in his words: "Ear plugs or cotton smeared with Vaseline can be used to cut off sound, and a sleepshade, blindfold, or meditation hood can also be used."

Elementary Technique

1. Sit in a meditative pose. Padmasana is preferred for those already experienced in Hatha Yoga, but Sukhasana or the Egyptian Chair Pose will be adequate for the beginner.
2. Raise the elbows level with your shoulders and at right angles to your body, jutting out on each side.
3. (a) Close your ears by inserting your thumbs in your ears.
   (b) Close your eyes with your forefingers by placing your fingers along the lower lids to trap the upper eyelashes.
   (c) Place your middle fingers on either side of the bridge of your nose, leaving the nostrils open for breathing.
   (d) Press your upper lip shut with the ring fingers, the fingertips touching each other.
   (e) Press your lower lip shut with the little fingers, the fingertips touching each other.
4. Breathe slowly and evenly while concentrating upon any visual images, spots, or colors that may arise. If spots appear, visualize them contracting and expanding.

The pose should be held for at least five minutes and maintained for up to fifteen minutes. You will notice that colors appear brighter after practice and a feeling of tranquillity ensues. Spend a week on this exercise before attempting the advanced technique.

> *Brahma verily is this whole world.*
> *The Brahma-knowing, Brahma indeed becomes.*
> — *Mandukya Upanishad*

YONI MUDRA POSITION

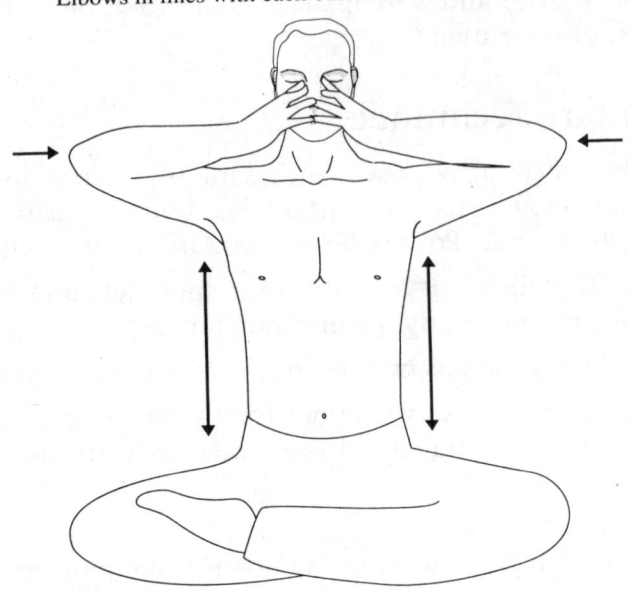

Elbows in lines with each other and at shoulder level

Chair or couch may be substituted

The initial conditioning involves learning to keep the arms up with the elbows straight out at the sides, at shoulder height. Discomfort tends to vanish within a week.

Yoni Mudra Special Instruction Chart for Thumb and Index Fingers

The thumbs may be used to block the ears in two ways:

1. When the thumbnails are short, smear both thumbs with saliva and insert them, with a forward corkscrew movement, into each earhole (External auditory meatus "B" on diagram).
2. With long thumbnails, press the tragus flap ("A" on diagram) firmly over the ear hole, using the ball of each thumb.

Inserting the wet thumbs into the ear canals provides the most efficient sensory isolation from sound vibration; indeed, the procedure provides a virtual waterseal.

Using the tragus as a "trap door" to occlude the ear canal is also quite effective, and in both methods it should be noted that a powerful stimulus is provided to the relaxation (parasympathetic) component of our autonomic nervous system, via reflex stimulation of a branch of the vagus nicknamed "Alderman's nerve." Yoga is sometimes defined by physiologists as "the cultivation of the parasympathetic nervous system."

The index fingers should be gently slipped down over the closed eyes (after the thumbs are blocking the ears) so that they secure the upper eyelashes over the lower eyelids. Be certain no pressure is exerted against the eyeballs by the forefingers.

Test this by gently attempting to open the eyes. If the index fingers are correctly placed, the upper eyelids should be softly sealed by the pressure of the forefingers trapping the upper eyelashes.

Advanced Technique

1. Repeat the elementary technique up to and including Step 3.
2. Commence alternate nostril breathing by pressing shut the left nostril with the left middle finger, and inhaling slowly and evenly through the right nostril. After a full inhalation, press the right nostril shut with the right middle finger, then open the left nostril and exhale slowly and evenly through it. Inhale slowly and evenly through left nostril, close it, open the right nostril and exhale through it, and continue repeating the cycle of alternate nostril breathing.
3. After firmly establishing the breathing rhythm, begin the mental repetition of the mantra

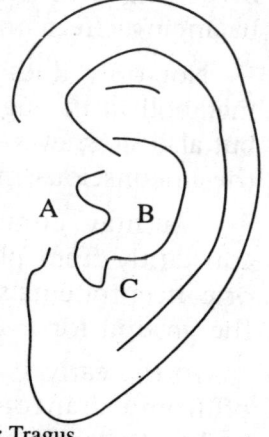

A: Tragus
B: External auditory meatus
C: Antitragus

So Hum. So is mentally repeated on the inhalation and *Hum* is mentally repeated on the exhalation. The *japa* (repetition) of the mantra is to be carried on in conjunction with, and while being mindful of, the alternate nostril breathing. This particular mantra will have a deep effect upon the subconscious as well as quieting the conscious mind.

4. Absorb yourself deeper and deeper in the exercise with the object of experiencing what might be best described as a conscious moment of "No-Thought."

This advanced stage should be performed for fifteen minutes and a goal set of thirty minutes.

IMPLICATIONS OF THE NEW STEPS

Let us discuss the implications of the new steps in the advanced stage.

The addition of alternate nostril breathing has a profound effect upon the body-mind relationship. As we will discuss more fully in a later section, the respiratory cycle is a major link between the physical and mental activity of humans. A person who is emotionally aroused, angry, or frightened will also breathe rapidly. Obviously, any attempt at controlling the breathing will simultaneously produce a tranquilizing, balancing effect on both body and mind.

Not only does the physiological effect of a harmonized metabolism through controlled respiration induce relaxation, but also slow, even breathing signals tranquillity and peace to the unconscious mind.

We may compare the mind to a monkey jumping constantly from place to place, never stopping to regenerate or concentrate its scattered energy unless a pole is placed into the ground for it to climb upon and rest.

In the early stage of Yoni Mudra the mind has been shut off from extraneous sensory stimulation and mental agitation and further calmed by deep, even respiration. It is now that the mind needs a "pole," i.e., a concentrative point, if it is to climb into higher states of consciousness. The pole, or focal point, is provided in the form of the mantra So Hum, which means "He I am."

"He" is the eternal source of all being, Brahman, the Paramatman, the Absolute. You could not have a more powerful pivot or focal point from which to spring into higher states of consciousness. Through this *audgita* (silent chanting) you pass from Pratyahara proper into Samyama (concentration, contemplation, and meditation).

Yoni Mudra is one of the most suitable methods in Hatha Yoga for passing into Antaranga, the higher branches dealt with in Raja Yoga. It should be mentioned that just as Shavasana is the hidden key to Yogic trance states, so Yoni Mudra is the key to the *siddhis* (psychic powers) of clairvoyance and clairaudience.

NEUROLOGICAL BASIS FOR PSYCHOSO-MATIC ACTION OF YONI MUDRA

The thumbs indirectly inhibit sensory stimulation of the eighth cranial nerve. This is the purely sensory acoustic nerve.

The fifth cranial nerve, the trigeminal, is the primary nerve affected by pressure of the fingers in Yoni Mudra. The trigeminal is the largest cranial nerve. The trigeminal divides into three major branches: the ophthalmic (sensory), the maxillary (sensory), and the mandibular, one branch of which is sensory.

During the performance of Yoni Mudra, the first fingers touch over the infratrochlear branch of the ophthalmic and the infraorbital branch of the maxillary. The middle fingers depress the nasal rami (branches) of the infraorbital nerve. The ring fingers press upon the superior labial rami of the infraorbital nerve. The little fingers affect the inferior labial branch of the mandibular nerve (sensory branch). (Note: The nerves pressed by the fingers are tactile.)

The second cranial nerve, the optic, is indirectly affected by the closure of the eyes and thus a saving of body energy is brought about by Yoni Mudra.

PSYCHOSOMATIC EFFECTS OF YONI MUDRA

1. The mind is brought to a point of relaxed absorption within itself. Pratyahara, or sense withdrawal, ensues. This state is probably produced by the pressure of the fingers upon specific nerves as outlined. Such pressure would result in:
   (a) Inhibition of some of the afferent or sensory impulses which normally disturb, stimulate, and distract the mind.
   (b) Induction of a slight dullness in tactile and pain afferent impulses of the skin which would further increase the psychological feeling or tendency toward introversion and abstraction from the external environment.

   The combination of these two factors would aid in placing the mind into a state of monoideistic equipoise such as usually results from the practice of Yoni Mudra.

2. Yoni Mudra rejuvenates the nervous system and gives the illusion of sharpening sensory perception. This may be attributed to the conservation of energy through shutting off afferent impulses to the optic nerve coupled with the psychological awareness of becoming slowly active after an enforced period of temporary inactivity.

3. Heavy perspiration and disturbance of heart rate sometimes occurs. This may be the result of oculo vagal reflexes such as occur after pressure upon the eyeball in an incorrect Yoni Mudra.

4. Stimulation of the vagal nerves (tenth cranial) is reflexively encouraged by pressure upon the ear canals with the thumbs. Vagal stimulation, thus initiated, safely encourages dominance of the parasympathetic nervous system, reducing heart rate, blood pressure, and encouraging digestive processes.

5. The position of the arms encourages neuromuscular coordination and improved ideo-motor discipline.

Yoni Mudra Neurological Chart

Pressure from	Nerve affected	Effect
First fingers	Infratrochlear ophthalmic	Tactile dullness*
	Infraorbital maxillary	Tactile dullness*
Middle fingers	Nasal rami infraorbital	Tactile dullness*
Ring fingers	Superior labial rami	Tactile dullness*
Little fingers	Inferior mandibular labial	Tactile dullness*

Pressure from	Nerve affected	Indirect influence
First fingers	Optic second cranial	Nervous energy conserved
	Oculomotor third cranial	Perspiration†
	Oculovagal reflex	Heart disturbed†
Thumbs	Eighth cranial	Inhibition Afferent impulses

YONI MUDRA PRESSURE POINTS

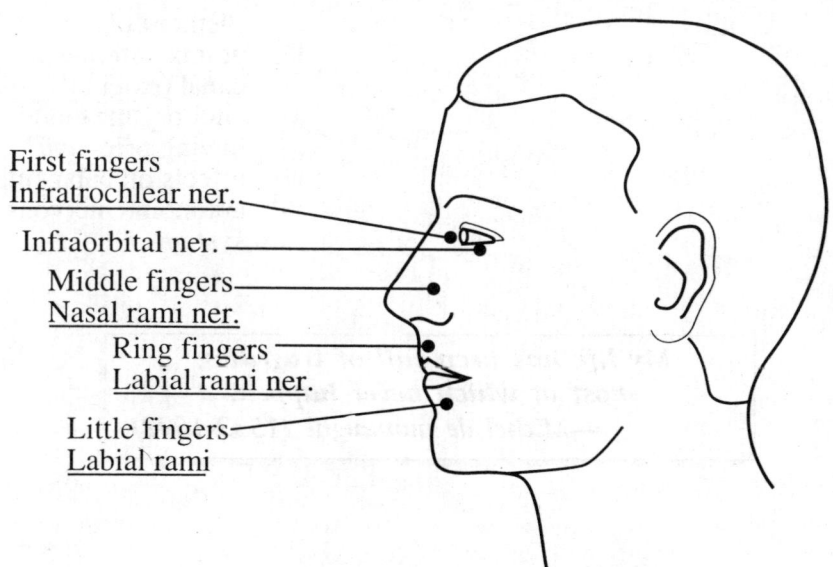

* This is composed of blockage of temporary sensory impulses and pressure of the fingers producing a slight numbing effect.

† Difficulties of this type may warn the student that the pose is incorrectly performed. Such disturbances may also have something to do with changes in blood pressure due to the position of the arms.

ACUPUNCTURE POINTS STIMULATED DURING YONI MUDRA

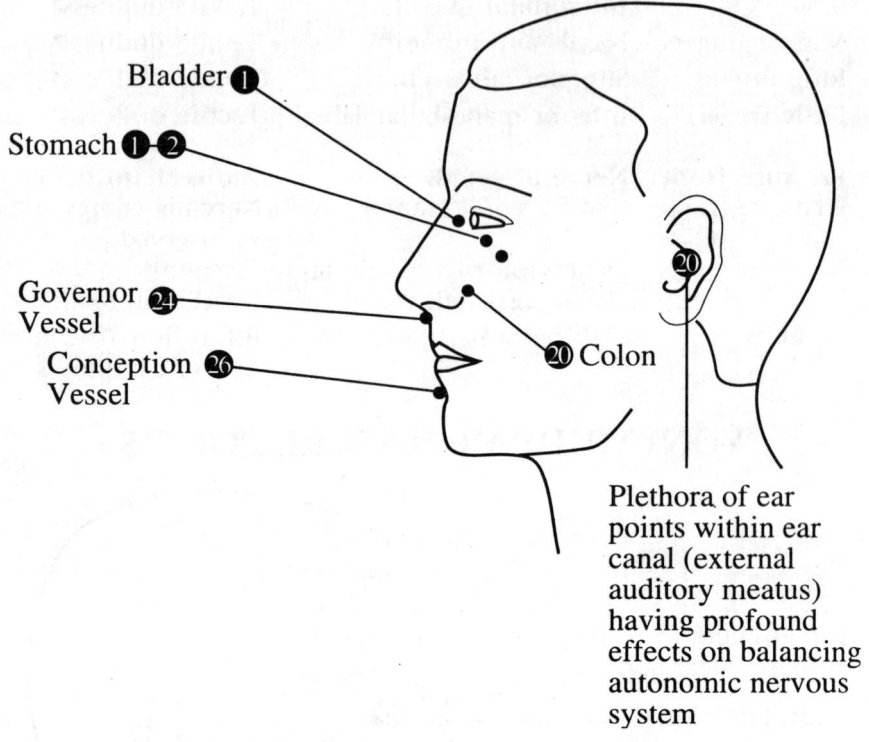

> *My life has been full of tragedies, most of which never happen.*
> —Michel de montaigne (1533-1592)

★★

Part Two

Raja Yoga for the Mind

In shallow souls, even the fish of small things can cause a commotion. In oceanic minds, the largest fish makes hardly a ripple.

— Hindu proverb

Chapter Four

Polarization

> *The wise man is like a blacksmith's anvil on which many experiences are hammered out without change in the anvil itself.*
>
> — Hindu proverb

"Raja" means "king," thus Raja Yoga is the "Kingly Yoga" or "Royal Way." The "King" or master in our lives is the mind, and it is the control of mind that Raja Yoga teaches.

Patanjali's *Yoga Sutras* is considered the classic text on Raja Yoga. Its four chapters deal with the discipline of the mind and psychic potential. *Ashtanga Yoga,* as Patanjali's book is often called, is a specific study of the inner or esoteric four limbs of Yoga. These four limbs are *Pratyahara* (sometimes considered a part of *Bahira-anga* or as the transitory stage from *Hatha* to *Raja*), *Dharana* (concentration), *Dhyana* (Contemplation or sustained concentration), and *Samadhi* (states of ecstasy, realization, and cosmic consciousness).

SUPERNORMAL ABILITIES

We are going to be primarily concerned with Dharana or concentration. Concentration is the key to the *siddhis,* the so-called supernatural powers (really supernormal abilities latent within us all) such as photographic memory, self-anesthesia, mental calculations, etc. According to tradition, Raja Yoga confers upon the student the more spectacular psychic powers in the form of telepathy, clairvoyance, psychometry, and related phenomena belonging to the field of parapsychology.

Raja Yoga may be defined as the science of concentrating and focusing the conscious mind upon the unconscious mind until a merger takes place between them, resulting in a new superconscious state of mind. As you have gathered by now, Raja Yoga deals exclusively with the mind and may therefore be considered as applied Eastern psychology.

In this age of Western psychologists, psychiatrists, and social workers, a few words would not be amiss concerning the essential differences between Eastern psychology, as typified by Raja Yoga, and contemporary Western psychology.

Modern Western psychoanalysis may be said to have really commenced with the work of Freud, some ninety years ago. The psychology of Raja Yoga, as expounded by Patanjali, is nearly 2000 years old and the source from which Patanjali drew his material is even older.

Western psychology is based upon theory proved empirically by tests which have provided statistical data. Eastern psychology has as its fundamental basis personal, subjective experience. The Eastern student does not rationalize truth—he or she experiences it. It is an Eastern maxim that the student accepts nothing as true until he or she validates it by personal experience.

DIFFERING METHODOLOGY

Western and Eastern psychology both have the goal of aiding people to solve their problems. Where they differ is in methodology.

What is needed is a synthesis of the best of Eastern and Western psychology. Where Eastern psychology lacks objective data for providing empirical proof, Western psychology lacks objective techniques which will produce subjective changes within the patient or student.

The emergence of the "Trans-personal" psychology movement in the eighties is certainly a promising amalgamation of East and West. Let us hope this trend continues through the nineties, as it is certainly a healthier perspective than the "pop" psychology fads espoused by some. The one thing certain in Western clinical psychology is that this year's theory will be replaced by a new one next year.

Raja Yoga, as taught by a competent teacher, has two aspects which are emphatically denied as impossible by Western psychologists.

First, through graded steps in visualization, the development of a photographic memory is ensured. Second, the raising of an individual intelligence quotient to well above average and perhaps even genius level can be done.

Keeping these claims in mind, the student can see just how interesting the implications of an East-West psychological synthesis would be.

WORRY-ABSORBING EXERCISE

We finish our "fifty-minute hour" with the psychiatrist and once again find ourselves alone to face the worries, frustrations, and problems of our lives. What have we gained, that we personally may apply, in the way of a concrete technique for self-help? Raja Yoga fills the gap of Western psychology with a worry-absorbing exercise that we call polarization.

Let us use an analogy as an aid to understanding the mechanics of polarization. Suppose we have a magnet and an ordinary piece of iron bar and desire to magnetize, or polarize, the metal. You will recall enough of elementary science to know that the molecular arrangement of a magnet is in alignment, so that a single force field is produced. This is not the case with the unmagnetized iron bar as its molecular structure is not harmoniously patterned, and consequently the individual force fields of each molecule are working at cross purposes to each other.

If we commence, slowly and systematically, to stroke the iron bar with the magnet, we shall gradually align the bar's molecular structure and a state of polarization will result, turning the bar into a magnet.

The magnet represents the mind, while the iron bar symbolizes the emotional and psychic aspects of the physical being. Raja Yoga teaches polarization as an exercise that brings about harmony and balance between all positive and negative aspects of the body-mind system. It is suggested that just as we may magnetize a piece of iron with a magnet, so may we magnetize or polarize the body with mental currents. Yoga teaches that this is possible through the functioning of the psychic nerves or Nadis.

A short trial of the psychological rejuvenation brought about by this exercise will convince the student that it is one of the most valuable techniques in Raja Yoga.

Specific Advantages

1. Practiced regularly, polarization will give relief from anxiety and mild depression. The mind is forced to absorb itself during the exercise and thus the "worry circle" is broken up.
2. Polarization may be practiced to induce Yoga Nidra, and therefore is useful in conjunction with Shavasana to ease exhaustion and insomnia.
3. Concentration and visualization are greatly increased; at the same time, internal awareness of the body is developed.
4. Yoga theory suggests that the psychic nerves are purified *(nadisuddhi)* through direct control of the nervous energy or prana within the body.

Technique

1. Lie supine (face up) on the floor upon a folded blanket or mat. The body should be so oriented that the head is north and the feet south. This is again the Yoga principle of taking advantage of natural forces—in this case, the earth's magnetic field.

2. Place the feet together and the hands palm up, close to the body (actually touching the sides).
3. Start polarization proper by visualizing—on a slow, even inhalation—positive, pranic, sun energy, warm and golden yellow in color, being drawn through the top of the head, down through the body, and out of the soles of the feet.
4. On a slow, even exhalation, visualize negative, apranic, moon energy, cool and blue in color, being drawn up through the soles of the feet, through the body, and out of the top of the head.
5. If you are practicing polarization for the relief of anxiety, neurasthenia, or insomnia, prepare yourself by doing Shavasana in reverse. Start with the vital zones of the head and work down to the feet, maintaining consciousness and not falling into Yoga Nidra.
6. Continue the respective visualizations of inhalation and exhalation, and at the same time try to feel the passage of these energies sweeping the body and producing a sensation similar to an electric current.

With the colored inhalation feel a tingle vibrate from head to toe, and from toe to head with the colored exhalation. Synchronize the breath, visualization, and sensation of energy flow.

THE FLOW OF THE SUN AND MOON ENERGIES

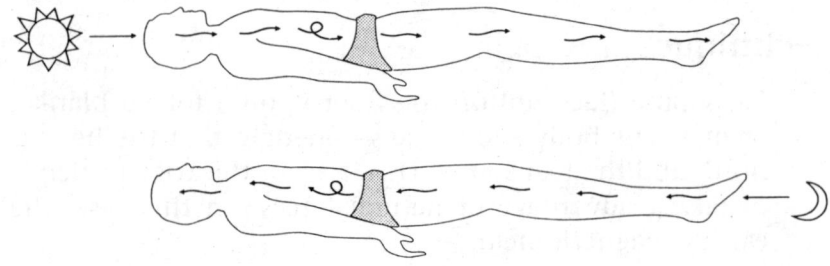

Ancillary Technique Considerations

1. Polarization may be done in bed, on a couch, or even sitting up in the Egyptian Chair Pose. In the case of sitting up, it is usually done for concentration purposes; the emphasis is on developing an electric, "pins and needles" (paresthesia), tingling effect.

2. Some students will find it more beneficial to break each of the two phases into inspiration-expiration cycle by themselves, i.e.:

    (a) On inspiration, draw golden solar energy through the top of your skull to your solar plexus. The solar plexus is located under the diaphragm, above the navel, and just below the tip (xiphoid process) of the breast bone.

    (b) On expiration, push golden energy down through the remainder of your trunk, through your legs, and out the soles of your feet.

    (c) On the following inspiration, draw blue (or silver) moon energy up through the soles of your feet to the solar plexus region.

    (d) On the subsequent exhalation, draw the blue-silver energy up through your chest, neck, and out through the top of your skull.

Continue the above sequence until the proper result has been acheived.

> *Men suffer from thinking more*
> *than from anything else.*
> —Leo Tolstoy (1828-1910)

REAPING THE BENEFITS

For the treatment of psychological symptoms, remain absorbed in the exercise until you lose consciousness and drop into the refreshing state of Yoga Nidra.

For improvement of concentration and visualization, keep the conscious mind focused on visualization and internal sensations without permitting sleep to ensue. Polarization should be practiced fifteen to thirty minutes each day for at least a week before adding new exercises.

The first indication of mastering this technique will be the intensification of concentration to the point where you feel a distinct electric current running through the body with each inhalation and exhalation. This is a sensation which must be experienced to be understood.

The commencement of study in Raja Yoga makes it possible to refine the Hatha technique of Shavasana, a method of achieving physical relaxation with inevitable mental relaxation following. We can now begin distinguishing between physical tension and mental tension.

As a rule, Shavasana and polarization may be used together to ensure the attainment of Yoga Nidra. The stipulation is that in cases of mental tension (namely anxiety and worry), Shavasana must be done from the head down rather than from the feet up. This is for the simple reason that we unconsciously and consciously associate our mental activity (and hence our mental tensions) with the head region. It is obvious that mental tension is better relaxed by carrying our conscious awareness away from the skull area and down to the feet.

---

*The mind is no more in the body
than music is in the instrument.*
— Robert Anton Wilson

*The self is no more in the mind
than the wind is in the trees.*
— Swami Anandakapila Saraswati

★★

Chapter Five

Concentration

The mind during meditation should be like a lamp in a windless place, where the flame does not flicker.

— Hindu Proverb

Concentration is a focusing of the mind by the mind. In other words, concentration always involves an internal adjustment. Most people forget, however, that just as a delicate, high-powered microscope must be gently brought into focus, so gentleness is a prerequisite for true concentration. Yoga emphasizes *Ahimsa*, or nonviolence, whatever the nature of the activity.

DHARANA YANTRA

How may we test for a relaxed state of mind ready to begin Dharana or concentration practice? Close your eyes and deliberately create a warm, smooth, velvety darkness as if you were looking up into a moonless, starless tropical night. The more tense your mind is, the more your inner blackness will be disturbed by colors and white spots.

It was to aid in gaining the necessary relaxed state of mind that Yogis recommended meditation in dark caves, monastery cells, and similar places. The creation of a pure, black field of mental vision will often so relax the mind that pain sensations from tension headaches are inhibited. (Recall in earlier chapters that we mentioned the meditation hood and also suggested the use of a sleeping mask for this purpose.)

The student may be wondering what specific result was gained by Dharana in the Yoga scheme of self-development. The mind may be thought of as a wave-covered (emotionally turbulent) lake. Such stormy waters perturb boats (the external objects perceived through the five senses) and also obscure the view of the lake bottom.

Through concentration, the waters of the mind are calmed and we achieve a clear focus upon the boats or objects of the senses. At a later stage (Dhyana), we focus within our own being and catch a glimpse of the pearls lying upon the lake bottom of our lives.

Specific Advantages

1. Develops concentration to the level required in Raja Yoga.
2. Increases the ability to visualize by transferring an external image to the inner mind's eye.
3. Facilitates unconscious access by opening a "tunnel" within the stilled conscious mind.

Preparation

It will be necessary for the student to construct a special Dharana Yantra or concentration diagram (a Yantra is a geometrical figure used for concentration purposes). The Dharana Yantra is made by pasting a two-inch square of white paper upon the center of a black piece of paper of average writing size.

Technique

1. Assume a meditative pose or sit in a chair facing a blank, light-colored wall at a distance of two or three feet.
2. Pin the Dharana Yantra diagram (see page 70) upon the wall in such a fashion that the center of the white square is at eye level. Have sufficient light thrown upon the wall from behind you to see the diagram clearly.

3. Close your eyes and spend two or three minutes creating a warm, velvety blackness. Relax and gently push all disturbing or distracting images aside by repeatedly creating the black field in your inner vision.
4. Open your eyes and perform Tratak, or fixation, on the center of the diagram for three to five minutes. Gaze steadily and firmly, inhibiting the blinking reflex somewhat (but avoiding strain), until an aura forms around the edges of the white square.
5. Slowly and without strain transfer your gaze to a blank portion of the wall on either side and concentrate upon the afterimage (a black square) which should appear on the wall. Hold your concentration for as long as the image is perceptible. When it becomes faint, use your imagination to strengthen it.
6. When the afterimage has faded completely again, close your eyes and mentally recreate it. Attempt to hold it as steady as possible on the screen of your conscious mind.

The practice of Dharana Yantra should be continued for at least a week before starting the technique for Internal Dharana. Practice time should be extended to fifteen minutes, and you should spend as much time upon each stage of the exercise as is necessary.

OPEN-EYED PRELIMINARY PRACTICE YANTRA FOR INTERNAL DHARANA

This Yantra is constructed using color patterns opposite to the ones you will visualize with your eyes closed. The chart may be used as a preliminary stage to Internal Dharana.

Gaze upon the white circle until a rim aura has begun to show around the edges. Wait at least a minute after the first appearance of the rim aura, and then close your eyes. The afterimages will manifest in the correct sequence of black background, white square, and black circle.

Note: The ability to retain an afterimage can become a barometer of your degree of mental relaxation. Western psychophysiology has only recorded the variables of stimulus strength and length of stimulus exposure in regard to afterimages, and the time span the afterimages can be seen by the subject. A variable that is known in the East is depth of mental relaxation. By increasing your depth of relaxation as soon as the afterimage starts to fade, you can perceive it longer.

Specific Advantages

1. Develops concentration and visualization to the point where a photographic memory becomes a distinct possibility.
2. May be specifically used to stimulate latent memory tracts of the subconscious and thus recall forgotten material.

Technique

1. Lie down, supine, in a semi-dark room.
2. Close your eyes; with great care create a mental field of warm, velvety blackness as in Step 3 of Dharana Yantra.
3. Project upon your black field a white square about the size of writing paper and centered ten to twelve inches from your eyes. Concentrate upon holding the image steady and prevent it from moving to either side or up and down.
4. Holding the image of the white square framed by the black background, imagine a black circle or black hole in the center of the white square. The black spot should be roughly the size of a fifty-cent piece. Concentrate upon the black circle while maintaining the composite visualization of the black background, white square, and black center.
5. End the exercise by suddenly releasing the entire visualization and watching the images that may flash across the mind's eye.

This particular form of Internal Dharana may be cultivated to the point where you close your eyes for a few seconds and instantly recall the desired material that had slipped beyond conscious recall.

The Secret of Instant Recall

All forgotten memories have simply passed from the conscious mind into the subconscious storehouse. When we forget something, in an examination for instance, what has happened is that the conscious mind has frozen momentarily and thus shut off communication with the memory tracts of the brain. This exercise "thaws out" the conscious mind by relaxing the tension and permitting a free flow along the association stream of preconscious and subconscious memory reservoirs.

Note: If recall does not come after fifteen to thirty seconds with your eyes closed, *break your pattern!* Open your eyes and focus on your fingers flicking in front of you. Get up and walk around. Do a clean-up task (dishes, filing, taking the garbage out, dusting, etc.). Later, the memory will flood back.

The next time you forget a desired fact or name, close your eyes, give yourself the sharp mental command that you will remember, and then absorb your mind in this Internal Dharana exercise. After completing the visualization, concentrate intensely upon holding it steadily for a few seconds, and then shatter the picture and wait (with eyes still closed) for the desired association to pop itself into your conscious mind. With practice, recollection will take place in ten to fifteen seconds.

The SCM Formula

The ability to create intense mental images is half the key to memory power. This ability is easy once you understand the fundamental mechanics of visualization.

CONCENTRATION
DHARANA YANTRA DIAGRAM 1

CUT ALONG DOTTED LINE

This diagram is designed, along with the one on the other side of this page, to be cut out. It may be enlarged by a photocopier to the desired size and used as per instructions.

CONCENTRATION
DHARANA YANTRA DIAGRAM 2

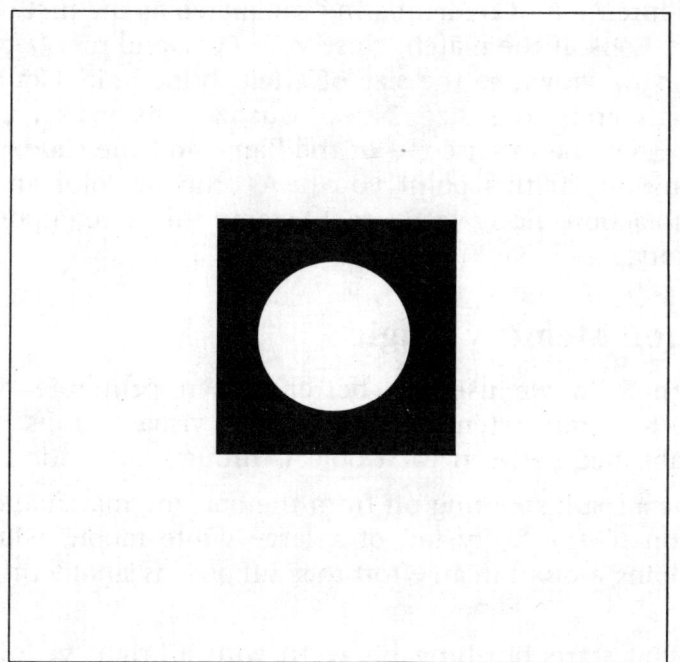

CUT ALONG DOTTED LINE

This diagram is designed, along with the one on the other side of the page, to be cut out. It may be enlarged by a photocopier to the desired size and used as per instructions.

SCM stands for size, color, and motion, the three requirements for successful mental imaging. If we are to leave an impression upon our memory we must do it by administering a triad of shocks to the mind. The best example is that of the advertising psychologist who stamps impressions upon the mind by the skillful use of large billboards, vivid colors, and flashing neon lights.

Take a simple object, like a match, and attempt to visualize it with the intention of remembering the match as the first of five objects. Look at the match, close your eyes, and mentally see it as having grown to the size of a telephone pole. Get a feeling of its enormous size. Now visualize this match as igniting and see the intense red of the flame and the sudden flare of ignition. At this point you have brought color and motion into action, along with size, to stamp the match upon your memory.

Association Memory Magic

Along with SCM we use the better-known principle of association to permit retention of a series of visualizations. A link is established between each object through association.

Imagine a spark shooting off from the burning match and dropping on to the fluffy tail of a large white rabbit, who begins hopping around in an effort to snuff out his smoldering tail.

The rabbit starts brushing his teeth with a bright yellow oversized toothbrush. Upon finishing, he throws the toothbrush into a river which is rushing by rapidly. A deer comes down to drink from the river.

You should now find that you have effortlessly memorized five items, namely match, rabbit, toothbrush, river, and deer. It is as easy to link together twenty objects as it is five. The student is encouraged to experiment with this.

★★

Chapter Six

Pranic Rejuvenation: The Key to Psychic Healing

*As a man sucks water through a lotus stem
so should breath be drawn in as immortal elixir.*

— Amrita Nada Upanishad

Yoga has always had very definite theories concerning mind and its potential uses. The Yogi considers mind to be the highest evolution of energy, and this theory is not limited to just individual mind but is applied to the universe as a whole. Yoga suggests that the ultimate and original state of the universe is energy in the form of Cosmic Mind, which permeates everything conceivable; as a result we are said to be surrounded by mind, much as goldfish are surrounded by water.

When Cosmic Mind manifests itself in building matter, the fundamental energy involved in such phenomena as cohesion, electricity, magnetism, etc., is termed *prana*, the basic kinetic energy of the universe. Such a cosmology naturally leads to the theory that since mind is all and a fundamental form of it is called prana, then each individual's mind should be able to control the prana or nervous energy within the individual physical body. Contrary to Western science, Eastern science claims that nervous energy within the body may be increased, stored up, and controlled at will by the mind.

This control of energy (prana) is learned through mastery of Pranayama (energy control) involving breathing exercises.

It is postulated that breath brings prana into the body as well as oxygen. This is the essence behind many so-called "supernormal" powers.

Raja Yoga holds the key which explains the apparent failure many people experience with Pranayama. The key is concentration of the mind upon the body while performing Pranayama. Just as the blood circulates through the body, so Raja Yoga teaches that the mind may be made to circulate consciously throughout the body.

> *As blood is the vehicle of oxygen, so mind is the vehicle of prana; this is the whole secret of revitalizing and rejuvenating the body.*

The practice of Shavasana has taught you to carry the mind through and to any of the Marmasthanani, while Polarization started you on the first experiments in controlling pranic energy. You are now ready for an effective rejuvenating technique that requires no mastery of a difficult Pranayama exercise, but only the comfortable retention of breath, coupled with intense concentration upon the basic sixteen Marmasthanani or vital zones.

Specific Advantages

1. Increased oxygen absorption as breath retention has a tendency to contract the spleen, throwing more red blood cells into circulation.
2. The full inhalation required enlarges the chest cavity, improving the heart action, and aiding the suction return of venous blood (deoxygenated red blood cells in the circulatory system) to the heart and lungs.
3. Prana, or hypothetical life force, is consciously infused into the body; this results in the recharging of organs, tissues, and cells.
4. Considered a psychic healing technique for any part of the body.

5. A specific antidote for quickly counteracting mental fatigue and physical exhaustion.

Technique

1. Lie supine (face up) with your feet comfortably together (allowing the toes to fall outward), your hands comfortably by your sides with palms up, or as close to this as is comfortable.
2. Inhale a slow, even, deep breath and hold it as soon as the lungs feel full. Retain the breath as long as is comfortable.
3. While retaining the breath, mentally become aware of the feet (first vital zone), and visualize golden pranic energy saturating the area with stimulating, tingling energy.

   Tip: Use your imagination to actually see the area glowing, scintillating from the inside out, filled with sun-gold vitality, forming an aura surrounding the Marmasthanani.
4. Slowly exhale, relaxing the intensity of concentration.
5. Inhale again, retain the breath, and move to the next Marmasthanani, the shins, and repeat your concentration.
6. Work up the body, retaining the breath and concentrating at each of the basic sixteen vital spots until you finish at the head.
7. If necessary, go over the entire body several times until you feel a distinct glowing and tingling from toe to head.

Allow at least fifteen minutes for the exercise. In that time you should be able to go over the body once or more, depending upon the retention period. The student should strive for thirty seconds *kumbhak,* or breath retention, at the end of several months' practice. The key point is to become so consciously aware of each of the zones that your awareness creates a tingling indicative of the successful infusion of prana into that zone.

Before proceeding to practice, we need to do a more detailed analysis of the Marmasthanani list given in Chapter 2. Each zone focused upon must be "sensed" as three-dimensional layering. Often the area involves a bone, so we cultivate the feeling of golden prana being taken into the lungs (subtle energy extracted from the air by the alchemical "will" of your mind) and then transported by consciousness to the body part concentrated upon. At the site of concentration, visualize the bio-energy diffusing from marrow cells through bone cells, blood vessel cells, muscle cells, skin cells, and outward for several inches, forming a force field.

Pranic rejuvenation, when used in conjunction with other exercises, is excellent for bringing the consciousness back from a deep state of introspection. You will discover that not only are physical results apparent with this technique, but also psychological effects appear in the form of a calm, relaxed mental state. This is due to the respiratory process acting as a psychosomatic link between mind and body, as discussed in the chapter on Yoni Mudra.

Pranic rejuvenation may be practiced daily and there are virtually no contra-indications, provided we always adjust the breath retention in terms of avoiding strain.

CLASSICAL MARMASTHANANI CHART

Body part	Area included and internal organs
1. Feet	Toes to heel, ankle joint, sole of foot to dorsum, all tissues.
2. Shins	Area between ankle and knee joint. Again, concentration is from the marrow out.
3. Kneecaps	Entire knee joint from popliteal space beneath knee through to patella (kneecap).
4. Thighs	Between knee joint and groin. Focus from inside out.

5.	Abdomen	Groin to a little above navel, lower poles of kidneys, genitals, bladder, small intestine surrounding large intestine. Also includes buttocks and front abdominal wall.
6.	Solar plexus	Navel to tip of breast bone. Spleen, upper poles of kidney and adrenals. Pancreas, stomach, gall bladder, liver.
7.	Upper chest "Brahma Dandu"	Tip of breast bone to top of breast bone (jugular notch), diaphragm, lungs, heart, thymus gland.
8.	Spine	Follow spine down from cervical region (starting where neck bones join skull) to coccyx (tailbone).
9.	Hands	Fingertips to wrists and inclusive of wrist joints.
10.	Forearms	From above wrist joints and inclusive of elbow joints.
11.	Upper arms	Above elbow joints and inclusive of shoulder joints.
12.	Throat	Thyroid gland, parathyroids, voice box, trachea, all tissues.
13.	Back of head	Occiput (heavy bone protecting the back of the head). Posterior half of brain.
14.	Jaw	Lips, gums, teeth (upper and lower), throat, face.
15.	Eyes	Eyes, nose, forehead, pituitary gland, anterior or front half of brain, ears.
16.	Scalp ("Brahmapura" or "God's City")	Bones on top of skull, superior or top portion of brain, pineal gland.

Note: Area boundaries and organ allocations may overlap in some cases, so this is a rough guide only.

ORGANS FROM MARMAS 5 TO 7

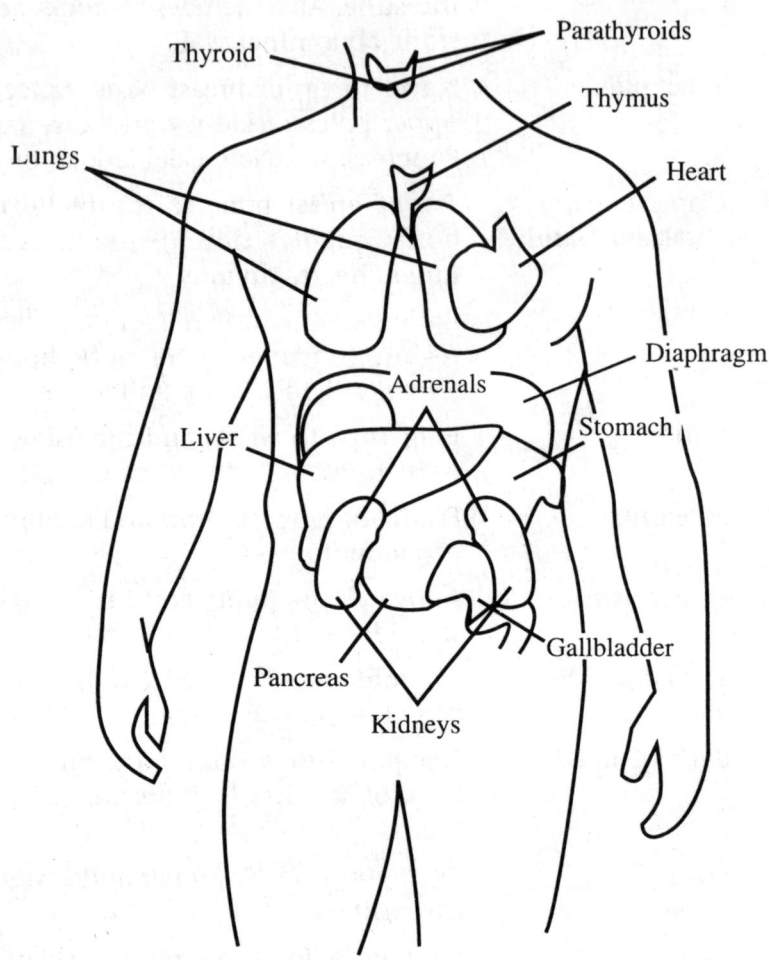

★★

Part Three

Laya Yoga for the Super-Sensible Body

Over it shines the sleeping kundalini, fine as the fiber of the lotus stalk. Like the spiral of a conch shell, her shining snake-like form goes three and a half times 'round Shiva and her luster is as that of a strong flash of young lightning. Her sweet murmur is the indistinct hum of swarms of love-mad bees. She maintains all the beings of the world by means of inspiration and expiration, and shines in the cavity of the root chakra as a chain of brilliant lights.

— Shatchakra Nirupana
Verses 10, 11

Chapter Seven

Laya Yoga: The Psychic Centers

> *Now I speak of the first sprouting shoot [of the Yoga plant] of the complete realization of the Brahman, which is to be achieved by means of the six chakras in their proper order.*
>
> — Shatchakra Nirupana
> Introductory verse

Laya Yoga is the science of unleashing latent energy hidden within the human nervous system. As we have evolved from a primarily physically motivated animal to a mentally motivated animal, we have lost much of our physical strength and capacity for endurance. It could be that the strength and endurance of our cave-dwelling ancestors still lies locked within our central nervous system (namely, the brain and spinal cord) in the form of potential energy. Laya Yoga is the key that attempts to unlock these hidden energy reserves. (Carl Weschcke has pointed out how the archetypal dream of primal power release has been evidenced in the former popularity of the television series *The Incredible Hulk*.)

This latent energy is called *kundalini* and is symbolized by a snake coiled three-and-a-half times. The symbology of the snake gives us the secret implications of kundalini.

The snake has been a sexual symbol from time immemorial, and this tells us that kundalini is intimately connected with the sexual expression of humanity. Indeed, sexual activity springs from the stream of kundalini force and is the most concrete example we have of a latent energy lying within us that has far-reaching effects in our life. The orgasm of sexual union is said to be similar to the trembling and bliss of kundalini rising.

This connection between sexual activity and kundalini has led to the development of two distinct schools of thought. The Tantra school teaches the rise and release of kundalini by using the physical act of intercourse as a channel for this energy to express itself. The Yoga school teaches that sexual activity should be curtailed (Brahmacharya), thus suppressing kundalini until the pressure becomes sufficiently strong for kundalini energy to force itself into arousal. Both schools of thought have half the key in their respective viewpoints, and the result has been that both schools have thoroughly confused Westerners who have taken to practicing the exercises prescribed by each tradition.

WISDOM OF MENTAL CONTROL

The snake, as well as symbolizing the procreative urge, symbolizes wisdom—the wisdom of mental control. This is a hint that if such an energy as kundalini does exist, it may be released only through the mind exerting careful stimulation at the points where kundalini is most apt to manifest. The individual who would awaken or arouse kundalini is advised to first gain control through Raja Yoga disciplines.

The last point that should be brought to the student's attention concerns the fact that the snake is always shown as coiled. This coiling of a snake is preparation for striking out, and it is in just such a manner that kundalini lies within us, compressed like a spring, ready to change from potential static energy into kinetic manifestations under the proper conditions. The coil of three represents the three states of energy (positive, negative, and neutral), while the half coil represents kundalini as always on the verge of changing from static to kinetic manifestation.

It is taught in the East that just as the snake-charmer must first become immune to the poison of the snakes, so the student of Laya Yoga must be prepared for the shock of arousing kundalini.

PROCESS OF INTROSPECTION

The ancient Yogis obtained their remarkable knowledge of the human body largely through a process of introspection. By Raja Yoga they became so intensely aware of themselves that they internally felt, rather than saw, the major blood vessels, nerves, and organs. Out of such introspections grew a theory concerning the existence of certain nadis, or psychic nerves, through which kundalini could manifest.

The three most important of these astral channels were called Ida, Pingala, and Shushmna. Ida and Pingala are said to run up the left and right sides of the spine (corresponding with the sympathetic nerve ganglion on either side of the spine), while Shushmna runs between them in a position corresponding to the spinal cord.

Ida carries feminine, lunar, cooling energy, while her partner, Pingala, conducts hot solar energy. This allocation is transcultural, as exemplified by the alchemical art of Renaissance (and earlier) Europe. In alchemy the same polar juxtapositions occur: via Sun and Moon, King and Queen, hot, burning sulphur (the Soul) and cooling, liquid mercury (the Spirit).

Allegorically, Sushumna is said to represent the channel of "Christ Consciousness" in us all which is kept vacant, or "crucified," by the emotions running rampant in Ida and Pingala (the two thieves hanging on either side of the crucified Christ).

Albrecht Durer, generally acknowledged as the greatest of German Renaissance artists, has a magnificent portrayal of the Crucifixion, with the thieves hanging on either side of Christ.

The Sun (Pingala) is above the thief on the right, while the Moon (Ida) crowns the thief hanging to the left.

Kundalini is stored at the base of the spine in the egg-shaped Kanda, from which is said to emanate 72,000 psychic nerves including Ida, Pingala, and Shushumna. The object of Laya Yoga is to bring about quiescence of Ida and Pingala and arouse the fire of kundalini so she ascends Sushumna, awakening various vital centers *(chakras)* situated along the way, and finally uniting with the top center, Sahasrara, where a union takes place between Kundalini Shakti (feminine receptive) and Shiva Shakta (masculine projective).

This concept may be taken as either symbolic or literal. Each chakra, or psychic center, as it is touched by the ever climbing flame of Kundalini, has the particular God and Goddess dwelling within consummate. This is the story of the union between the solar (logic) and lunar (emotion) aspects in our life, which takes place upon the ascent into spiritual consciousness.

Laya Yoga is transcendental alchemy. The body becomes both Athanor (Furnace) and Crucible (Latin cross + thurible, back to Greek "sacrificial cross"). The fire of kundalini calcinates (purifies) the salt (material aspects), sulphur (Soul), and mercury (Spirit).

Ultimately, with repeated purifications and extractions, transmutation and reconstitution into a more perfect being occurs. The spagyric of Body, Soul, and Spirit manifests and the alchemist/Yogi becomes the "Lapis Philosophorum."

BASIC CHAKRA CONCEPTS

Most commonly, it is taught that the human body contains seven major psychic centers, five situated along the spine and two found within the head. These centers are called chakras or *padmas*. Chakra means "wheel," and thus it is implied that these centers are moving or active. Padma means "lotus," and as a lotus, like any plant, is something that grows, so the

THE CRUCIFIXION

psychic centers are not fully developed in us but have yet to open their "petals" into full bloom.

The Greek mystery schools espoused the same idea of inner growth potential when they called their first degree initiates "Neophytes," or literally "New Plants." The European alchemical and Rosicrucian analogous lotus was the rose, the color coding of red, yellow, or white signifying the degree of opening in the psychic centers. The Western equivalent to the implication of chakra, i.e., movement, was the concept of planets orbiting within the microcosm-man himself.

The flower is a particularly powerful feminine symbol of cup-like receptivity to impregnation by fire power (focused attention).

The six-petaled lotus is the macrocosm (Universe at large), sacred to Vishnu, the Preserver. Within this context, kundalini becomes the functional equivalent of an insect insuring cross-pollination with each padma.

The flower sacred to Shiva is the hibiscus—five-petaled, representing the five senses of the human person, and is therefore analogous to the microcosm. The God (Deva) and Goddess (Devi) in each chakra/padma respectively become the stamen (lingam) and pistil (yoni), and hence the inherent potential for cohabitation with each psychic center when stimulated by kundalini.

Even more importantly, the hibiscus is sacred to Shiva's Shakti, whose many names include the epithet Kali. Enoby Kali is the timeless mother of all manifest (Prakrit) matter. The blood red of the hibiscus is her sacred menstrual fluid and is also symbolic of the Rajasic or active principle of nature.

> *A psychic center (chakra/padma) is a whirling vortex of energy situated at the conjunction point of the body and mind.*

THE PARTS OF A HIBISCUS FLOWER

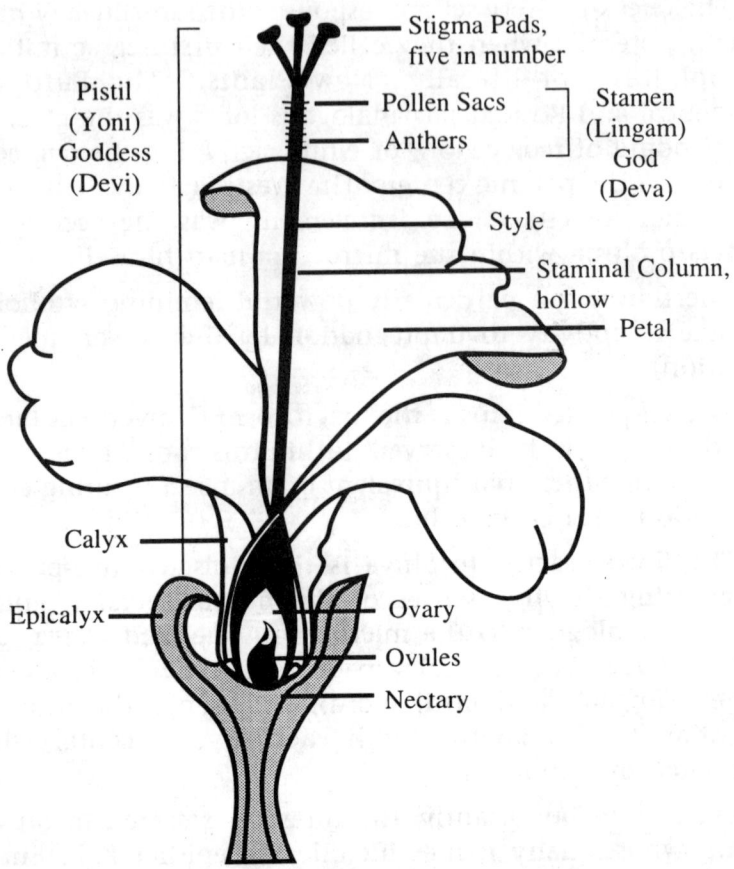

The hibiscus is a genus of plants profuse in warm, temperate regions of the Northern hemisphere. They are known as rose mallows (family: *Malvaceae*) and the hibiscus syriacus is even called "Rose of Sharon." Colors range from yellow to red, purple, and white.

The Laya Yoga teaching of chakras is in reality an abstract 2,500-year-old Eastern theory only recently rediscovered in the West as psychosomatic medicine, and most recently as psycho-neuro-immunology. Located in a psychic body, or considered as a reaction of the pituitary-adrenal axis, the chakra concept is a holistic map reuniting mind and body, in defiance of the Cartesian dualism that has plagued Western science for the last few hundred years.

The chakras are transducers (shunt points) for stepping energy up or down, and Laya Yoga is an ancient "unified field theory" yoking all existence beyond individuality of organisms and matter. At the purest level, we no longer can acknowledge that "I don't mind and you don't matter."

Returning to our definition of a chakra: "A chakra is a whirling vortex of energy at the conjunction point of the mind and the body." Translate this into Western anatomy and physiology and note that the traditional location of each chakra correlates with a major gland, or glands, and a main autonomic nerve plexus within the body. By some coincidence or method of analytical introspection now lost to us, the point where each chakra is located corresponds with the points in the body where psychosomatic illness most commonly manifests.

1. **Muladhara** means "root support," is situated at the base of the spine in the coccygeal region, and is physically manifested through the gonads and the pelvic plexus. Traditionally this chakra controls the sexual functions in humans (a responsibility shared with the next chakra), and therefore is implicated with sexual dysfunctions. Muladhara is said to influence the legs and has a relation to the sense of smell.

2. **Swadhisthana** means "one's own place." All fluids in the body are balanced through this center. Physiologically related to the adrenal glands, kidneys, and hypogastric plexus, Swadhisthana has its root in the first few vertebrae of the sacral region. Classic teaching relates malfunctioning of Swadhisthana to fluid disturbances such as edema, anemia, anuria, polyuria, etc. Sexual fluids, the arms, and the sense of taste are also connected.

3. **Manipura**, or the "gem city" center, emerges from the lumbar region of the spine and is physically evident as the solar plexus. The glands most often connected with Manipura are the pancreas, spleen, and liver. The solar

plexus ("sun center") has often been called the second brain; its importance psychosomatically is readily appreciated by anyone who has ever suffered stomach cramps, "butterflies," etc. The Indians believe that, according to your date of birth, some are more prone to feel emotional tension in this area. The theory is that sustained tension here may elicit anything from ulcers to gallstones. The anus and the eyes are also influenced by Manipura.

4. **Anahata**, the center of "unstruck sound," comes out between the upper thoracic vertebrae and manifests through the cardiac plexus and the thymus gland. Heart problems such as palpitations, tachycardia, up to angina pectoris and even cardiac infarction have been suggested as falling within the domain of Anahata. Secondary factors include any disorders of the lungs. Anahata also encompasses the entire tactile response from the skin and the procreative genital function.

5. **Vishuddha**, or "with purity" center, is the last of the chakras rooted upon the spinal column (cervical or neck vertebra, in this case). The thyroid and parathyroid glands, as well as the pharyngeal plexus and vocal cords, are associated with Vishuddha as physical vehicles. Thyroid over- or underactivity will be accelerated in some people by stress, as well as speech disorders and deafness. (Vishuddha has the ears as a sensory input.)

6. **Ajna**, or the center of "command," is stated to be situated about where the eyebrows cross, if extended, and internally where the pituitary gland rests in the "Turkish saddle." Ajna is the Third or All-seeing Eye and may logically be related to the nasociliary plexus and frontal lobes of the brain. This is interesting when we consider the pituitary gland as the overseer of most of the other

> *The old question/conundrum*
> *"WHAT-IS-MATTER?" "NEVER-MIND!"*
> *"WHAT-IS-MIND?" "NEVER-MATTER!"*
> *has become totally irrelevant.*

ductless glands. It should be stated that the pineal gland is also considered related to this chakra.

7. **Sahasrara** chakra means the "thousand-petaled" center. This is a reference to the thousands upon thousands of brain cells contained within the cerebrum, with which Sahasrara is related. The gland connected with Sahasrara is the pineal—about which we know too little.

It is said that when kundalini rises and unites with Sahasrara, the resulting shock to the nervous system awakens the pineal gland from its dormant state and we find ourselves possessed of *siddhis*, or psychic powers. These siddhis represent dormant sensory faculties within us that have been lost through disuse.

Australian aboriginals, for example, are still capable of appearing to track by smell, much as a dog does. The native senses water in desert areas and generally displays an acute sensitivity to the environment which is lacking in his or her modernized counterpart. The native's siddhis, like those of an animal, have remained active through force of circumstances.

CHAKRA CHART I

Sanskrit	English	Body root	Plexus and gland
Muladhara	Root support	Coccyx	Pelvic plexus Testes and ovaries
Swadhisthana	One's own place	Sacral vert. Navel (below)	Hypogastric plexus Adrenal glands
Manipura	Gem city	Lumbar vert. Navel (above)	Solar plexus Pancreas and liver
Anahata	Unstruck Sound	Thoracic vert. Heart region	Cardiac plexus Thymus gland
Vishuddha	Purity center	Cervical vert. Throat area	Pharyngeal plexus Thyroid gland Parathyroids
Ajna	Command	Nasion Between eyes	Nasociliary plexus Pituitary gland
Sahasrara	1,000-petaled	Bregma Top of head	Cerebrum Pineal gland

At this point I must emphasize that Westerners, over the last hundred years, have launched a momentous rationalization in attempting to correlate the chakras with physical correspondences. This is best exemplified by careless "snap" allocations of the endocrine glands to the padmas. For example, Swadhisthana is aligned with the adrenal glands (more properly in primates, the suprarenal glands). But Swadhisthana is below the navel; if you should have your adrenal glands that low you are in serious trouble and need to consult an endocrinologist!

Yet consider this: the Tantric Yogis matched Swadhisthana with the sensory input of taste (gustation), the element of water (fluid), sexuality, and the moon, and related it intimately to Muladhara chakra (earth, salt—"Salt of the Earth!")

I will vastly oversimplify the suprarenal glands by designating them as the SSSS glands (salt, sex, stress, sugar). Underactivity of the suprarenals (Addison's disease) produces taste hyperacuity and inadequate reabsorption of water and salt (specifically sodium). Alternatively, overactivity of the suprarenal cortex (Cushing's disease) results in "moon face," excessive reabsorption of water and salt (sodium), diminished taste sensitivity, and excessive production of androgens (sex hormones).

Comparing the chakras with the endocrine glands is strictly an Occidental habit of logical materialism and popular copycat convenience—few people, Eastern or Western, are capable of any real thinking or originality. All endocrine correlations with the chakras should be approached from a physiological, functional stance and never from an anatomical, structural stance. Further evidence of the subtle, intuitive genius displayed by the Hindu sages may be found in "A Tantric Synoptic Commentary on the Shat Chakras" in my book *Ecstasy Through Tantra*.

I have by no means exhausted the material available on the theory of Laya Yoga, but have been concerned with only what is pertinent to the purpose of this book. Above all, I have concentrated upon rationalizing all such theory into a more or less acceptable form.

Regarding the theory as a whole, the reader will readily discern two points:

1. The theory may be taken as an allegory of the ascent and transmutation of human consciousness into divine consciousness.
2. This ancient theory contains material which has an undeniable implication for and relationship with the hypothesis of modern psychosomatic medicine.

A TRANSCULTURAL ALCHEMICAL ALLEGORY

At the base of the spinal cord (Sushumna) is the conus medullaris: an inverted witch's hat containing a cone of astral power. Here sleeps Shakti (Sleeping Beauty) awaiting Shiva (Prince Charming). Shiva's kiss of consciousness can release her from trance, allowing them to ascend into the medulla oblongata ("oblong cube" or Mason's "Ashlar"). They consummate within the cranial nuptial chamber, termed by anatomists "thalamus" (Greek for "bed chamber").

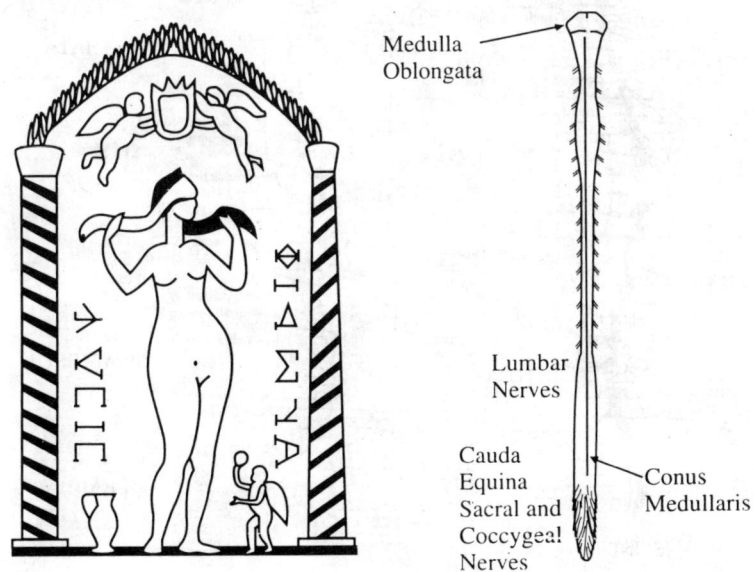

Shakti is a widow (Isis); a virgin (Snow White—served by the seven chakras, "dwarfed" in the unawakened).

She is the bride Cinderella (i.e., "Lady of the Cinders") whose latent alchemical fire is tended at the fireplace (kanda), ever ready to ignite as kundalini blazing up the chimney (Sushumna).

She is the lady of the lake, constantly bathing her hair (cauda equina) in a cistern of alchemical water (cerebrospinal fluid), and one day she will thrust up Excalibur to be received by Arthur. This is both a reference to the ancient Vedic horse sacrifice and the secret contractions of the Yogi.

THE CHAKRAS AND THE BODY ZONES

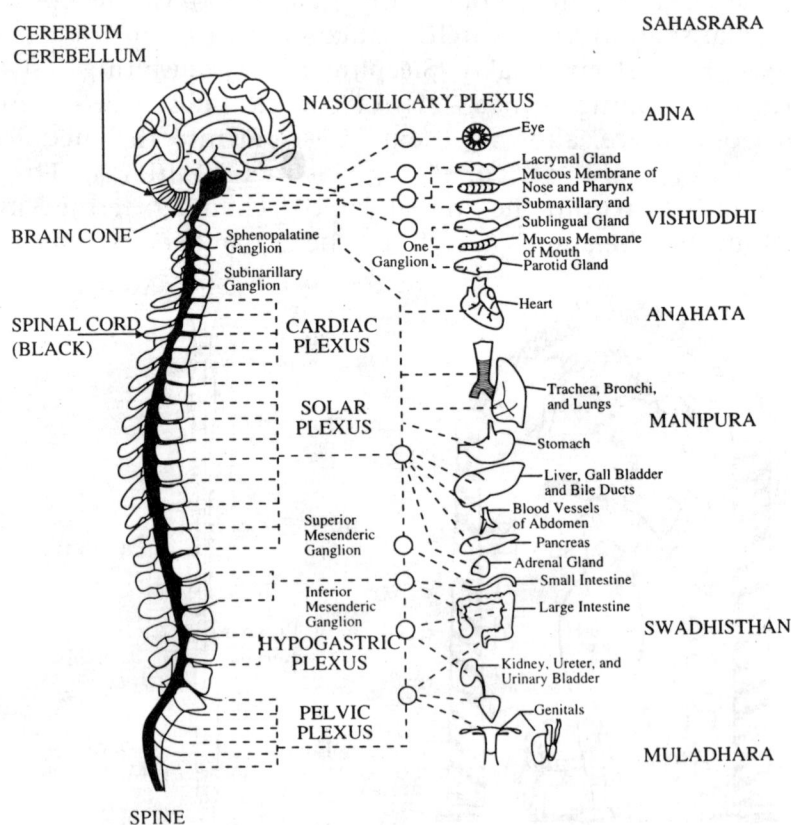

LOCATION OF ORGANS AND GLANDS

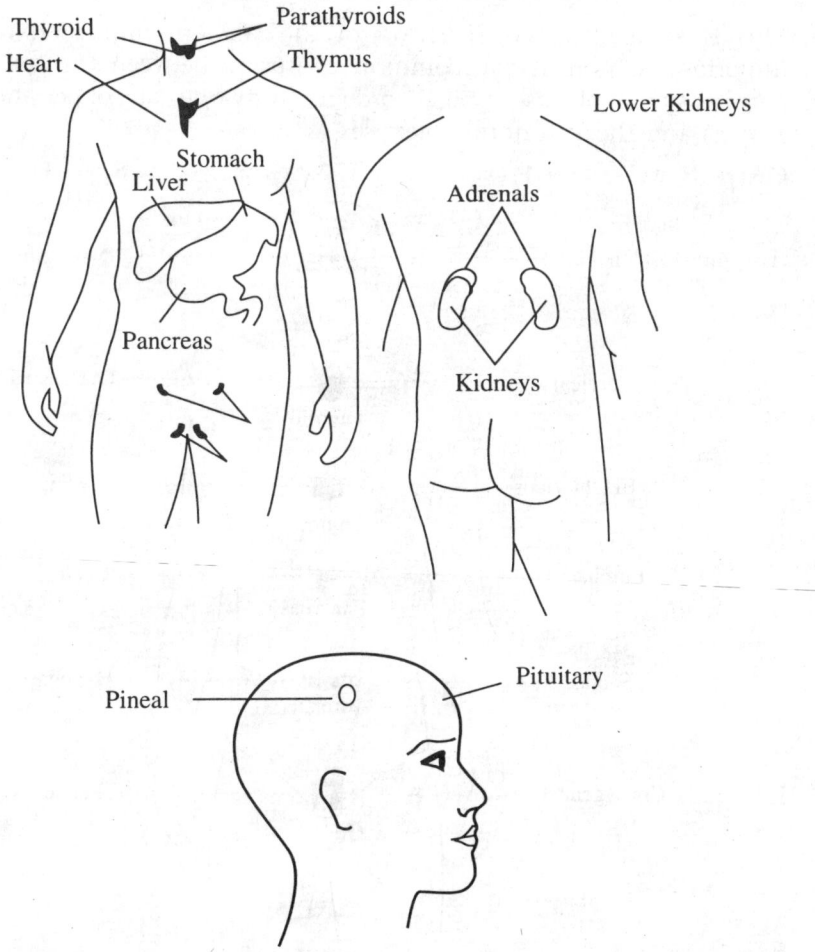

Shakti is not only a widow, a virgin, and a bride but also a wife, mother, and divorcee: humankind has forgotten the Athanor within the sacred sacrum foundation of the body temple. This microcosmic furnace extracts gold from sulphur, silver from mercury, unites (yokes) the sun and the moon, the red rose and white rose, distills the tincture from the principles, the quintessence from the elements, and gently heats the "Philosophers Egg" within the alembic of the skull, ultimately manifesting the Lapis Philosophorum.

CORRELATIVE NEUROANATOMY OF THE CHAKRAS

This is an artifical construction of the Western mind. What is important to note is the common confusion between the central nervous system plexuses (spinal cord and thirty-one pairs of peripheral nerves) and the autonomic plexuses.

Central Nervous System Plexuses*		Autonomic Nervous System Plexuses
Trigeminal Ophthalmic (cranial nerve V)		Naso-ciliary
Cervical	Thyroid	Pharyngeal
Brachial	Thymus	Cardiac
Lumbar**	Pancreas	Coeliac
Sacral**	Adrenals	Hypogastric
Coccygeal**	Gonads	Pelvic

---

*Formed from anterior rami, peripheral nerves of the spine.

†The trigeminal nerve ("Three Twins") reflexes from the mouth to the frontalis muscle of the forehead: consequently a very cold substance ingested into the mouth (e.g., ice cream) may produce a reflex pain between the eyes (Ajna chakra). Swami Gitananda always suggested marking the site of the pain, indicating each individual's trigger point for Ajna.

**Lumbar, sacral, and coccygeal plexuses are subdivisions of lumbo-sacral plexus.

ORGAN EQUIVALENT CHAKRA CHART WITH ALTERNATIVE CHAKRA NAMES

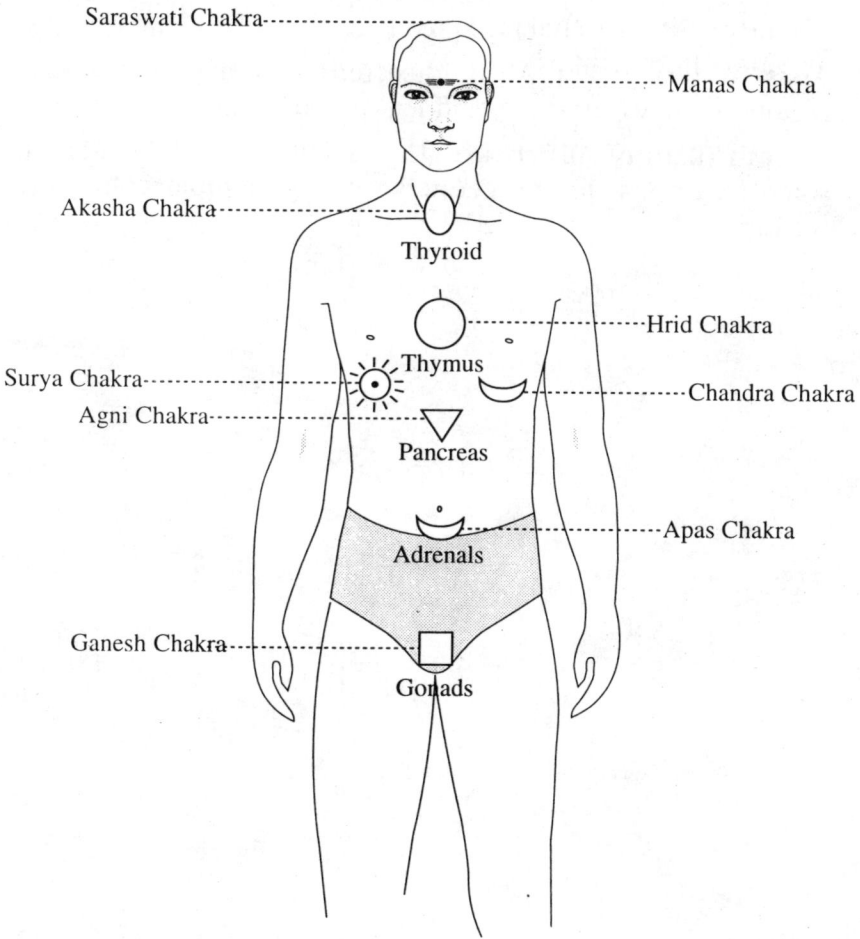

Saraswati (Goddess of Wisdom) chakra: Cerebral cortex, sensory and motor strips, frontal lobes.

Manas (Mind) chakra: Optic chiasma and visual cortex.

Akasha (Void) chakra: Larynx.

Hrid ("Heart" as the English "hearth" derivative) chakra: heart and lungs.

Agni ("Fire god;" English derivative "ignite") chakra: Pancreas and stomach.

Surya (Sun) chakra: Liver and gall bladder.

Chandra (Moon) chakra: Spleen.

Apas (Water) chakra: All fluid secretions of abdominal-pelvic region (kidneys, ureters, bladder, and urethra).

Ganesh (Lord of All) chakra: The "Elephant God," related, in some traditions, to the genitals, uterus, sigmoid colon, and rectum.

Chapter Eight

Chakra-Dharana: Focusing Psychic Power

We may say that a Yantra is an instrument, designed to curb the psychic forces by concentrating them in a pattern, and is such a way that this pattern becomes reproduced by the worshipers visualizing power.

— Heinrich Zimmer, Ph.D., Indologist

Humankind has always been aware of the existence of certain vital areas in the human body. The use to which the esoteric knowledge of these nerve zones was put varied from civilization to civilization.

The work we are embarking upon relates to the shat-chakras, or six centers. Be aware that doing visual Yantra and color awareness classically involves the five primal elements:

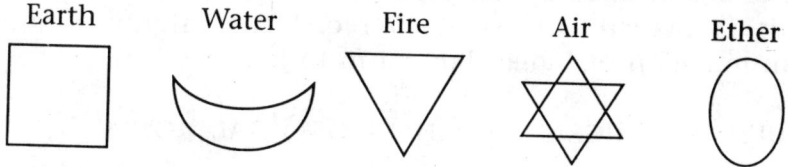

Earth   Water   Fire   Air   Ether

Or, as represented in Western alchemy:

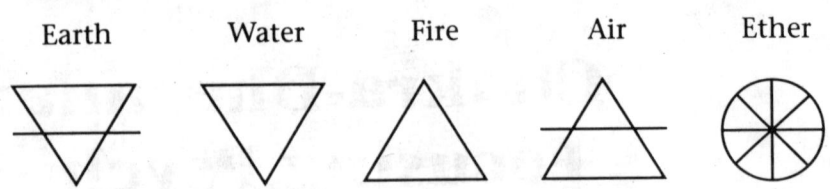

Hence, the exercises are *panch* chakra (five centers) only. Ajna and Sahasrara open automatically when the first five centers are stimulated. However, we will deal with the sixth center, Ajna, in Chapter 13, and answer your inevitable questions about the seventh, Sahasrara, in that chapter as well.

The student will be interested to note that a correlation exists between the chakras of the Indian Yogi and the *kyushos* of the Japanese Judo expert. The seven most deadly kyushos (jiu-jitsu pressure points) taught in *Atemiwaza,* one of the esoteric branches of Judo, exactly correspond with the traditional positions of the seven chakras. While the Indian mind used this knowledge for spiritual and psychic purposes, the Japanese mind used the same knowledge for concrete physical purposes, namely, the induction of unconsciousness or even death (Atemiwaza) and the revival of those who had been so disabled *(kwappo).*

There is evidence to indicate that the martial arts originated in India, and were taken up by the Tibetan monks as a means of self-defense (their religious vocation forbade the carrying of arms) and spread from Tibet to China, where they were picked up and developed by the Japanese in the fifteenth century. This is plausible if we also recall the migration and transmutation of Indian Buddhism to Japanese Zen.

CULTURAL MIGRATION CHART OF VITAL ZONES

Race	Major Emphasis	Occupation
Indo-Aryan	Meditation	Priests/Yogis
Chinese	Acupuncture healing points	Physicians
Japanese	Martial arts striking points	Soldiers

Note: This chart only denotes a trend, as each race also had meditation, acupuncture, and martial arts utilization of vital zones.

If you are in doubt about the existence of an ancient Indian martial art, then I must inform you that it is a living tradition in South India today. Not only does this art exist, but ear acupuncture and control of the elephant through 90 vital points has been an established Indian medical science and everyday practice by the *Mahout* (the elephant driver) for 2500 years.

MARMA POINTS OF AN ELEPHANT

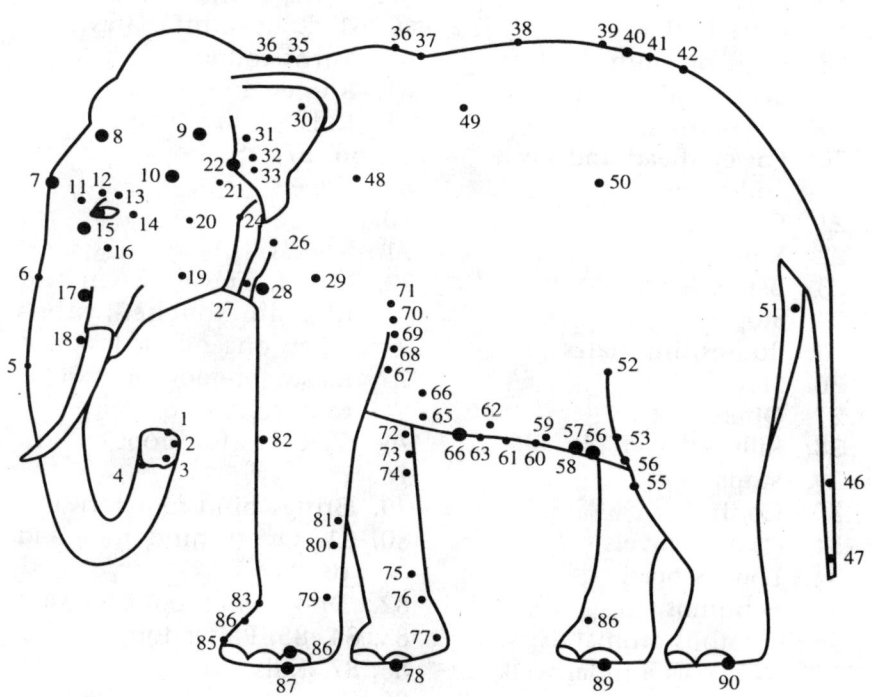

(Courtesy of L. S. P. S. S. Publications, Madras, South India, from *Marma Chikitsa in Traditional Medicine.*)

Specific Functions of the Elephant's Marma Points

1. Twists trunk
2. Straightens trunk
3. Frightens
4. Frightens and makes trumpet
5. Frightens and makes animal trumpet and stop
6. Controls
7, 8, 9, 10. Kills
11, 12. Controls
13. Rouses
14. Controls
15. Kills
16. Kneels
17. Goes backwards
18. Controls animal while being tied to a tree
19. Gives his shoulder
20. Lowers head and neck and stops
21. Controls
22. Kills
23. Bends head
24. Stops
25. Rouses, infuriates
26. Stops
27. Offers seat
28. Kills
29. Stops
30. Controls
31, 32, 33. Travels
34. Lowers head
35. Benumbs
36, 37. Stops animal as well as makes animal walk
38. Lowers seat
39, 40, 41. Frightens
42. ?
43, 44, 45. Walks
46. Stops
47. Travels
48. Stops animal, and makes it walk
49. Offers seat
50. Stops without fidgeting and puts trunk to ground
51. ?
52. Gets up and runs
53, 54, 55. Turns round
56, 57. Kills
58. Drops to ground
59. Turns round
60, 61. Rouses, infuriates
62. Turns round
63. Rouses, infuriates
64. Kills
65, 66, 67, 68. Stops
69. Kneels
70. ?
71. Kneels
72, 73, 74. Travels when two nila are touched; stops when one nila is touched
75. Raises forefoot for mahout to mount
76, 77. Gives fore foot
78. ?
79. Brings hind foot forward
80, 81. Offers hind foot and twists
82. Draws hind foot backward
83, 84, 85. Raises forefoot
86, 87. Kills
88. ?
89, 90. Kills

In February 1993, I returned to Pondicherry, South India, after twenty-two years to see my beloved mentor, Dr. Swami Gitananda. He was sponsoring a Yoga World Earth Summit and I was one of the keynote speakers.

There I met a South Indian martial artist, and later, back in Madras, he shared some information with me. The fighting arts, taught even today, are known as *Marma* or *Varami (Varma AsSaan)*. In the villages, knowledge of these zones is used for healing and has been passed down, parent to child, and provides the backbone of an indigenous rural healing system.

South Indian ancient palm leaf manuscripts, proudly possessed by masters of various South Indian martial schools, often have a picture of Laotzu engraved on the front—an indication that the art, perhaps, was transferred to China several hundred years BC, and then migrated back to India with the addition of some Chinese innovations.

The remarkable concentration I saw exhibited by practitioners of Varami in focusing energy into a single blow upon a vital zone involves simultaneously:

1. Visualizing a Deva or Devi (god or goddess) sitting within the opponent's vital zone.
2. An invocation (mantra) to the god or goddess, invoking their power.
3. Contacting the zone on the opponent's body with an awareness of prana *(Chi* or *Ki)* exploding there.
4. The split-second withdrawal of the fist, elbow, knee, or foot striking the surface, leaving the shock waves, psychic and physical, to cause havoc.

As a final comment, my first serious introduction to Varmannie was in New York, 1965, where I had gone to see the World Fair. I met Swami Vyragiananda and the following quotation from the news story by Sidney Fields in *The New York Mirror*, September 10, 1959, will indicate just how early Varmannie migrated to North America—admittedly only taught as a recondite art.

SWAMI FLIPS TOPS WITH VARMANNIE

Only Human
By Sidney Fields

The little man over in the Broadway studio who calls himself Swami Vyragiananda says that trying to compare Varmannie to Ju-jitsu is like comparing bird watching to the medieval torture rack.

Courteously, but with doubt, I said, "Show me the difference." The Swami is only five feet, two-and-a-half inches tall, weighs 140 pounds, and is 69 years old. He led me to the mat, and recalled that once, while demonstrating the art of Varmannie at a doctors' convention, one doubting physician used a sudden Ju-jitsu hold to floor him and sat triumphantly on his chest. "I gave him the warning he didn't give me," the Swami said. "I asked him: 'Are you ready?' and when he was, he flew off my chest in a second. Come on, I will show you how." He let me get a double wrist lock on him, force him to the mat, and sit on his chest, still holding the wrist lock. "Are you ready?" he asked. I nodded. He just pressed against my elbow. I flew off his chest, and my arm felt like it was leaving my shoulder. "If you wish to enjoy a happy confidence in life you must learn to defend yourself," the Swami said, helping me to my feet, while I rubbed my arm and shoulder. "With such confidence you can use all your mental power to enjoy life and not waste it with unnecessary fear and worry."

He offered to demonstrate a few Varmannie holds: Serpent Clinging, Arm Saw Cut in Belt, the Elephant Grab, or the Breath Plugger. I took the last one with the understanding he wouldn't plug the breath off completely. He agreed graciously, allowed me to put a tight hammerlock on him from the rear. Up went his rump, jarring me, and up went his fingers deep under my chin and deeper into my throat.

"Uncle?" he asked.

"Uncle," I wheezed. He led me to a chair.

"In Varmannie," he soothed, "we use the enemy's strength and weight to disable him. The simple way you can apply Varmannie

VARMA POINTS FRONT OF BODY

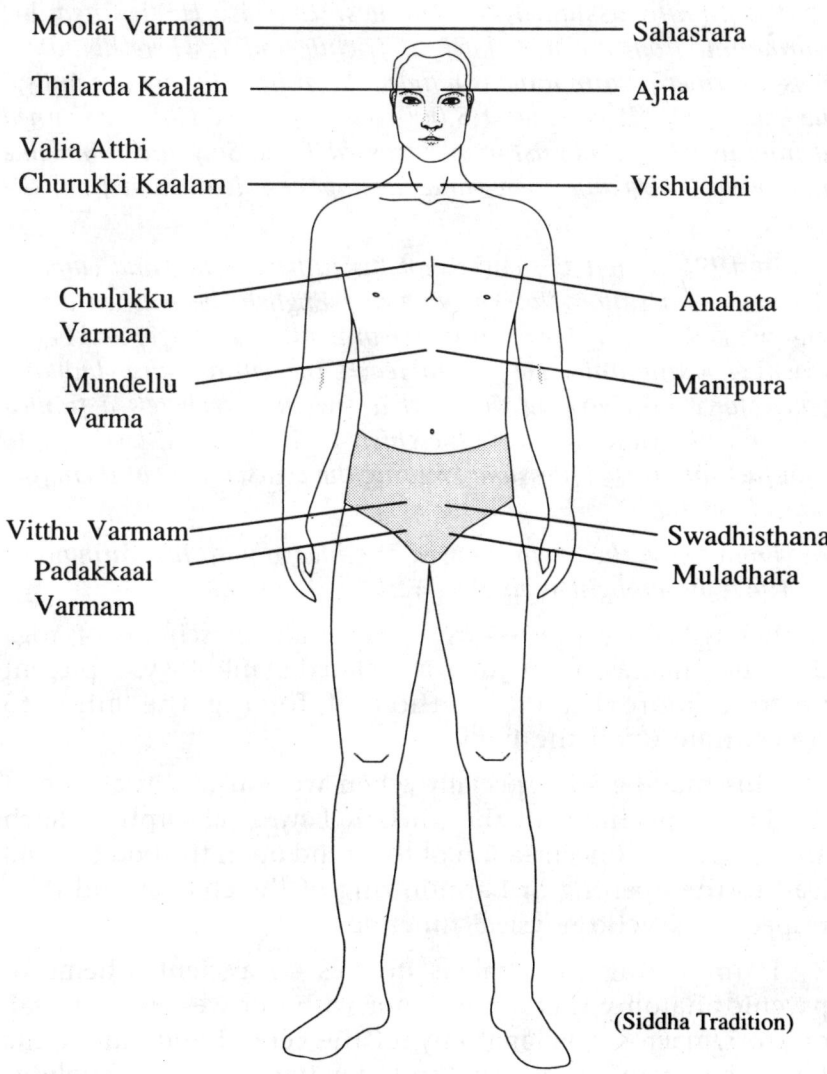

Japanese Judo Atemiwaza Striking Points — Yoga Chakras

- Moolai Varmam — Sahasrara
- Thilarda Kaalam — Ajna
- Valia Atthi Churukki Kaalam — Vishuddhi
- Chulukku Varman — Anahata
- Mundellu Varma — Manipura
- Vitthu Varmam — Swadhisthana
- Padakkaal Varmam — Muladhara

(Siddha Tradition)

is the nice part. I would like to show you now the Skull Cracker Throw."

"Let's talk for a while," I countered.

Swami means teacher, and Vyragianand is "joy of determination" or "drunk with spirituality," and he admits humbly that both are assumed—the names, that is. He learned his Varmannie from an uncle back in Trichur, India, where his father was a farmer. "Varmannie is handed down from family to family," he explained. "It is at least 5,000 years old. The Chinese learned it from us when Buddhist monks crossed Tibet. So you can imagine how weak it became there, and the Japanese learned it from the Chinese."

In 1921 he left the poverty of his father's farm, and came to America as a sailor. Not knowing any English, he washed dishes and worked with a shovel until he learned the language, and began teaching Varmannie. He got to teach the entire Gary, Indiana, police force by throwing the chief a few times. There's a framed letter on his wall, signed by the chief, L. T. Studness, testifying to that fact and this confession: "During the course, none of them [the police] got hurt."

From Gary, the Swami moved to Chicago with his Varmannie; in 1941, he brought it to New York.

It has been suggested by several modern schools of Yoga that the chakras, with their associated symbology, represent nothing more than a method of forcing the mind to concentrate upon the body.

This may be so, especially when we consider that one of the literal meanings of the Sanskrit *Laya* is absorption. Such absorption, or concentration of the mind upon the body, would lead to the opening or harmonizing of the chakras and their respective psycho-physical functions.

Harmonizing the chakras implies an ancient scheme of psychic anatomy that corresponds with our western physical, or gross/macroscopic anatomy, of the central and autonomic nervous systems. Consider the following correlative analysis.

CHAKRA DHARANA COMPARISON CHART

Japanese Judo Atemiwaza Striking Points   Yoga Chakras

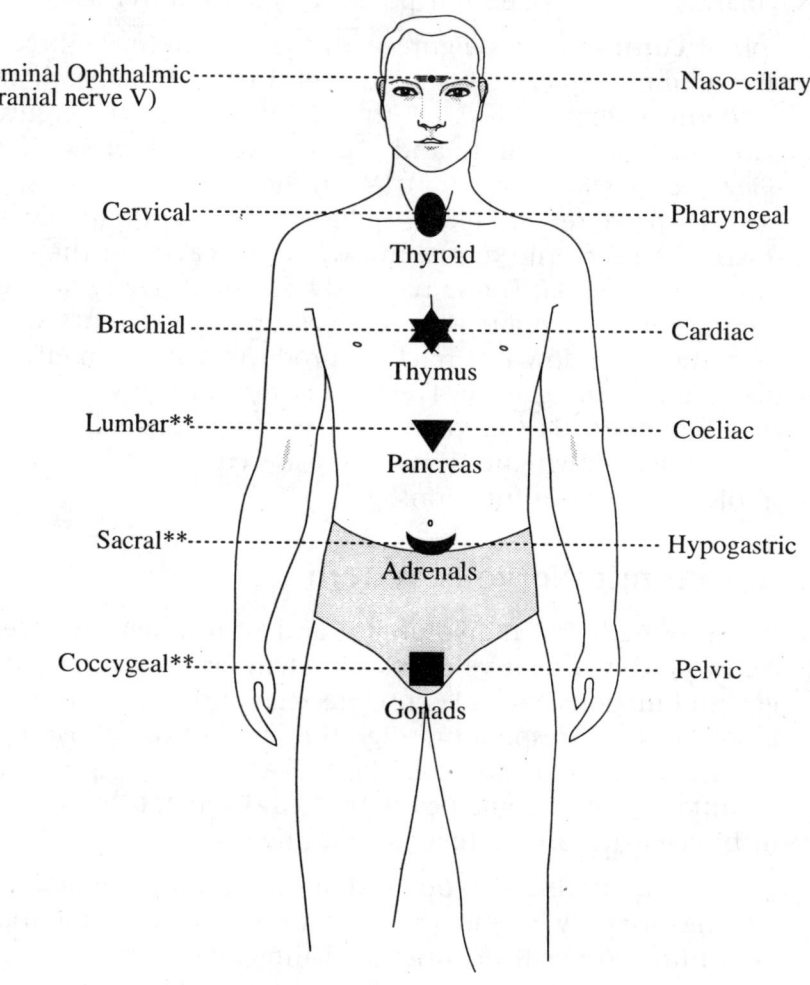

Central Nervous System

Divided into brain and spinal cord.

Brain: Cerebrum and cerebellum. A midline sagittal slice resembles the fetus, symbol of latent growth, the neophyte, or Sahasrara padma—i.e., full potential yet to be released.

Spinal cord: Averages eighteen inches in length. Eighteen is the Hindu number of completeness. In the *Mahabharata* we note the eighteen days of the Great Battle, the eighteen battalions that fought, and the eighteen chapters of the *Bhagavadgita* ("Song of God"). When the spinal cord is dissected out of the vertebral column, along with the brain cone, it resembles a serpent (kundalini), while the cavity of the spinal canal is Sushumna. The spinal cord transmits sensory (afferent) messages to the brain and receives motor (efferent) signals from the brain down its tracts to produce changes in effectors (i.e., muscles and glands). The sensory nerve tracts of the spinal cord represent Ida (receptive, passive) functions while motor nerve tracts down the spinal cord are equivalent to Pingala (projective, active) functions.

Autonomic Nervous System

It was formerly called involuntary, and even earlier (nineteenth century), the vegetative nervous system, as it was thought to govern functions beyond conscious regulation—e.g., heart rate, blood pressure, respiration, digestive functions, etc. However, by the 1970s Elmer Green, Ph.D., was able to prove that voluntary control could be established through a combination of biofeedback and autogenic training.

The autonomic nervous system divides into two sections which constantly interact with each other, either for dominance (according to need) or functional integration.

Sympathetic branch: Left and right chains of ganglion, tethered to the spinal cord but running down each side of the anterior bodies of the vertebral column, and averaging twenty-two ganglion a piece, spread out from the coccyx up to the cervical vertebrae. This symmetry is reminiscent of Ida and

Pingala with Sushumna, the spinal canal, as the "Middle Pillar" of Western magical practice. The twenty-two ganglion represent the number of the Avatar, or coming savior in Hinduism, and in Western occult anatomy the twenty-two ganglion correspond to the twenty-two paths on the Qabalistic Tree of Life, twenty-two letters of the Hebrew Alphabet, twenty-two bones of the skull (used as a "communion cup" as in the Nordic Skoal), and the twenty-two cards of the Major Arcana in the Tarot. Functionally the sympathetic nerves most often act as an accelerator, producing Pingala reactions, an extreme example being the so called "fear, fight, flight" syndrome.

Parasympathetic branch: The major section comprises a pair of vagus (in English, "vagrant") nerves, which emerge from the base of the skull to wander down the neck, through the chest, and deep into the abdominal cavity. Again remember the symbolic twins: Boaz and Jachin, Ida and Pingala. Parasympathetic branch fibers constantly meet with sympathetic branch fibers to form plexuses, the major ones on the physical plane representing the materialization of the non-physical chakras. Functionally the parasympathetic nerves most often perform braking actions; I call them the "rest, relaxation, recuperation" fibers, and hence they may be allied to Ida reactions.

Now examine, on the following page, the anatomy chart we first presented in Chapter 7.

A few simple examples may help us relate to the autonomic nervous system in a meaningful way.

Organ or system	Sympathetic Action	Parasympathetic Action
Pupils of eyes	DILATE: Better to see with if interested or frightened.	CONSTRICTS: No threat, so every photon of light not necessary.
Heart rate	INCREASED: Tachycardia. If frightened or anxious, more oxygen and glucose pumped around faster.	SLOWED: Bradycardia. Safe to relax and rest.

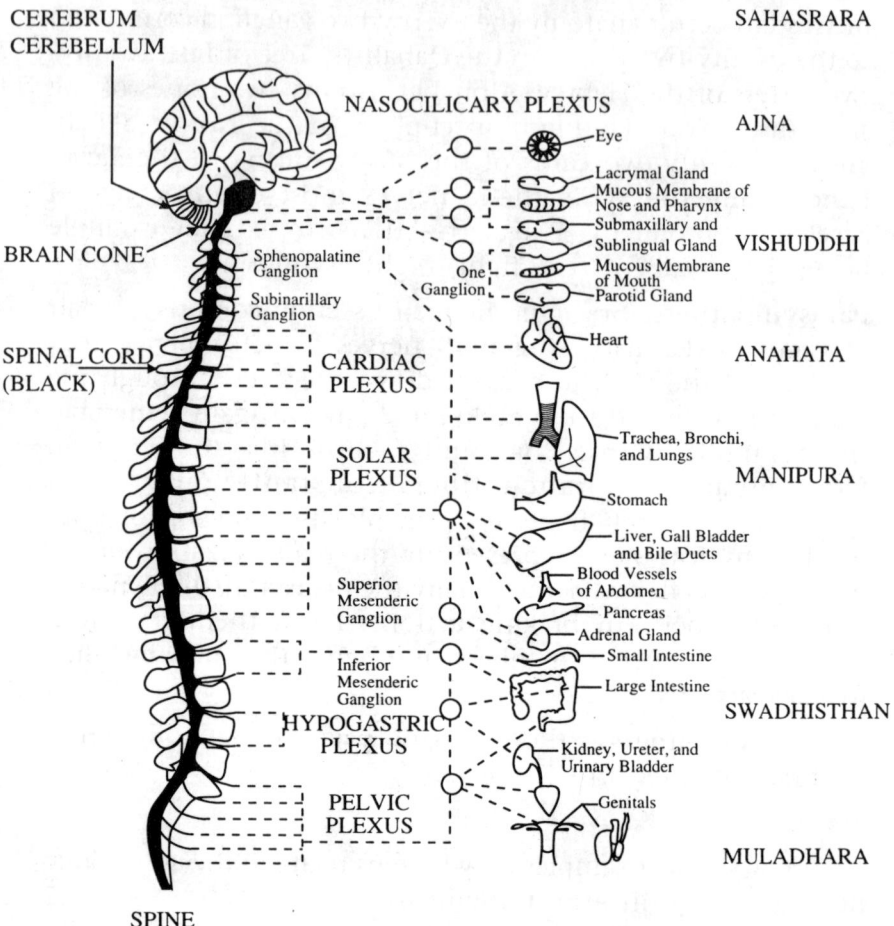

Hand temperature	COLD: principle of "Brain sparing." Blood is withdrawn from extremities and saved for the heart and brain.	WARMED: Vanishes cold hands. Many types of meditation do this.
Sleep	HYPER-ALERTNESS: anxiety, insomnia.	Deep sleep comes easily.

MALE SEXUAL FUNCTION

Erection	Inhibits if nervous, as arteriole blood supply constricted to penis.	Allows full erection.
Ejaculation	Sympathetic arousal at right level is necessary for ejaculation.	Inhibits ejaculation.

FEMALE SEXUAL FUNCTION

Vaginal lubrication	Inhibits	Promotes
Nipple tumescence	Inhibits	Promotes
Clitoral tumescence	Inhibits	Promotes

Note: Overarousal of the sympathetic may lead to premature ejaculation and also ejaculation without erection.

The above examples demonstrate a delicate "union," or Yoga, that must occur between the sympathetic and parasympathetic branches of the autonomic nervous system. In the sexual example, we could express it in Laya Yoga terms and say that a fine balance is necessary between Muladhara and Swadhisthana, and between the God and Goddess cohabiting within each chakra.

The discussion of the nervous system has been vastly oversimplified but it can form a solid physical matrix to build a much more subtle base for inner concentration. Someone once defined Laya Yoga as autonomic nervous system gymnastics.

Indeed, more specifically, we could define most meditation as parasympathetic gymnastics. Examining the above sympathetic-parasympathetic action chart, it will become apparent why Dr. Swami Gitananda will not commence EEG or ECG readings in male subjects until their nipples are erect.

Examine the chart below. Some parasympathetic branches have been placed on the left and sympathetic on the right. Realize they constantly intertwine; this device allows us to perceive their delicacy a little more easily. On an etheric plane the ramifications are even more intricate, but regardless, we can learn to control the physical more easily by focusing upon the chakras.

SCHEMATIC DIAGRAM OF PARASYMPATHETIC AND SYMPATHETIC NERVOUS SYSTEMS

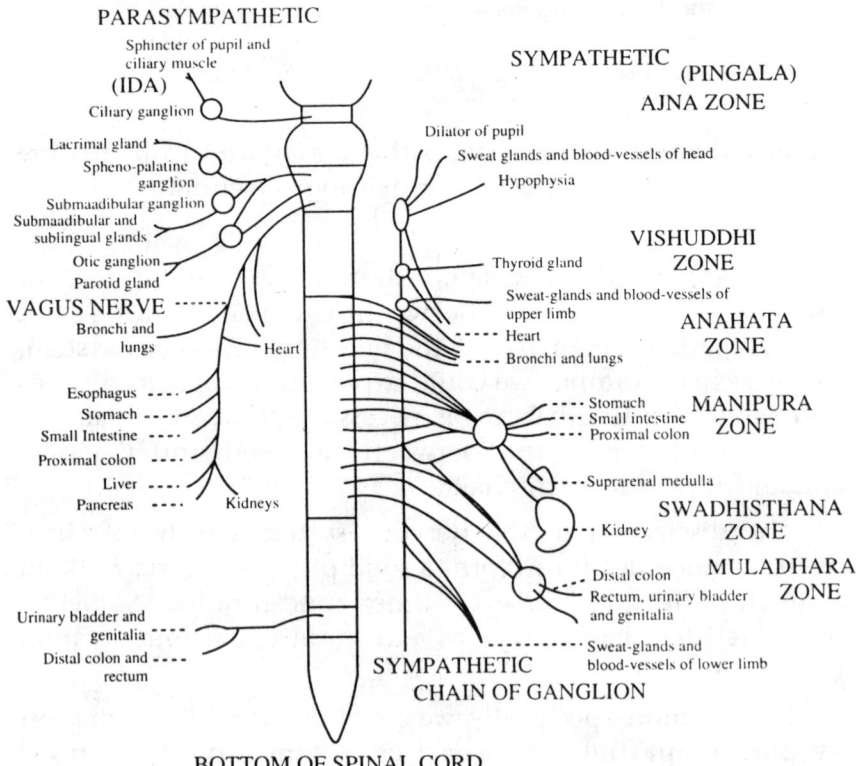

INTRODUCTION TO CHAKRA DHARANA

Yoga postulates that the focus of psychic power may be developed through concentration (Dharana) upon the chakra zones. The result is dispersion of psychosomatic tension that so often occurs at one or more of these vital zones.

An analogous situation is autogenic training, developed in the early part of the twentieth century when the German psychiatrist Dr. Johannes H. Schultz amalgamated Yoga methodology with a then current European fascination—hypnosis. For example, concentrating upon the hands, visualizing them flushing red with blood, and telling yourself they are getting warm will actually raise the hand temperature by as much as ten degrees Fahrenheit, depending on your starting point.

This type of autogenic training is a form of "Western Yoga" and works exactly the same way as most meditation methods. The sympathetic nervous system is dampened, allowing the peripheral arterioles to dilate and flood the extremities with blood. By now you will have empirically discovered that successful meditation is always accompanied by an end result of warm hands and feet.

In the initial stages, the mind is best trained by giving it something concrete upon which to concentrate. This is the purpose of the elaborate symbology. Each chakra has a certain number of petals, and each petal is inscribed with a letter of the Sanskrit alphabet (this is for awakening the chakra through Mantra Yoga), an animal, a god and goddess, a geometric form, a color, and a *Bija*, or seed, mantra.

All that will be necessary, for our purposes, will be a knowledge of the last three symbolic components: color, form, and Bija mantra. Students who wish to learn the full symbolic implications of each chakra are encouraged to peruse Arthur Avalon's classic study of Tantra, *The Serpent Power*.

The form and color of the first five chakras represent the Tattwa, or element, assigned to each. The Bija mantra is a basic sound which groups or awakens the dormant energy of the individual chakra.

A special comment about the sound vibrations or Bija mantras is required. Learning Yoga from a book can be a delicate matter; in fact, Indians are quite sarcastic about it, and refer to many self-styled Western "experts" as "Kitab (book) Yogis." In a market inundated with Yoga books written by people who have not trained in India and have no knowledge of Sanskrit pronunciation, errors can occur in the intonation of sounds. I was myself guilty, in early editions of *Psychosomatic Yoga,* of neglecting to clarify the pronunciation of the Bija mantras, and since an integral part of this approach involves very specific vibratory patterns during the intoning of the mantras, I have to address this issue now.

The five primary Bija sounds we are concerned with are, to be simplistic, consonants. In Sanskrit every consonant has an inherent "a" vowel. The five consonants are:

L V R Y H

Or, when transliterated with the inherent vowel:

La Va Ra Ya Ha

It looks straight-forward enough; however, there are two forms of "a" in Sanskrit—one short and one long—and without getting complicated, suffice it to say that neither "a" in Sanskrit sounds like the English "a" as in "apple." Without trying to be a Sanskrit pundit (which I am not!), or merely pedantic, the vibration we are after more closely approximates the "a" as in the English "father" or the "u" in "up."

Irrelevant? Consider the following: When we chant or silently vibrate these Bijas, each consonant now correctly ends with either a "NG" (nasal-palatal) sound, or an "M" (labial) sound. This is called the *Anuswara* (literally "little heaven"), and heaven, after all, is a state of mind! Chanting aloud we attach the "NG" sound, and meditating mentally we attach the "M" sound. Since the whole Bija acts as a fish-hook for the unconscious mind, we want to be careful of English associational words.

For instance, assume the "a" has the value of English "a" as in "apple," and we are mentally repeating the Bijas with an "M" ending:

LaM — The message might be construed, by the unconscious mind, as instruction to flee or hide as in "go on the lam," or perhaps you may develop a problem with sheep.

VaM — Straight into vamping or maybe vampires? Note: "v" in Sanskrit sometimes sounds like "w," but with the Bija it is "v" as in "Victor."

RaM — Be careful you don't starting bashing into things, or attract a frisky male goat.

YaM — Perhaps a strange urge will emerge: to dig obsessively in the earth for a root vegetable.

HaM — Meditations may be disturbed by uncontrollable visions of smoked pork.

We will now replace the inherent "a" of each Bija with an "u" as in the English "up" ("yuppie," "rut"). I am only employing an artificial device which will get us within the correct intonation range. Therefore, we have:

LuNG — Audible chant as in English "lung."
LuM — Mental repetition as in English "lumbar."

VuNG — Audible chant as in English "vulcan."
VuM — Mental repetition as in English "come."

RuNG — Audible chant as in English "rung."
RuM — Mental repetition as in English "rummage."

YuNG — Audible chant as in English "young."
YuM — Mental repetition as in English "yummy."

HuNG — Audible chant as in English "Hungarian."
HuM — Mental repetition as in English "humming."

There exists a consensus of opinion amongst scholars that Sanskrit is a perfect language, having an exact representation for nearly every possible intonation. This device of using "u" with the Bijas is a practical scheme I have devised to avoid technicalities. The "u" is a connective bridge between the consonants and the Anuswara "NG" and "M." Almost no accent should be placed on the "u," and in fact, if you imagined it there, we could safely write:

| LNG | VNG | RNG | YNG | HNG |
| LM | VM | RM | YM | HM |

Symbology of the Chakras

Muladhara: A yellow square representing Prithivi, the Earth Element. The Bija mantra is "LuNG" (audible) and "LuM" (inaudible).

Swadhisthana: A silver crescent moon representing Apas, the Water Element. The Bija mantra is "VuNG" (audible) and "VuM" (inaudible).

Manipura: A red triangle, apex down, representing Tejas, the Fire Element. The Bija mantra is "RuNG" (audible) and "RuM" (inaudible).

Anahata: A blue hexagram composed of two interlocked equilateral triangles representing Vayu, the Air Element. The Bija mantra is "YuNG" (audible) and "YuM" (inaudible).

Vishuddha: A black or dark indigo oval egg representing Akasha, the Ether (sometimes called Spirit) Element. The Bija mantra is "HuNG" (audible) and "HuM" (inaudible).

The procedure of Chakra Dharana is based upon a form of concentration known as *Saguna* meditation, or meditation upon concrete qualities as expressed through color *(raga)*, form *(rupa)*, name *(nama)*, geometric shape *(yantra)*, and vibration *(mantra)*.

Chakra Dharana divides into two phases: External Chakra Dharana and Internal Chakra Dharana. External Chakra Dharana is an open-eyed Saguna two-dimensional meditation, while Internal Chakra Dharana is a closed-eyed Saguna three-dimensional meditation. Focus is upon color, geometric shape, mantra, and ultimately upon the physical space within the body.

Chakra Chart

Chakra	Two-dimensional geometric form	Color	Body space
Muladhara	Square	Yellow	Gonads, pelvic floor
Swadhisthana	Crescent moon	Silver	Between pubic bone and navel
Manipura	Triangle, apex down	Red	Between navel and breast bone tip (sternum)
Anahata	Hexagram	Blue	Behind breast bone, roughly on a line between the nipples
Vishuddha	Oval (egg)	Black	Inside "voice box" (thyroid cartilage, "Adam's apple")

Specific Advantages of Chakra Dharana

1. Concentration and visualization are improved.
2. Eastern occult theory states that this technique of concentration is one of the safest and most natural ways of gently awakening and harmonizing the psychic centers.
3. Relaxation of psychosomatic tension, in any specific chakra body space, develops by focusing upon that chakra within its area.
4. Traditional psychological characteristics are encouraged by meditating upon chakra areas with the appropriate color, sound, and shape.

Psychological Attributes of the Chakras

Chakra	Three-dimensional geometric form	Psychological attributes
Muladhara	Cube	Solidarity, cohesiveness, integration
Swadhisthana	Crescent (like a melon slice)	Diplomacy, flexibility, equanimity
Manipura	Tetrahedron, inverted	Power, passion, energy, motivation
Anahata	Hexagram	Compassion, tolerance, understanding
Vishuddha	Egg	Empathy, communication, freedom

The list of psychological characteristics as chakra attributes is not a sophisticated summary, but only intended as a guide to possibilities.

PREPARATION FOR EXTERNAL CHAKRA DHARANA

Reference to the diagram on the following page will provide a clear picture of the symbolic representation of each chakra through its Tattwa, or quality. To produce models for these yantras suitable for use, the student will require a selection of yellow, silver, red, blue, and black drawing paper such as is commonly given to children for cutting and pasting.

With a ruler and compass, construct each geometric figure upon the correct color of paper: the square is inscribed upon yellow, the crescent upon silver, the triangle (apex down) upon red, the hexagon upon blue, and the oval upon black. It is now a simple procedure to cut out each pattern and paste it on the center of a larger square of black paper (with the exception of the black oval, which needs a white background). The final result is a set of five Tattwa yantras which may be affixed to the wall for the technique of External Chakra

Dharana. Alternatively, the student may find it advantageous to mount each Tattwa yantra on a cardboard backing for durability and ease of handling. It is then easy to stand the Tattwa yantra card selected against any stable object on a table or desk top for the Dharana exercise.

CHAKRA TATTWA YANTRAS

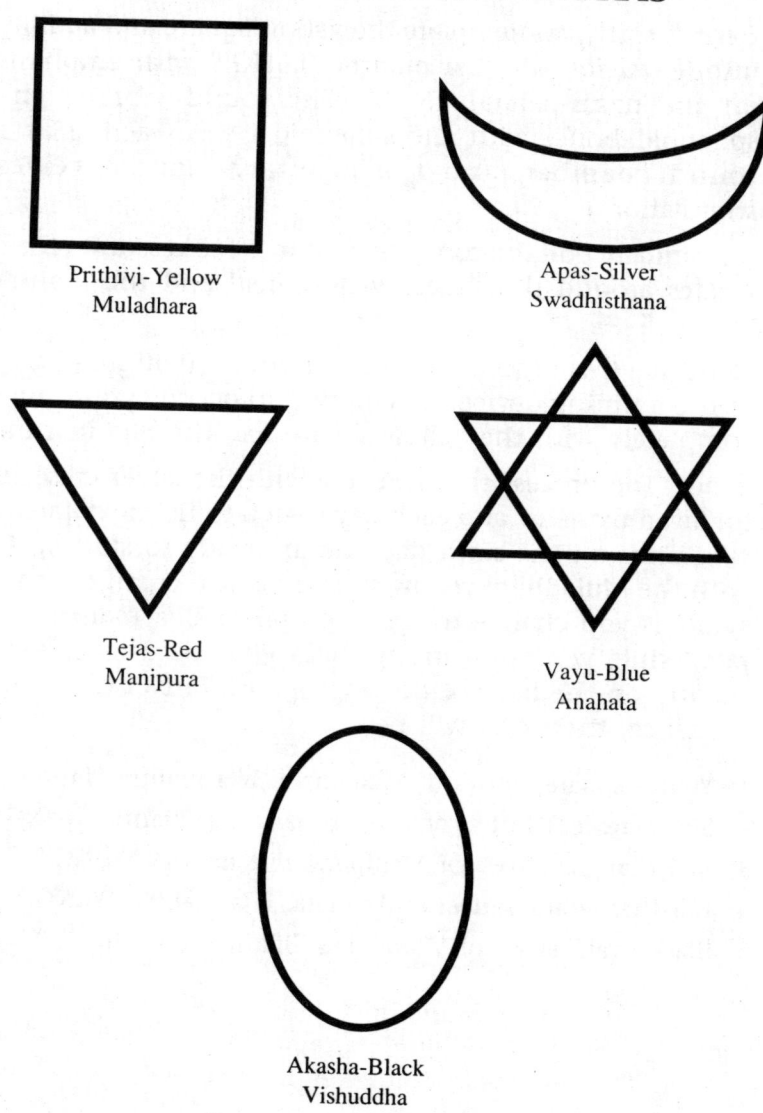

Prithivi-Yellow
Muladhara

Apas-Silver
Swadhisthana

Tejas-Red
Manipura

Vayu-Blue
Anahata

Akasha-Black
Vishuddha

Technique for External Chakra Dharana

1. Sit in a meditative posture or in a chair, in a room lit by a candle.

2. Place before you the yellow square Tattwa of Muladhara chakra, with the candle on one side so that the diagram is illuminated.

3. Gently, softly, contemplate the yellow square and audibly intone *(udgita)* the Bija mantra "LuNG," with emphasis on the nasal-palatal "NG." (The sound vibrates the sphenoid bone, with the sphenoidal sinus acting as a sound chamber, and the pituitary gland receives stimulation.)

4. Continually pull the consciousness into focus so awareness rotates around the square yellow field and the mantra "LuNG."

5. Continue this procedure for five minutes (you may want to use a timing device), attempting to occupy your mind completely with the yellow square and the Bija mantra.

6. Repeat the process the next day with the silver crescent for Swadhisthana, and each day switch to the next Tattwa card until on the sixth day you are ready to start again with the Muladhara yellow square. As you change Tattwa symbols you change to the appropriate Bija mantra—in fact, while you are learning them you could write each mantra on the back of the appropriate Tattwa card. The sequence, therefore, will be:

Day 1: Yellow square Tattwa of Muladhara. Bija mantra "LuNG."
Day 2: Silver crescent Tattwa of Swadhisthana. Bija mantra "VuNG."
Day 3: Red triangle Tattwa of Manipura. Bija mantra "RuNG."
Day 4: Blue hexagram Tattwa of Anahata. Bija mantra "YuNG."
Day 5: Black oval Tattwa of Vishuddha. Bija mantra "HuNG."

Special Considerations with External Chakra Dharana

Three rotations of the five Tattwa cards takes fifteen days; this is suggested as the minimum before progressing to the advanced Internal Chakra Dharana.

The object is to quiet the consciousness by becoming more and more imbued with the geometrical shape seen, entranced with the color related to the form, and entrained by the Bija mantra reverberations.

Do not gaze intently at the Tattwa, as in the fixated gaze of Tratak. Blink when required and if the color field starts to change, look away until the eyes readjust. The External Chakra Dharana is not intended to produce afterimages through ocular fatigue as is the case with Tratak.

The word "Sanskrit" means "perfectly formed," and this is a hint about how scientifically the language was structured 2500 years ago. Each of the thirty-three consonants is carefully grouped according to the parts of speech used in the production of its spoken vibration. An additional tip about the Bija mantra for Manipura ("RuNG") is worth noting: The Sanskrit "r" is normally untrilled, the psychic effect may be enhanced by trilling somewhat as in Russian. "R" in Sanskrit is designated as a cerebral, along with five other consonants. A cerebral sound is one which is produced by the tip of the tongue retroflexing or flapping its underside against the palate (roof of the mouth). The result is that a vibration is sent through the skull bones affecting the frontal lobes of the cerebral cortex. If you place one hand on the top of your forehead and strongly trill the "r," you will feel the frontal bone momentarily shake with the sound; needless to say this effect is physiologically and psychically beneficial so it is worth emphasizing the trill in "RuNG"—if you can. Unfortunately, some people cannot trill, and if that is the case, just get as close to it as you can.*

---

* If you look at a chart of the Sanskrit alphabet you will find "r" grouped with "y," "l," and "v" as semi-vowels. Such charts often fail to show you that each of these letters is often subgrouped according to the position of the tongue when the letter is pronounced: thus "ya" (palatal), "ra" (cerebral), "la" (dental), and "va" (labial).

Each technique in this book is carefully designed to be synergistic and is firmly grounded in classical Yoga. By the same token, I have not hesitated to use contemporary innovations when they enhance the value of these practices. It is important that the exercises in any given chapter are not hurried and that ample time is given to practicing initial forms before moving to the more advanced phases.

PREPARATION FOR INTERNAL CHAKRA DHARANA

Find the complimentary color Tattwa yantra plates in this book. They may be cut out, or you may prefer taking the book to a copying or quickprint place and having color copies made, and even enlarged, for your use.

The principle with Internal Chakra Dharana is that we start by performing fixed gaze Tratak on the complimentary color Tattwa yantra in order to fatigue specific color cone receptors at the back of the eyeballs. When the eyes are then closed, an inner experience of the correct color will be perceived.

For example, the square of the Muladhara complimentary color Tattwa yantra is blue—consequently, after a minute or two of gazing at it, when you close your eyes the complimentary color of yellow will manifest as an after-image.

Technique for Internal Chakra Dharana

1. Sit in a meditative posture or in a chair, with a desk lamp available to illuminate the Tattwa yantra. Ideally, this should be the only light as this exercise is best undertaken in the evening, and you should be able to switch the desk lamp off so you can enjoy relative darkness.
2. Place before you the blue square complimentary color Tattwa yantra of Muladhara and arrange the desk light so it is fully illuminated. The card may be on your lap, or perhaps mounted on the wall at eye level.

3. Inhibit your blink reflex and gaze fixedly at the black Bindu, or spot, in the center. Continue gazing (it may take one or two minutes) until a rim aura of light starts to appear around the edges of the square and the blue color starts to pale. While watching, focus the inner self upon the silent repetition (Audgita) of the Bija mantra "LuM." Many students find that this mantra recitation naturally accompanies the breathing.

4. When the rim aura is well manifested, simultaneously switch the light off and close your eyes. Continue the silent repetition of the Bija mantra "LuM" while gently looking through your forehead and closed eyelids. With relaxation, a yellow square will gradually emerge, floating in the dark space in front of you. Watch the yellow square, constantly adjusting the focus of your attention, in order to perceive the afterimage as long as possible.

5. When the afterimage has totally faded, proceed to the final step by imagining you have moved the Tattwa symbol down into its appropriate space in your body. In this particular case (for Muladhara), visualize the yellow square as level with the base of your spine and occupying the pelvic floor.

6. Now, turn the two-dimensional square into a three-dimensional solid gold cube. Your unconscious mind will determine the size, and this image is uniquely yours. Continue concentrating on this for at least ten minutes. Be patient with fluctuations and simply recreate the cube each time it fades, distorts, or changes. Throughout this portion of the technique you will be still repeating the Bija mantra "LuM" to yourself.

Special Considerations with Internal Chakra Dharana

All of the geometrical yantras, when internalized, should be formed in three dimensions. You will imagine ("image-in") this by changing your perspective, with the following guidelines:

INTERNAL CHAKRA DHARANA YANTRAS

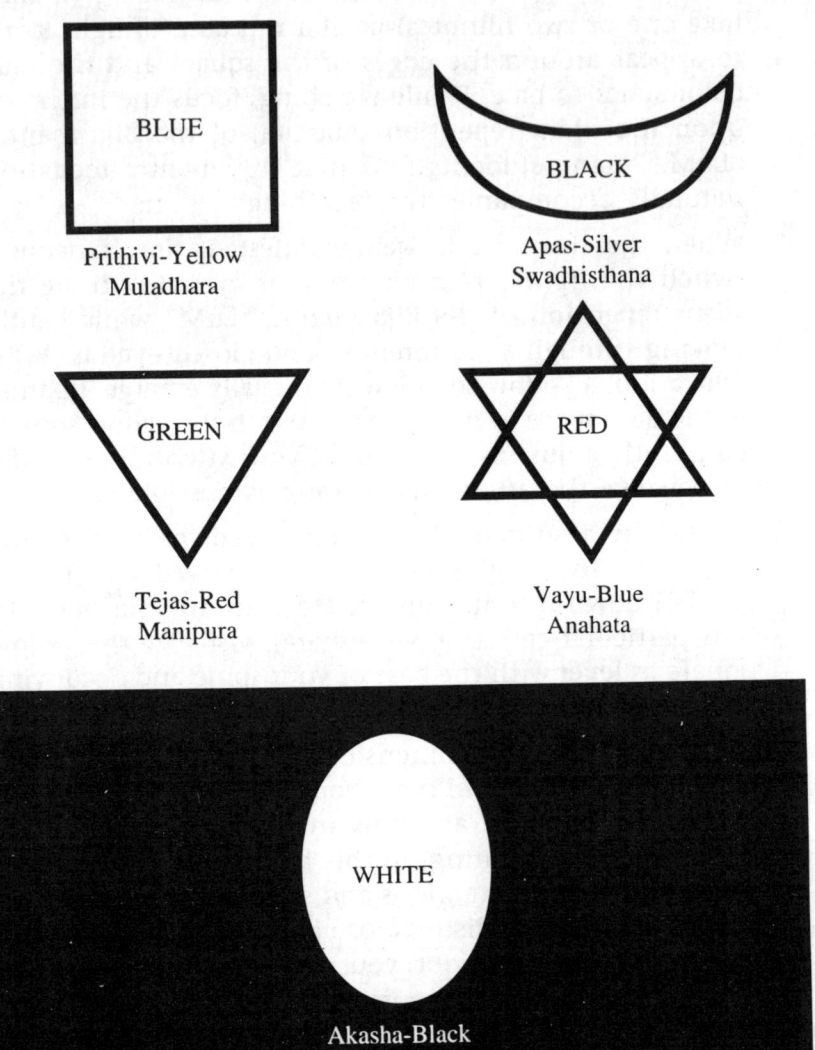

Muladhara	: Yellow square converts to golden cube.
Swadhisthana	: Silver crescent converts to silver melon slice.
Manipura	: Red triangle converts to ruby red tetrahedron (an upside down, three-sided pyramid).
Anahata	: Blue hexagram converts into six-sided blue star carved out of blue sapphire.
Vishuddha	: Black oval converts into a black marble egg.

Remember that the appropriate Bija Mantra with the "M" ending is used at all stages of Internal Chakra Dharana.

Practice Routine

The technique of Chakra Dharana should be practiced for ten minutes or more each day. Begin with Muladhara chakra the first day, Swadhisthana chakra the second day, and so on, doing each chakra in turn until you return to Muladhara and start the cycle over again.

After the first two or three weeks, you may dispense with External Dharana in the form of concentration upon a Tattwa diagram and may proceed with just Internal Dharana upon the chakra symbols within the body.

With practice, a sensation of physical stimulation will be produced by mentally moving the Tattwa symbol down into its proper position along the spine and concentrating upon the area. The yellow square of Muladhara should be visualized as at the base of the spine; the silver crescent of Swadhisthana is two inches below the navel; the red triangle of Manipura is about three inches above the navel, level with the pit of the stomach; the blue hexagram of Anahata should be visualized as level with the heart; and the black egg of Vishuddha chakra is level with the Adam's apple.

In essence, Internal Chakra Dharana is the familiar Tantric technique of internalization of gods, colors, forms, etc.

★★

Chapter Nine

Solar Plexus Charging

> *Above it, and at the root of the navel, is the shining Lotus of ten petals. Meditate there on the region of Fire, triangular in form and shining like the rising sun.*
>
> —Shat-Chakra Nirupana
> Verse 19

The student has now reached the point of introduction to pure *Laya* technique. I must, however, warn that the material presented in this chapter is beyond rationalization, although I will not hesitate to draw some correlative comparisons with Western anatomy.

The absolute and sole purpose of Laya Yoga, Kundalini Yoga, or simply Yoga is to induce a profound altered state of consciousness that I will describe as a singular grasp of multiplicity. This is a concept beyond the dogmatism of both Western science and orthodox religion, East or West. The end "goal" of Yoga has nothing to do with the plane of material existence, and that this is so can only be appreciated from the perspective of mysticism, and in particular the most profound aspects of traditional Indian mysticism.

I will affirm that mysticism is the immediate experience of Ultimate Universal Unity. Mysticism is the direct apprehension of "reality." The word "apprehension" deserves definition as I am using it in a specific philosophical and psychological context.

Philosophical: "The act of mentally grasping or of bringing before the mind; specifically, a perception that is comparatively simple, direct, and immediate and has as its object something considered to be directly and non-discursively understandable."

In traditional logic: "That one of the three operations of thought by which one grasps what is expressed by a term or a name—contrasted with judgment or reasoning."

Psychological: "The observing of an object as a whole without distinguishing its parts."

— Webster's Third New International Dictionary

Advanced Laya exercises are couched in terms of awakening the chakras and arousing the kundalini to the point at which the practitioners experience definite subjective and objective changes taking place within their bodies—yet such manifestations are only penultimate; the ultimate is solipsistic and transcendent.

KRIYA

The Laya *kriyas,* or techniques, bringing about, in symbolic language, the ascent of kundalini up Sushumna are among the most closely guarded secrets of Laya Yoga, and yet, like the alchemical *prima materia,* they could be freely displayed and go unnoticed by the world.

I am deeply indebted to my mentor and guru, Dr. Swami Rishi Gitananda of Pondicherry, Tamil Nadu, South India, for initiating me into a set of six Bengali Laya kriyas in 1958. These cannot be passed on in a book; however, the first kriya is what will herein be described as "Solar Plexus Charging." I should remark that even if the aspiring student had access to the mechanics of the five succeeding kriyas, it would be of little value as the degree of concentrative ability required to bring about results would, in all probability, be beyond the student's present stage of development.

Just as certain pathological conditions produce distinct signs and symptoms permitting an accurate diagnosis, so the arousal of kundalini is traditionally marked by specific signs and symptoms. The first definite indication that latent energy is being successfully released into the body is the appearance of psychic heat.

At first, this is subjective and the student simply becomes aware of warm currents running up and down his or her spine and circulating in the region of the solar plexus. Later the currents become hot, and anyone passing a hand along the student's spine will feel distinct heat waves emanating from whatever chakra region the kundalini energy has ascended to. As kundalini rises, the heat waves move from the base of the spine to the top cervical region.

Tibetan Yogis make particular use of this psychic heat in a process called *tummo*, mastery of which permits wandering naked in the snow-covered Himalayas.

My friend, the Belgian writer on Yoga, Andre Van Lysbeth, shared with me the superb description of tummo given by Professor Jacques Keyaerts. This excerpt is from the article "Glances at Tibetan Yoga," which I have translated from the French.

The Gtum'mo (Tummo)

The Gtum'mo is perhaps the form best known in Europe of all Tibetan practices. Its fame had already passed beyond the frontiers of Asia under the Roman Republic, proof that it is antecedent to the introduction of Buddhism into Tibet. Cicero mentions it in his Tusculana. In the twentieth century, Madame A. David-Neel is giving it wide publicity. It concerns the creation of physical heat which allows the adept to live almost naked in the most rigorous cold. Most often he clothes himself in a long cotton garment, whence his name of rasp'a (repa): "dressed in cotton." The principle presiding over the training is simple enough to seize for one familiar with Yoga. Evans-Wentz sums it up exactly: "According to the secret teachings, the word 'gtum'mo' indicates a method for extracting prana from the inexhaustible reservoir constituted by nature and for storing it up in the battery of the human body, then for using it for transforming the seminal liquid into a subtle energy by which an internal psycho-physical heat is produced and circulates in the channels of the psychic nervous system." In other words, the practice of gtum'mo allows the initiate to accumulate cosmic energy within which acts on the sexual force. This latter undergoes a transformation; it is turned aside from its habitual end and produces, by circulating in the psychic body, an important release of heat. Exact or not, this doctrine allows the adept to obtain spectacular results. The Yogi succeeds not only in resisting the most intense cold without suffering from it in the slightest degree, but can also make the snow melt around him and dry wet sheets covering his body.

Unfortunately, the gtum'mo implies a rigorous asceticism, a long training under the guidance of a qualified master (and there are hardly any in the West), as well as a kind of life incompatible with an organized society. Only a hermit can hope one day to reach the goal. Such is the present situation. This, of course, does not preclude an Occidental from one day being able to extract a practical recipe by reconsidering the question from a personal point of view.

Specific Advantages

1. The solar plexus storehouse (Manipura chakra) overflows with pranic energy; this surplus is automatically distributed wherever needed.
2. The arousal of kundalini and the resulting heat produced will surely change the student's attitude toward cold. Once it is experienced, the body never really becomes cold again.
3. The mind becomes deeply absorbed in the exercise as the production of heat increases.

What is the Solar Plexus?

Defining the solar plexus as a psychic reservoir is a bit like the experiential definition of Valium: "Valium is that substance which, when ingested or injected, vanishes the subjective state called anxiety."

And thus: "The solar plexus is an autonomic neural conglomerate, which is, with the possible exception of the pineal gland, most talked about as a psychic appendage."

Given the difficulties, this is actually quite a good definition. Our Occidental, left-hemisphere dominant thought processes are really doomed in any attempt to rationalize Indian metaphysical conceptions. The word "rationalize" comes from the root "ratio," which means "to divide or break up," and once you have broken something, you no longer can easily grasp the whole.

When we equate Manipura chakra with the solar plexus, the reality is, at best, that we are only constructing analogies, correspondences, metaphors, similes, etc. In truth, when we equate any of the chakras or kundalini with anything, we are only constructing relationships. We cannot help ourselves, and even to invoke the argument that the human brain is "hard-wired" for making sense out of nonsense is a rationalization (i.e., a rational lie) that is part of an infinite regression.

And yet we need a "conception" to occupy the void, until a moment of meditation can provide an existential, experiential state of "Being."

Classical Tantric literature suggests that Muladhara, Swadhisthana, and Manipura chakras are interconnected in an intricate web of fibers (Nadis), and that they function both synchronistically and synergistically. (The ultimate seduction is always to find physical parallels which objectively exist in the physical body.)

Early anatomists must have considered the term "solar plexus" a fitting description of the ganglion, wrapped around the abdominal aorta as it exits through the diaphragm, in view of a severe blow to it inducing "lights out!" (unconsciousness). Remember, Manipura is allocated to fire, heat, metabolism, energy, and light.

The autonomic nervous system powerfully innervates the solar plexus. Sympathetic "fear, fight, flight" fibers (Pingala?) cohabit with parasympathetic "recuperation, rest, relaxation" fibers (Ida?) in an influential net that spreads down the abdominal cavity, to interconnect the hypogastric plexus (Swadhisthana?) and the pelvic plexus (Muladhara?).

The solar plexus is also called (most correctly) the coeliac plexus with its subdivisions, the coeliac ganglion. "Coeliac" stems from a Greek root meaning "cavity, hollow," and, distantly, "heaven."

Finally, consider "abdominal brain," an interesting term suggesting an auxiliary control center—perhaps, as Dr. Douglas Baker once suggested, "an evolutionary remnant of the pelvic brain of the brontosaurus."

The Technique for Solar Plexus Charging

1. Lie supine, with your head north and feet south, in a semi-dark room, with your legs folded as in Sukhasana (as if you had fallen backward while in Sukhasana) and the hands clasped over the solar plexus.

2. On a slow, even inhalation, visualize warm, golden pranic energy being drawn in through your head (as in polarization) and down the body into your thighs and lower abdominal region, where it is prevented from escaping by your crossed feet and is therefore stored.

3. On a slow, even exhalation, bring the accumulated prana up and around the solar plexus in a series of clockwise circles (as if you had a clock dial, the size of a dinner plate, centered over the navel with twelve o'clock at the chest and six o'clock at the groin).

4. Making as many circles as possible, while exhaling concentrate upon feeling an internal heat develop with each visualization of energy sweeping around the solar plexus.

The exercise should be carried out for a minimum of thirty minutes. Once the student succeeds, he or she will be surprised to realize that the inner psychic heat produced is not the result of self-hypnosis. The mechanics of the exercise, when analyzed, reveal several interesting theories peculiar to Yoga.

THE SOLAR PLEXUS/COELIAC GANGLION

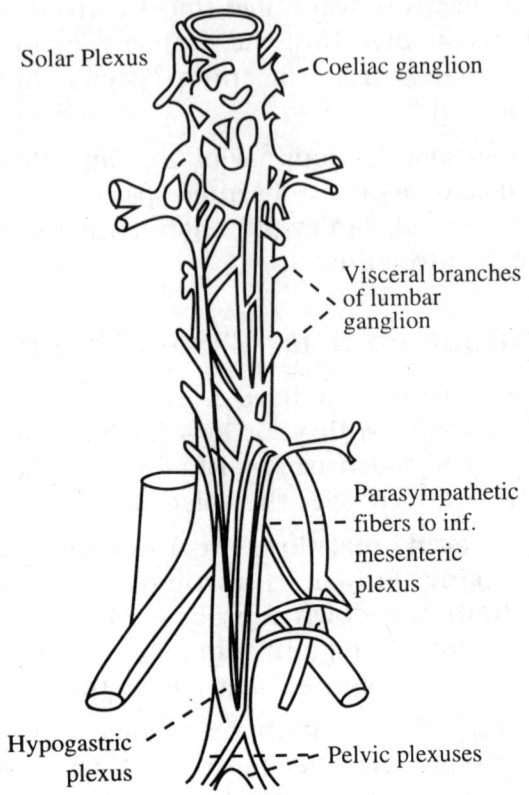

> *I don't know anything about anything except anything I know anything about!*

Yoga physiology maintains that the hands and feet are terminals through which the body throws off psychic energy in the form of prana. The crossing of the feet and interlocking of the hands short-circuit the escape of prana and results in an additional source of energy for solar plexus charging. The crossing of the feet relaxes sexual tension as well, and thus

SOLAR PLEXUS CHARGING

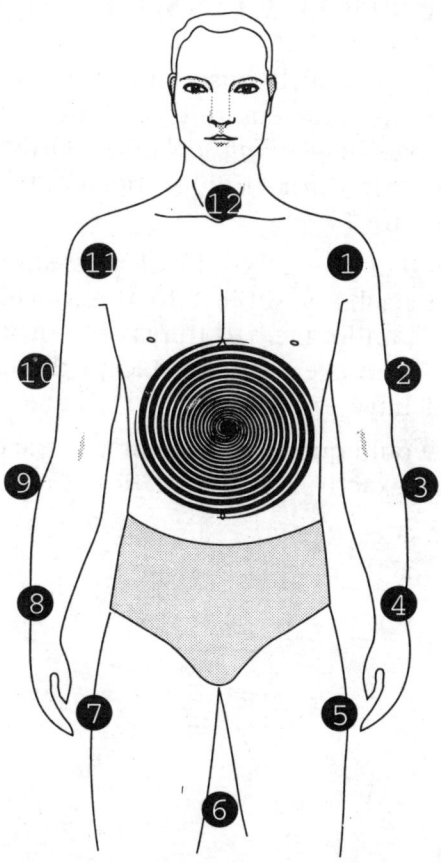

another possible source of energy waste is prevented. It is with this kriya that we realize the need for a new physiology capable of explaining the release of hitherto unsuspected energy reserves.

Once the induction of psychic heat is accomplished, the student will find his or her mind becoming more and more absorbed in the performance of this type of kriya. The student will come to understand that Laya truly means absorption and rhythm such as can be found only within the eternity of one's own consciousness—the link with Universal Consciousness.

LAYA YOGA AND SELF-REALIZATION: SOME FINAL CONSIDERATIONS

The European medieval alchemists constantly reiterated to their apprentices that no one could tell them the secret of the Philosopher's Stone, *Lapis Philosophorum*. Only the individual could find the secret for him or herself through diligent applications of "fire."

This mystery of the Elixir must be searched for in the moment, and in a body subject to the vicissitudes of time; often, as a physician I have had to reassure others, and myself, that we recover from every disease except the last one. For the last ten years, I have explained:

Those who would quench their thirst at the ocean of Indian metaphysics are exactly in this position.

★★

Part Four

Siddha Yoga and Supernormal Powers

The third center, Manipura, is located in the region of the navel. Here dwells the Realized Being, giver of all auspicious things, named Rudra, "Lord of Tears."

— Shiva Samhita 5, 104-105

Chapter Ten

Yogic Power Flows

> The Yogi, focusing always on Manipura (Fire) chakra, achieves all attainments. Pain and disease vanish, every desire is fulfilled, and time defeated.
> — Shiva Samhita 5:106-107

The *siddhis* represent suprasensual and suprasensory controls bestowed upon the Yoga adept as the result of *sadhana* or practice. Mcdonell's *Sanskrit Dictionary* defines siddhi as "hitting of a mark, accomplishment, performance, fulfillment, complete attainment, success, getting the better of, cure (of a disease), attainment of one's aims, success, fortune, personal perfection entailing the acquisition of supernatural powers, magical power (magic is the art of causing changes to occur in conformity with the "will" or Itcha Shakti), efficacy, efficiency, skill, demonstration."

The demonstration of siddhis is a by-product of one-pointedness *(Ekagrata)* and neural equilibrium (Yoga), through years of technique (Kriya).

MIND-BODY DURABILITY

Over the decades a constant source of personal excitement for me has been the exploration of my own mind-body durability against the fundamental elements of nature; fire, blood, and steel. We are conditioned from infancy to fear fire, blood, and steel, and the conquest of such fear is symbolic of the ascent of spirit over matter. For my own mastery, I am indebted to a series of adepts both Eastern and Western. Indeed, in India some of the secret Siddha Yoga Kriya is inherited from father to son and may be passed down generation after generation. Immunity to fire and pain is not a trick in the sense of sleight of hand or mirrors, but rather the ultimate confidence trick.

Confidence literally means a mental state of togetherness (Greek prefix *con*) in perfect trust, faith, and fidelity (Latin *fides*) to one's own true self—in short, "trance-consciousness" or transcendence of the little self which is so habitually filled with doubts and insecurities.

Even a momentary lapse of such confidence (Yoga) during a demonstration can mean a trip to the hospital or morgue for the foolhardy and unenlightened. The three chakras below the diaphragmic partition give control over fire, blood, and steel, as follows.

Muladhara Chakra

Opening of Muladhara gives power over all the elements of the earth, including metals (particularly steel) and the earth part of the person, or flesh.

After the opening of Muladhara, pain control becomes a reality with the skewering of the flesh, spiking, the oft-joked about "bed of nails" (everyone's life!), and ultimate crucifixion preceded by the crown of thorns (opening the Sahasrara chakra) producing "at-one-ment."

Swadhisthana Chakra

Mastery of the blood flow in the *deha*, or physical body, of the Yogi arises with the opening of this force center. Vasoconstriction and vasodilation of the arterioles at will and even cessation of capillary oozing occurs. Stigmata or the percolation of blood through the skin to the outside environment can also be demonstrated.

Swadhisthana is the fluid control point for the entire system. With the opening of Swadhisthana, the inherent "swami" or water-walker of each man and woman emerges.

Manipura Chakra

This is the center of the salamander, fire-walker, and fire-breather, whose inner life is sustained by the primal heat element. The fire-walkers of North India who tread across beds of glowing embers and the Pacific islanders who walk upon white-hot stones employ the Manipura chakra, as do those who lick white-hot bars.

So-called "fire-eaters" unwittingly use the Manipura chakra in conjunction with the Anahata chakra (air or pranayama center) to perform their feats.

Simultaneous mastery of earth, water, and fire with subsequent immunity to pain and searing of flesh by heat is accomplished through juggling of the forces inherent in the first three chakras blossoming upon the tree of life. Classical demonstrations include dipping the hands into boiling water, boiling oil, molten lead (lead melts at three times the temperature of boiling water), and molten steel—also bathing in and drinking these substances.

Tongue Piercing

In the Hindu tradition, siddhi rituals are a religious act of supplication to the goddess Durga for karmic purification. All ceremonies begin by piercing the tongue with a dirty, non-sterile spike or skewer. This results in the reflex awakening of the Swadhisthana chakra, permitting "fire to be fought with water."

Just transfixing the tongue alone is no petty feat, for although the sensitivity to pain varies in different body areas, the tongue—along with genitals, eardrums and the eye cornea—shares the distinction of being one of the most painful and sensitive regions in the body. (Remember the last time you bit your tongue?)

A group of medical doctors investigating Hindu torture rituals in Fiji stated:

> *The piercing of the tongue, however, is a different matter. It is a very sensitive organ. The participants maintain that no pain was felt when the tongue was pierced, and that no bleeding took place. There was certainly no sign of either. Whereas the absence*

of blood during skin puncturing can perhaps be explained in other terms, the piercing of the tongue cannot. It is blood-filled and tender. There can be no doubt that the normal bleeding reaction, as well as the normal pain reaction, was successfully overcome by whatever processes are involved in the rituals.

— *Holy Torture in Fiji,* Pacific Publications, Sydney, Australia

HINDU TORTURE RITUAL

Gnosticon 1977 Twin Cities, MN USA
South India Fire Ritual

Swami Anandakapila commences the ritual with the traditional piercing of the tongue to open Swadhisthana chakra. A skewer is thrust through the tongue into a lemon.

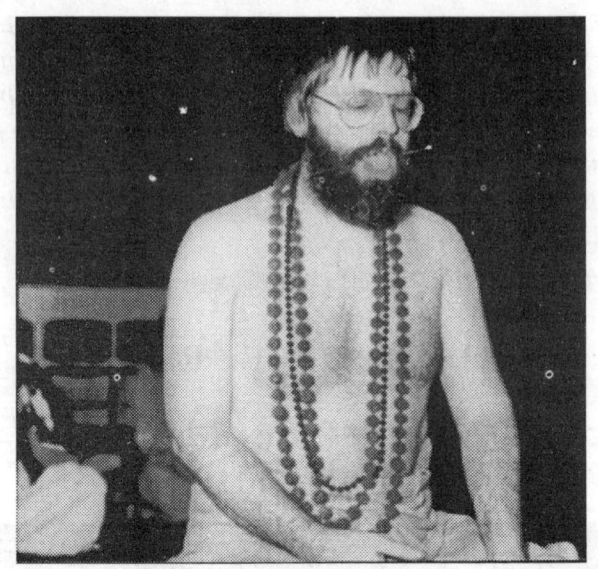

The swami in trance, having conjoined steel (Muladhara) with flesh (Swadhisthana) to evoke and invoke the Water element in preparation for Fire (Manipura).

Preparing to heat the steel bar to the white hot stage.

Margery and Robert using a mantra to transcend fear, pain, and heat.

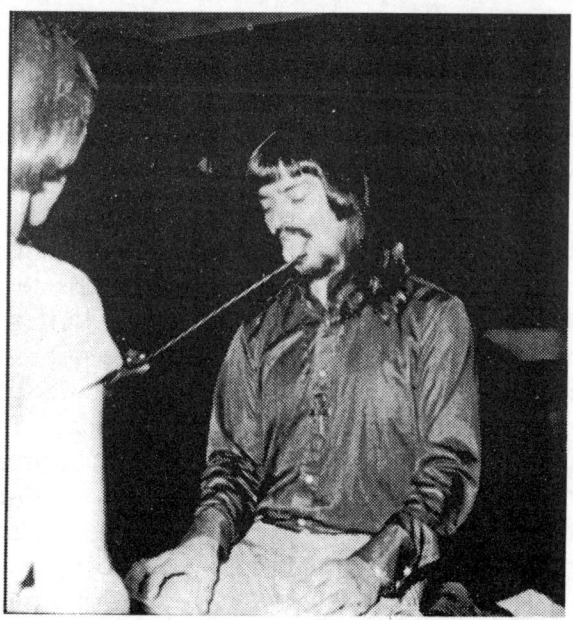

Robert licking a white hot steel bar, impervious to fire, beyond fear, and immune to pain.

An ounce of practice is worth a pound of theory, one picture is worth a thousand words—one demonstration a year is worth eleven lectures. The purpose of unleashing psycho-physiological power through the siddhis is to create a psychic shock in the witnesses, so that a momentary realization of life's potential is experienced. Such demonstrations provide TAN-gible proof of the TRA-nscendence possible through TAN-TRA.

TANTRIC SEXUALITY

In 1975, my book *Sexual Occultism* was published by Llewellyn Publications. An enlarged edition retitled *Ecstasy Through Tantra* has since been published. The introduction states: "It is my profound hope that encouragement will be given to all, through this book, for utilizing the sexual dimension as a key unlocking joyous power."

In these purportedly enlightened times let me make several flat statements at the very outset of this section.

All Yoga is really derived from Tantra. Gurudev Satyananda says: "Yoga is an offshoot of Tantra" *(Tantra-Yoga Panorama)*. The scholastic proof of this is outside the scope of this section, but we will deal with it another time.

Westerners (who love gossip about sexual matters) equate Tantra with sexuality. This is incorrect, as sexual considerations form but a small fragment of the total Tantric teaching and indeed sexual references are sparse in the Tantra Shastras—most of which have not yet been translated into European languages. However, the attitude in Tantra toward sexual expression is one of liberation and reality rather than repression or suppression. Quoting my friend Dr. Sinha (Director of the India Institute of Yoga, Patna) writing in his book *Yoga, Meaning, and Values:* "According to Yoga, sex is not an evil nor a sin. It is neither degrading nor weakening. On the contrary, according to Tantra Yoga, sex is regarded as generative of vitality, energy, and power, and also as a harmonizer of the senses."

The zoologist Desmond Morris *(The Naked Ape)* ascribes ten distinct purposes to sexual experience. Beginning with procreative sex (the most primal of sexual functions—anyone who limits sexual activity to procreation needs a psychiatrist!), his enumeration includes physiological sex (relief), occupational sex (anti-boredom device), tranquilizing sex (anxiety-reducing), and status sex (aggression release), as well as five other categories. Using his brilliant analysis of sexual function from a biological viewpoint, we could add three further dimensions to sexuality which derive directly from Tantric wisdom.

1. **Sex for consciousness expansion:** An orgasm tends to automatically illuminate the nervous system in a way traditionally described as awakening kundalini. Nearly everyone can learn to deepen, prolong, and enhance this state, through some types of tantric methodology, using the orgasm as a springboard to transcendence.

2. **Sex for ESP development:** Sexual activity promotes sensory hyperacuity or sensory awareness (at least it should!). Tantric sexual Sadhana induces profound experiences of ESP ("extra sensual perception"), converting the whole skin into one extensive, massive, genital organ. (One meaning of the Sanskrit root *tan* is "to extend.") Humans are so out of touch with our own bodies that few ever even experience the two erogenic zones in each hand that are Tantric chakras. Those who open up the full potential of the five sensory gates through Tantric sexual Sadhana will immeasurably speed their psychic development.

3. **Sex for positive thinking:** Sexual arousal, culminating in a climax, is the key to attitude-changing or self-hypnosis. The English psychiatrist William Sargeant *(Battle for the Mind)* rediscovered the Tantric secret that a sexually aroused human is hyper-suggestible. Correct use and knowledge of this (sometimes called sex magic) allows an individual to consciously inculcate his or her unconscious with life-affirming—rather than life-negating—attitudes.

Sexual Terminology

Etymology and semantics, coupled with psycho-linguistics, reveal the esoteric and arcane function that the erotic impulse serves in the human organism. The following are a few examples taken from my book *Ecstasy Through Tantra*.

Climax: The word, which we use as a term for the desirable culmination of sexual stimulation, comes from the Greek *klimax* meaning "ladder" or "staircase to heaven." It indicates the inner significance of sexuality as a spiritual path. This is unconsciously implicit in the joke that a "run" in nylon stockings or pantihose is a "ladder to heaven."

Clitoris: From Greek through Latin, as in *clavis*, a "key." That part of the female vulva which unlocks her nervous system in the way a key unlocks a door. The central genital push-button for ecstasy.

Consummate: Used in the contemporary sense of completing a marriage through intercourse. The original Latin root is replete with the significance of the esoteric object of intercourse, for it means is to bring to completion (Yoga) or perfection, make perfect (siddhi), highest, topmost, utmost, and the crown. (The object of Tantric intercourse is to open Sahasrara, the crown chakra).

Create: From the Sanskrit root *kr* meaning "to make," through to Latin as *creare*, implying production, growing, to bring into existence. The close relationship between sexual fecundity and mental originality is demonstrated by our use of the word to denote both creation of life and artistic creativity.

The birth of ideas is analogous to physical birth. We interchange words like "conceiving" and "conception," using them both for either physical pregnancy or mental agility. We also speak of a "fertile woman" and a "fertile imagination."

Occult psychology views the mind as divided into the masculine active consciousness and the feminine passive unconscious. The art of mental creation is an alchemical process of impregnating the unconscious mind with a seed or germinal idea, grasped by the consciousness but ejaculated into the deeper unconscious realms for incubation. Gestation continues in the unconscious womb, until the sudden birth of the idea as "flash" or "inspiration" which emerges—fully formed—into consciousness.

Orgasm: Found in English, through French and Latin, from two closely related Greek roots; *orgio*, a sacred rite or sacrifice (of semen?) ceremony in the early Greco-Roman mysteries celebrating the feast of Dionysus or Bacchus, hence our expression "an orgy." The second related root is *orgasio*, meaning "to swell" with ardent desire, passion (expansion of the auric field in the way a balloon is over-inflated), "to burst;" namely, an experience of such intense excitement that the ego is momentarily fragmented, producing a nameless-formless inner state.

Venerate: Allied to the Sanskrit *van*, "to love or honor," but directly taken from the Latin *vener*, "to revere and love." Related words from the same Latin stem are venerable, venereal, and Venus (the Roman goddess of love). To venerate is to recognize the sexual parts as truly worthy objects of our adoration and awe.

In conclusion, let us realize that—contrary to popular belief and teachings —the sexual dynamics of life have by no means been neglected as a source of spiritual Sadhana in the Indian Tantra Yoga. In particular, the Tantrist worships woman as divinity personified, and sexual Sadhana is an oblation to the eternal female. It is the Mother Goddess sustaining manifest existence as eternal Shakti who is incarnate in each woman.

Secret Science of Hand Gestures

The word "mudra" (as applied to hand positions) has the multiple meanings of sign, symbol, and gesture. Mudra, in this context, is a secret sign language sending a message from the body to the mind via the nervous system and from conscious to unconscious spheres of existence.

A simple example of this occurs when practicing Shavasana (deep relaxation pose) lying supine with the palms placed uppermost in Shunya mudra or the "empty gesture," signaling the mind to become receptive (empty). Shunya mudra is that universal open-handed sign "I give in," "trust," "surrender," "relaxation," or "letting go."

Mudra also means " seal," "short cut," and "short circuit"— indicating an actual physiological basis for the effects of hand gestures by closing or uniting certain neurological reflex points which terminate on the surface of the hands.

The famous Gnana (pronounced "G-yan") mudra formed by joining thumb and forefinger, leaving the remaining three fingers gently extended, demonstrates the anatomical, neurological, and psychological principles of mudra. Gnana mudra means literally "the wisdom gesture." The Sanskrit Gnana gives rise to Greek *gnosis*, which comes through into English as "knowing." The person who meditates in Gnana mudra affirms a subsuming of all the wisdom of the universe, thus placing the mind automatically in an optimum state for higher consciousness. Why?

The Thumb: Humanity

Let us begin with the thumb, which is the digit symbolizing humanity: finite, limited, but at the top of the evolutionary phylogenetic scale as "the greatest of beasts." The characteristic of a human ("humus" or earth creature) is a developed mind (Sanskrit *manas*) coupled with a tool-making capacity or manual dexterity excelling that of all other animals.

This tool-making ability is due to the anatomical development of the saddle joint at the base of the thumb where it joins the wrist. The saddle joint allows the thumb to be placed firmly in apposition to all the other fingers, thus permitting manual flexibility and grasping to a degree not found in other mammals and primates.

MULADHARA TATTWA CARD FOR INTERNAL CHAKRA DHARANA

SWADHISTHANA TATTWA CARD FOR INTERNAL CHAKRA DHARANA

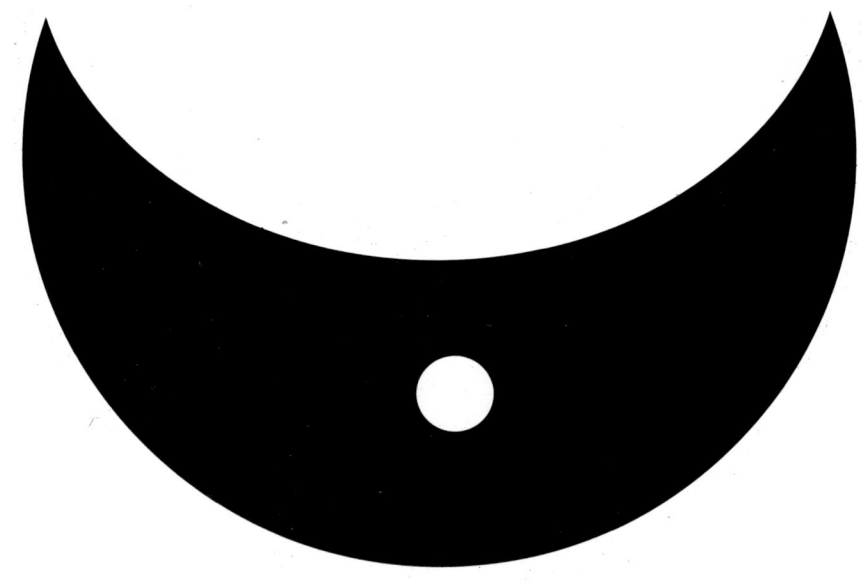

MANIPURA TATTWA CARD FOR INTERNAL CHAKRA DHARANA

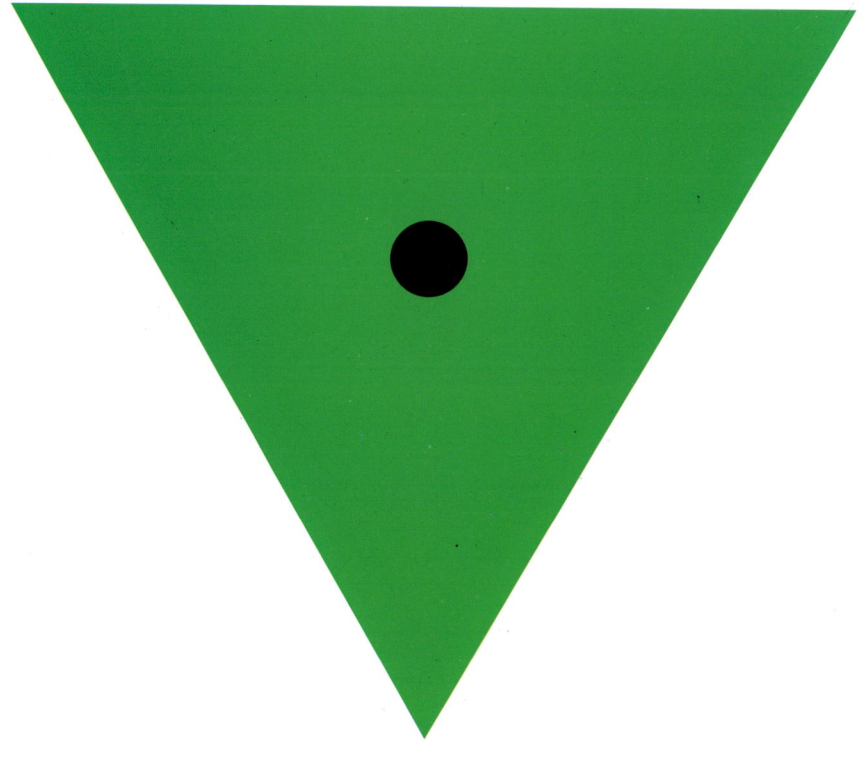

ANAHATA TATTWA CARD FOR INTERNAL CHAKRA DHARANA

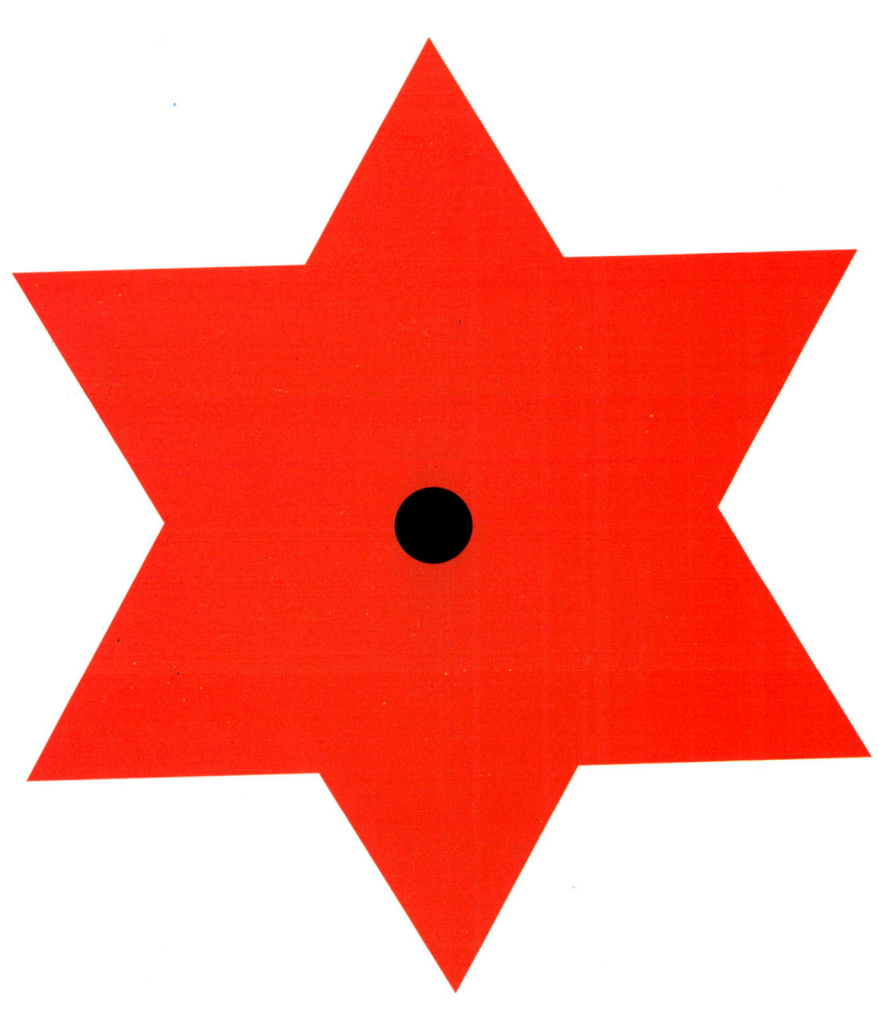

VISHUDDHA TATTWA CARD FOR INTERNAL CHAKRA DHARANA

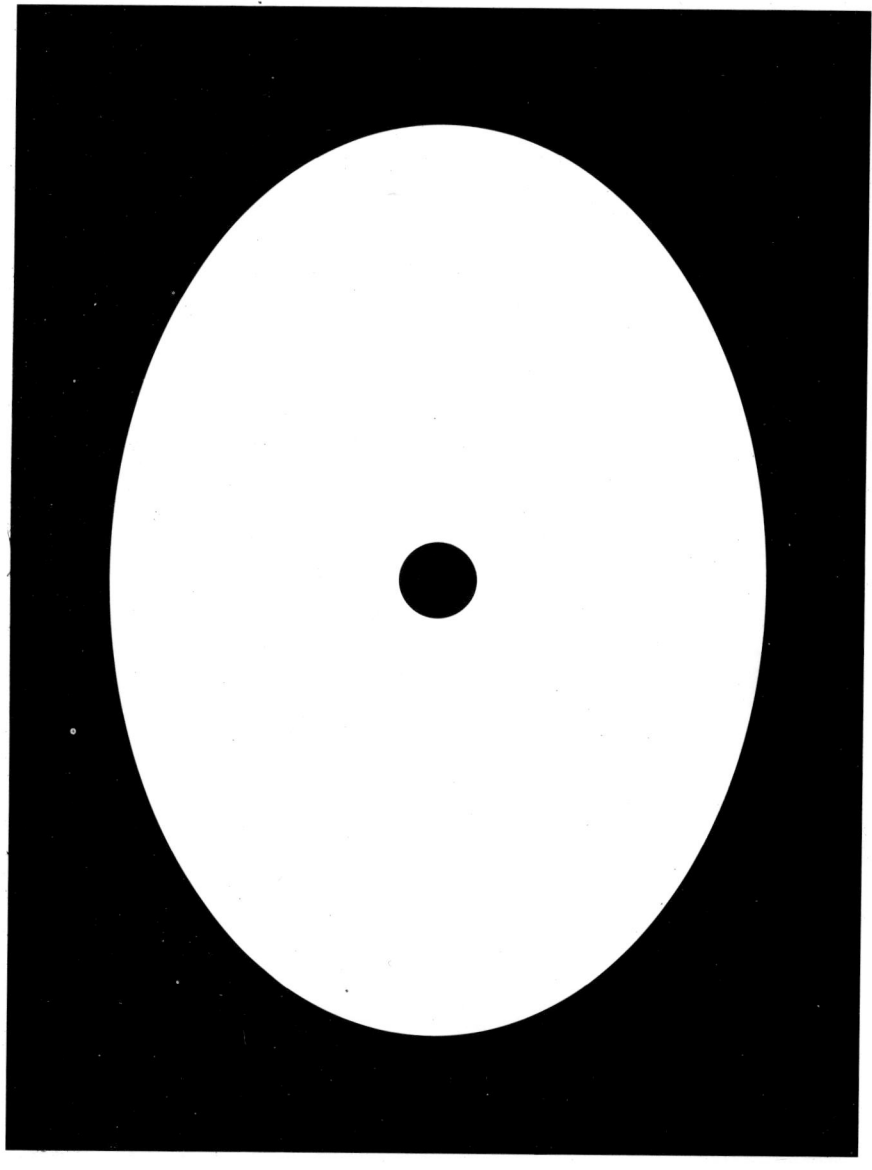

AJNA TATTWA CARD FOR INTERNAL CHAKRA DHARANA

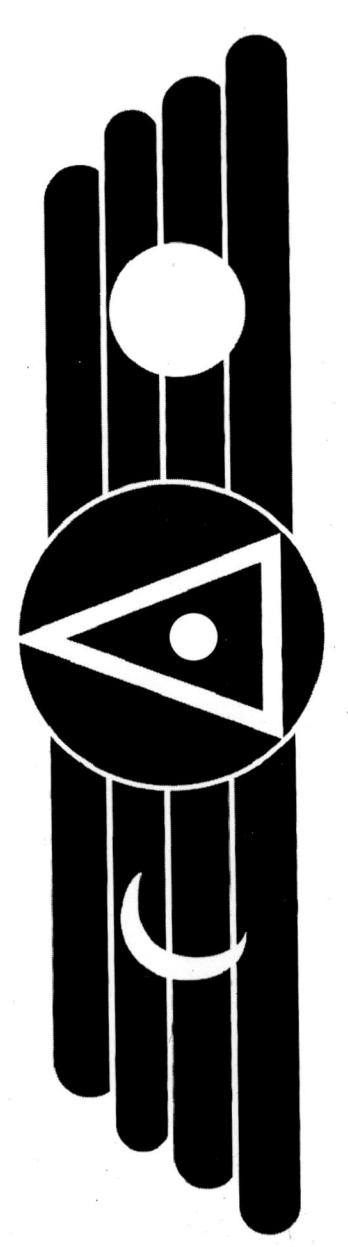

SAHASRARA TATTWA CARD FOR INTERNAL CHAKRA DHARANA

CAUDUCEUS CARD FOR INTERNAL CHAKRA DHARANA

The Index Finger: God

The index finger (so called because we instinctively "index" or classify all creation outside ourselves by pointing with this foremost or forefinger digit) represents God, the absolute sea of cosmic energy that is infinite, limitless, and eternal.

Uniting the thumb with the index finger forms a circle in which finite, limited humanity is linked with the infinite, unlimited absolute. The circle is a (w)hole, being both absolute zero and utter completeness. Pascal, the seventeenth-century French theologian, defined God as a circle whose circumference is nowhere and center everywhere.

It is incorrect to say that God exists; only humanity exists and the moment something exists it is already limited by form and name *(Namarupa)*. God subsists and persists but never exists.

Principle of Trinity

When forming the Gnana mudra gesture, the remaining three fingers represent the principle of trinity in major world religions. Christianity conceives the Father, Son, and Holy Ghost. Ancient Egypt immortalized Horus, Isis, and Osiris as a triplicity, while Hinduism rests upon a tripod of Brahma, Vishnu, and Shiva.

The gods and goddesses of theology esoterically represent—not persons—but rather forces responsible for the manifestation of all creation. Existence is the result of an interplay of three forces: positive, negative, neutral; male, female, hermaphrodite; the sun (positive), the earth (receptive), and the moon (neutralizing transformer).

In assuming Gnana mudra for meditation and Pranayama you have telegraphed to your unconscious that you possess all that can be known about life, yourself, and the universe.

Humankind has developed an intimate relationship between hands and brain, hence whatever we do with our hands affects, through the nervous system, the cerebral cortex and the associated conscious and unconscious layers of the mind.

In a general context, all hand mudra is a special category of body language which is instinctive and universal among both primitive and civilized races.

Hastha Mudras

A very interesting group of mudras are referred to as Hastha Mudras, which automatically gesture the breath into the abdominal ribcage or collar-bone area of the lungs. These special hand positions readjust the relationship between the pelvic girdle and the shoulder girdle in such a manner that expansion of desired lobes of the lungs occurs.

For the beginner in Hatha Yoga, the Hastha mudra technique is a dramatic introduction to Yoga breathing or Pranayama, bestowing breath control upon the merest tyro. At any given moment the position of our hands exerts a subtle but profound influence which actually determines the manner in which we breathe.

Mudra is the psychic science relating hand and brain, gesture and state of consciousness. Following the Hermetic axiom "as above, so below," our finger movements betray our inner state at an instant in time; hence, the nervous drumming with fingertips by the agitated or eager person is described as "itchy fingers." Conscious assumption of ritual mudra reverses this psychosomatic arc, molding mind, breath, and body into the willed or desired state required as a prelude to ultimate inner life experience.

★★

Chapter Eleven

Yoga and the West

The wise renounce the fruit of action and in so doing attain a state beyond all evil.

— Gita 2:51

The reward of a thing well done is in having done it.

— Ralph Waldo Emerson

Yoga is the world's oldest and most effective method of achieving total mental and physical health. The whole person is included in Yoga, all aspects of the self. What do we mean? The United Nations World Health Organization has defined health as "A condition of mental, physical, and social well-being and not merely the absence of disease." This statement is in perfect agreement with the goal and aims of Yoga in general.

Yoga is evolutionary in approach. Western science, from the time of Darwin, has accepted the principle that all living creatures have evolved their physical features over a period of time on the basis of adapting to change and survival of the fittest. In terms of the human animal, Western biologists consider that the body is fully mature and ceases growth around the age of twenty-five.

But what of the mind?

SELF-REALIZATION

Yoga has always taught that growth does not cease with maturity of the physical body. Each of us contains an unlimited potential for mental and psychic growth to influence our personalities. The individual who evolves wholly as a person will eventually experience a mental state that is called self-realization in Yoga. He or she will become fully aware of the inner possibilities and richness of the mind. Western psychologists belonging to what are sometimes called Humanistic Schools call this state "self-actualization."

Yoga is a technique that makes a better person of the Christian, Hindu, atheist, socialist, and agnostic alike. Better people make better communities, better communities make better nations, and better nations make a better world.

THE INDIAN ROPE TRICK

Who has not heard of the Indian rope trick? This legendary feat of Asian magic involves the magician throwing a coil of rope into the air. Suddenly the rope hangs erect, suspended by magic. A small boy appears, climbs to the top of the rope, and vanishes into thin air.

Everyone has heard of this trick but no one has ever witnessed it. Why? Because the trick is not a feat but an allegory or story about your life and mine. The magician is the creative power of mind, the unrealized or immature self. The rope is an astral umbilical cord, Sushumna or Jacob's ladder, giving access to heaven or the sky. ("Heaven" is a state of mind.) The whole legend is a statement about how we may use Yoga to rise above the earth or for escaping the pettiness of ego and limited self to find freedom of mind and body.

WEST MEETS EAST

In the summer of 327 BC, Alexander the Great invaded a small section of what we now call India. Having conquered the then known world, he ambitiously sought to subjugate the last unknown land. Alas, India was to become Alexander's "Russia"—his supply lines too long, the territory too vast—and by 325 BC he retreated with a shattered army.

Plutarch, the Greek historian, left a record of Alexander's experiences in India and thus gives us some idea of the cross-fertilization that occurred from the meeting of these two civilizations: the Western Greeks, with their love of philosophy, and the Eastern indians, possessed of an even deeper value for philosophy and for the introspective life.

As a boy, Alexander was tutored by Aristotle and inherited an appreciation for philosophical dialogue and a keenness to understand foreign religions. After one battle in which he nearly lost his life, he captured a group of ten Yogis. The Greeks called these ascetics *gymnosophists* ("naked philosophers," or, more literally, "nude sophisticates") and greatly admired their sagacity and perspicacity in giving pithy answers to impossible questions.

Upon pain of death for unsatisfactory answers, Alexander asked each of the Yogis a question. I will quote three of the questions and answers as particularly good examples of the inherent realism within Hindu philosophy—easily the equal of the shrewd Diogenes and the Epicurean school of Greek realism.

Alexander: "Which are the more numerous: the living or the dead?"
Answer: "The living, for the dead no more are!"
Alexander: "How long is it good for a man to live?"
Answer: "As long as a man thinks life better than death!"
Alexander: "Which is the stronger: life or death?"
Answer: "Life, for it endures so much misfortune!"

Alexander was delighted with all their answers and sent them away richly rewarded. However, he begged one of the Yogis to stay with him and become his teacher and advisor. The Yogi agreed and left India with Alexander.

After about a year, Alexander's personal Indian sage became ill and requested that a funeral pyre be built for him. The Greeks did so and the Yogi climbed atop the pyre, locked himself into the Lotus posture, and ordered torches put to the wood. As the flames mounted he gave one last glance at Alexander and said: "My Lord, in a year I will meet you at

Babylon." He closed his eyes and impassively allowed himself to be consumed by Agni, the fire god.

One year later, June 13, 323 BC, Alexander the Great was dead outside the walls of Babylon.

Yoga and Western Science

Yoga has been directly influencing Western medicine since physicians with the British East India Company first started publishing reports in Europe of Indian *faquires* demonstrating volitional controls beyond the then understood anatomical and physiological possibilities. This was first drawn to my attention by Dr. Elmer Green, who also noted the marriage of Eastern Yoga with Western hypnosis giving birth to autogenic training.

By the 1970s, Elmer Green, Ph.D., at the Menninger Institute began researching and documenting correlations between Yoga and biofeedback with accompanying measures of psycho-physiological parameters. The results, aside from his many published research papers, flowered in his magnificent documentary film, *Biofeedback: Yoga of the West*. In 1979, I attended one of his autogenic training workshops as a student, and the cross-referencing between Yoga and psychology was amazing. In 1982, I was able to catch up with his research at the Transpersonal Psychology Conference held in Bombay, India.

At the same time Dr. Green was exploring Eastern connections, Dr. Charles Tart, Ph.D. (University of California) was breaking new ground with research into brain tracings arising out of altered states of consciousness (he legitimized, for psychologists, the abbreviation ASC), as well as pioneering psychophysiological investigations of meditation, sleep, dreams, hypnosis, and parapsychology.

This efflorescence in the seventies also sprouted the best theoretical explanation, in my opinion, of kundalini. Dr. Lee Sannella, M.D., published his *Kundalini: Psychosis or Transcendence?* (1976). In the Spring of 1977, I had the privilege of spending a few days with Dr. Sannella in San Francisco, and experimenting with Itzhak Bentov's apparatus for measuring micromotion during meditation. It was impressive, to say the least, and I have not seen anything so clever since.

The list could go on endlessly. I have merely highlighted three Western scientists whose work influenced me.

YOGA AND INDIA IN THE 1990S

The Yoga Earth Summit (February 1993, Pondicherry, South India, organized and chaired by Dr. Swami Gitananda) brought academic delegates from all over India together.

Yoga is intrinsic to Indian culture, despite the fact that, as one of the six classical schools of Indian philosophy, it is hetero-orthodox in relationship to Hinduism.

An impression left deeply with me, as always when I am in India, is that Yoga is very much an Indian philosophy, science, and art—only capable of being appreciated fully by the Hindus themselves. A Western mind, even our best Indologists, probably never plumbs its depths completely.

I can report that many Indian medical schools, universities, and institutes are funded by the Indian government to establish full-time research departments devoted to investigating Yoga as a medical and psychological therapy for somatic (if there exists exclusively such an entity) and psychosomatic disease. The doctrine of Panch Kosha (five sheaths) denies simplistic separation of mind-body in terms of pathology, and the Yogis understand instantly our Western dilemma that "a specialist is someone who knows more and more about less and less, until ultimately, he or she knows everything about nothing."

Yoga was never intended as a therapy in classical India; however, beyond a doubt, it has therapeutic efficacy, including very powerful behavioral conditioning effects as well as allowing imagination to establish a healing bridge between the physical and mental realms.

The techniques discussed in the first nine chapters of this book may be formed into a loose and flexible Yoga therapy guide.

THE ESSENCE OF HATHA

The object of all Yoga is to induce a harmonious release of energy at the intellectual, emotional, and physical levels of being. In Hatha Yoga, the two syllables *ha* (Sun) and *tha* (Moon) refer to the inherent duality of all living organisms expressed as expansion and contraction, relaxation and tension, reflected down to the cellular levels of metabolic building up (anabolism) and breaking down (catabolism).

In terms of the gross energy known to Western science, Hatha Yoga practice achieves a correct balance of using sugar and oxygen for energy and throwing out carbon dioxide and water as breakdown products of this burning.

The effect of all *asanas,* or poses, in Hatha can be summed up once the principle that "nature tolerates no empty spaces" is understood. All twisting and bending of the body through asanas produce an internal compression massage of the tightly packed body organs, releasing vitality just as a sponge (or body organ—for example, the liver) can be cleansed by immersing it in a basin of water (the body and circulating fluids) and systematically squeezing and releasing it.

Every student of the philosophical life should find at least a few minutes daily for some of the classical life-affirming poses of Hatha. In lawrence Durrell's *Justine,* Balthazar—the cabalistic physician—comments: "...after all the work of the philosophers on his soul and the doctors on his body, what can we say we really know about man? That he is, when all is said and done, just a passage for liquids and solids, a *pipe of flesh.*" (My emphasis.)

The efficacy of Hatha Yoga maintains the "pipe of flesh" as the perfected vehicle of expression *(tha)* for the enlightened consciousness *(ha).*

YOGA THERAPY INDEX

This is a fragmentary hint of possibilities and in no sense is suggested as a substitute for treatment by a registered health-care professional.

Note that the word "therapy" stems from a Sanskrit root before it found its way into Greek, and on through the Indo-Aryan language tree for final deposit into English. The original Sanskrit root meaning is "to sustain, support, nourish."

Subject	Technique	Page
1. Anxiety	Polarization, Shavasana I and II	60, 25, 34
2. Circulation, poor	Shavasana II, Rejuvenation	34, 74
3. Concentration, scattered	External and Internal Chakra Dharana	66
4. Depression (mild)	Polarization, Rejuvenation	60, 74
5. Energy (low)	Shavasana II, Rejuvenation	34, 74
6. Fatigue	Shavasana II, Rejuvenation	34, 74
7. Hypertension, systolic	Shavasana I and II	25, 34
8. Insomnia (onset of)*	Polarization, Shavasana II and III	60, 34, 74
9. Insomnia (disturbed sleep)	Shavasana II, Shavasana III	34, 74
10. Meditation	Sukhasana, Yoni Mudra I and II, External and Internal Chakra Dharana	16, 49, 50, 66
11. Neurasthenia (Burn-out)	Polarization, Shavasana II, Rejuvenation	60, 34, 74
12. Neuromuscular and ideo-moto control	Sukhasana, Yoni Mudra I and II	16, 49, 50
13. Tension, muscular	Shavasana I and II	25, 34
14. Tension, mental	Shavasana I and II, Polarization	25, 34, 60
15. Visualization, to improve	SCM, External Chakra Dharana	69, 66

*Early morning sudden awakening with an inability to fall back to sleep may be caused by severe depression involving a disruption in brain biochemistry, and should be checked out with a doctor—especially if accompanied by ceaseless worry, feelings of hopelessness, and suicidal ideation.

YOGA THERAPY SUGGESTION

Some students may find it an advantage to drain their legs by elevating them using a large cushion or padded chair during certain practices in this book.

These practice include:
Advanced Shavasana (Chapter 2)
Polarization (Chapter 4)
Pranic Rejunvenation (Chapter 6)
Solar Plexus Charging (Chapter 9)

Note: In the case of Solar Plexus Charging place the right ankle over the left foot. This has an equivalent effect to lying supine in sukhasana; i.e. the terminals of the feet are short circuited.

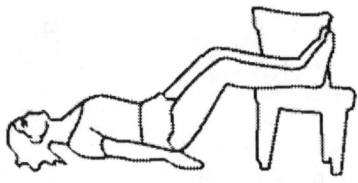

Alternative bent leg position for those with acute or chronic low back problems (Astronaut position)

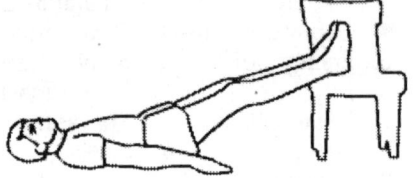

Normal drainage position

The above position is very helpful for those with:

1. Oedema (caused by fluid retention) of the ankles. Not a substitute for diuretics, where prescribed, but may be used in conjunction with them.
2. Tired, swollen feet from standing all day.
3. Varicose veins, for temporary relief (serious varicose veins are only fixed by injection of sclerotic fluid or surgery).
4. Restless leg syndrome.
5. Strained or sprained ankles.
6. Leg ulcers, to assist healing.

Finally, my personal aphorisms for your contemplation:

> ***Psychotherapy is anything that promotes faith, courage, and hope.***
>
> ***Nothing is never—and nothing is ever.***
>
> ***Care is essential to cure, and curing is caring.***

Part Five

Gnana Yoga for the Inner Life

He whose undertakings are all free from the will of desire, whose works are burned up in the fire of wisdom—him the wise call a man of learning.

— Gita 4:19

Chapter Twelve

Meditation and Inner Being

> *Having abandoned attachment to the fruit of works, ever content, without any kind of dependence, he does nothing though he is ever engaged in work.*
>
> — Gita 4:20

Yoga students are often confused about meditation. The *Oxford English Dictionary* states that to meditate is "having in mind to do or make, to ponder over, indulge in thought." This definition gives the impression that meditation is an active, ongoing process of the mind with many thoughts, like fish, swimming through the stream of consciousness. The implication is that meditation is a form of thinking; namely, a problem-solving activity. Nothing could be further from the truth!

The word "meditation" is inadequate to describe the higher mental states sought in Yoga. The object of Yoga exercises is to induce a state of mental quietness, of tranquillity, which is far removed from pondering or indulging in active thought. A state of "no-thought" better describes the result of Yoga.

The author of the world's first known text of Yoga was Patanjali, who defined Yoga as stilling the mind, making the consciousness motionless, and suppressing emotional fluctuations.

EIGHT PROGRESSIVE STEPS

Patanjali lucidly outlined eight progressive steps to be followed by those seeking experience of Yoga mental states. His system is termed Ashtanga Yoga, literally the eight limbs or branches leading to absolute integration of the self through fusion of the personality in trance consciousness.

The first two phases of Ashtanga Yoga are the Yama and Niyama, comprising ten rules of conduct or behavior for the student desiring a unified life. Western scholars have confused the Yama and Niyama precepts with the Ten Commandments of Moses, not understanding that the concept of sin or punishment is foreign to Yoga. Karma, the law of action and reaction, is impartial in Eastern teaching. Karma is the psychological equivalent of Newton's physical law that for every action there must be an equal and opposite reaction. The Yama-Niyama practices are based upon a knowledge of karma, and unlike the Ten Commandments, are devoid of moral or ethical meaning.

For example, "Ahimasa is the Yama of observing non-violence towards all creatures." This dictum is based on the knowledge that we pay for violent acts or feelings by the loss of our peace of mind. Mental agitation precludes higher psychic states.

Santosha, the cultivation of contentment, is the Niyama rule of living in the present time without brooding over the past or daydreaming about the future. Living in the present time conserves the psychic energy needed for meditation or superconsciousness.

The aim of these precepts is purely the maintenance of mental hygiene.

Yamas

1. **Ahimsa:** Non-violence.
2. **Satya:** Truth. Maintaining a lie wastes energy and disrupts internal states.

3. **Asteya:** Non-stealing. We have a right only to that which we have earned.
4. **Brahmacharya:** Sexual energy "response-ability."
5. **Aparigraha:** Non-possession or detachment from materialism.

Niyamas

1. **Saucha:** Purity of the physical body and freedom from toxic wastes.
2. **Santosha:** Contentment. Living in the "eternal now."
3. **Tapas:** Indifference to extremes or external change.
4. **Svadhyaya:** Self-development. When we cease learning we begin to die.
5. **Ishvarapranidhana:** Devotion to the philosophical life.

The third stage of Patanjali's classical system is asana, meaning any position which is relaxed and sustained, allowing the body to be held motionless while mental silence is sought. Body activity is linked with mental states and the object of asana is to reduce the tendency of the physical body to disrupt mental poise.

Pranayama (life energy control) is the fourth branch for mastery. It consists of breathing techniques resulting in controlled respiration which is characteristically deep and slow. Slow, full breathing, deliberately performed with conscious awareness, signals profound relaxation to the mind of the aspirant preparing for meditation.

HATHA YOGA

From the third and fourth stages of Patanjali's Ashtanga Yoga has arisen the well known and excellent school of Hatha Yoga with its postures and breath controls contributing to the maintenance of health or freedom from "dis-ease."

Hatha Yoga is designed to bring into reality the dictum of "mind over matter." Through Hatha Yoga, the consciousness gains rulership of its vehicle for expression, the physical body.

Pratyahara, the fifth step, is withdrawal of the senses from the stimulation of the environment as preparation for the journey into the mental space explored in meditation. It may be induced by fixing the attention upon a mental image so intensely that conscious recognition of impulses from the five sensory gates are excluded or diminished. Physical aids, such as retirement to a dark underground cave or blocking the body orifices with cotton wool, may facilitate Pratyahara.

The final three stages are the jewels of Yoga meditation. In these states the mind is cleared of the multitude of thoughts characteristic of normal consciousness, leaving the lake of consciousness placid.

This process is termed Samyama and may be likened to dropping a pebble (image concentrated upon) among a school of minnows (thoughts) with the result that the fish immediately flee, leaving the pebble resting on the bottom, visible through the clear, calm water of consciousness.

When the consciousness can contain a chosen mental image for approximately twelve seconds without interruption, the sixth stage of Dharana has been reached. This is more difficult than may appear. Subtle breaks in concentration occur, such as the thoughts "I am doing this well" or "twelve seconds must be up."

Dhyana, the seventh phase, is sustained Dharana (or steadiness of concentration) for over two minutes.

Samadhi: "With Pure Consciousness"

The last stage, Samadhi, may occur at any moment in a spiritual disciple's life or it may be the culmination of diligent practice of the previous seven steps. The word itself means with *(sam)* pure consciousness *(adhi)*. The Sanskrit root *adhi* has been compared with the Hebrew *adoni,* meaning "Lord," and hence Samadhi may be thought of as an experience of cosmic consciousness dwelling with God.

In this state, the Yogi becomes one with the object meditated upon and loses awareness of separateness between the self, the object of attention, and the process of attending. Samadhi is the return to paradise lost.

Patanjali's Ashtanga Yoga had been summed up by a very clever Englishman as simply to "Sit still, shut up, stop thinking, and go away." Excellent advice!

The technique of meditation is not difficult, but like any worthwhile practice it requires perseverance, effort, and time. Daily meditation is a vital necessity which is totally missing from our Western way of living.

Each day we waste our mental energies with negative emotions, useless daydreaming, and gossip. Even talking about projects—or intellectualizing—drains our energy, preventing us from actually doing or accomplishing in life. The philosophical student should be reminded of the injunction that what comes out of the mouth is more important than what goes into it.

Interior Depths

Yoga mind control offers a state of consciousness accessible to all, in which ceaseless mental chatter is finally stilled and we plunge into the interior depths of our minds to find rejuvenation of the nervous system and a new awareness of living.

Meditation takes us upon the journey into inner space which is as limitless and infinite as outer space. The particular method used—mostly concentration upon sound or visual imagery—varies in each tradition, but whatever the technique, it may be considered to be a navigational aid, bringing us to the shores of meditative experience.

Meditation is not one experience but many experiences. Bliss, creative thinking, meaningful emotional experience, and heightened sensory awareness all form some of the concrete results of meditation.

The criteria for validity of psychic or spiritual experience lies in the integrating, settling effect upon all levels of the meditator's personality. Those who experience real meditative states are loath to discuss their experiences, as opposed to those who manifest their personality disturbances, which they interpret as "spiritual experience."

We initiate in a particularly potent form of meditation known as Surya Shabda or "listening to the solar currents." These "currents" are inner, subtle sounds heard in the right hemisphere of the brain and related to the flow of certain nerve channels originating in the right sympathetic ganglion, which—together with the left sympathetic ganglion—form a "Jacob's ladder" to "heaven" on either side of the spine.

The classical texts compare focusing upon internal sounds in the head to luring a deer (the restless mind) with a hunter's flute (*nada* or inner music) into a snare or trap to be slain (thought dies).

Sound Has No External Reality

All sound exists only in the mind and has no external reality. If a tree falls in the forest without anyone being in the vicinity, does it make a noise? No! The tree drops as silently as a feather, for the movement produces air vibrations only—not sound vibrations.

Until shock waves traveling through the air are picked up by the ear and changed into mechanical vibrations, which in turn are converted into electrical impulses (in the temporal lobe of the brain), producing what we call "sound," nothing is heard. When we search for inner sound we force the awareness to cut through the twenty-seven layers of mind like a knife cutting through an onion to the center.

To begin practicing the most elementary aspect of the Surya Shabda kriya (or technique), sit comfortably in a quiet, darkened room with your elbows resting upon a table or your knees. Lick the thumbs (moistening them thoroughly) and then screw them firmly into the ears, letting the fingers cover the eyes without pressing upon the eyeballs. External noise and light should now be eliminated.

Focus your attention upon your right ear and begin listening for inner sound. Do not analyze the sounds you hear but simply accept them, searching underneath each manifestation for a yet more delicate sound, thus carrying yourself deeper and deeper within the cavern of the mind-brain complex.

As with all meditative kriya, initial patience and quiet perseverance is necessary. Practice for ten minutes the first week, increasing the time by five minutes each week to meet a goal of thirty minutes.

Ten Billion Cells

The human brain contains some ten billion cells, of which only ten percent (or one billion) are used in daily living. Surya Shabda, when fully practiced, opens up the "psychic" or dormant areas of the right cerebral cortex, raising energy levels throughout the mind-body maze and releasing fuller intellectual, emotional potential.

Personal initiation into Surya Shabda involves the giving of a *shakti* ("power") mantra which vibrates the cerebral area, making it literally "slop in" neuro-secretions, *soma, amrita* ("juices of immortality"), instantly relieving tension, dispersing negative emotion, and dropping blood pressure.

Initiates are taught the mapping of twenty-seven layers to the consciousness and the meaning of each type of sound heard while practicing Surya Shabda. As the meditation experience deepens, synesthesia (translation of one sensory modality into another), occurs—with the inner sounds becoming inner light, until ultimately Samadhi ensues.

YAMAS AND NIYAMAS

The doctrine of Yama and Niyama has been so crudely interpreted in popular Hinduism and in popular Western Yoga that it has been thought to be mere morals and dogmas. Such simplistic attitudes simply do not work.

When the Yamas and Niyamas are taken to be a set of rules for moral behavior, we are faced with a profound problem. It is not possible for people to be perfect in the moral sense. It is not in our nature. In every person, no matter how highly developed, there are the basic uncivilized instincts deep in the normal brain, and as long as they are there the possibility exists of the crisis situation which will release them.

I have found out two things about humans by my own personal experience: in every person there exist twin buttons. One of these buttons I call the "killer button" and the other I term the "Judas button."

The killer button is an emotional response for a certain area of the brain, and when it is found in a person (normally by pushing that button with words), you can turn the most innocuous, the most passive, the most harmless person into a killer. The Judas button is related to the particular flaw in each of us, which—when it is pressed—will lead us to betray the Christos, the higher consciousness that is within.

Subtle Inner Processes

This whole doctrine of Yama and Niyama is not a rule about moral conduct. It is a guide about subtle inner processes for controlling the ebb and flow of psychic content in the inner being. When we start analyzing them, we find they have a deeper meaning beyond the popular, external mass meaning.

If we look at the first Yama (control), it is Ahimsa, which literally means nonviolence. From a simplistic view it is equated with the Commandment "Thou shalt not kill." Yet within each one of us a button can be pressed in some crisis situation in life when we become capable of killing—Yoga or no Yoga.

One of the basic Buddhist injunctions is a form of Ahimsa: "Thou shalt kill no living thing." Yet if you take quinine to cure malaria, you kill certain parasites floating around in your bloodstream. If you are a Jain (who rings a little bell to scare away the insects as he treads on the grass), are you breaking your vows on nonviolence if you use penicillin to overcome the microorganisms causing an attack of pneumonia? If a person is in a position in life where he or she must kill, where the person feels that to kill is righteous or justifiable, is he or she breaking the rule of Ahimsa? Is Ahimsa meant literally—no physical killing?

Given a little thought, it is obvious that the whole thing is a joke if it does not mean a little more than that. What is it in humanity that is not to be killed? What nonviolence means, what Ahimsa means, is an attitude of mind—not a set of actions. It is the attitude in the mind, not the action, that determines the karma.

And what is it that each person is prone to kill? It is higher consciousness. What is the killer of the higher consciousness? It is negative emotions. One who esoterically practices Ahimsa tries not to permit violence against the higher consciousness or to kill it by the misuse and abuse of the emotional faculties.

Satya: Truth

The second Yama is Satya—Truth. It is a familiar moral injunction to always tell the truth—at an external level. Now humanity possesses a very curious thing. It is called the unconscious mind. As each of us reads this, we are operating with approximately one-tenth of our total mental activity, because—like an iceberg—nine-tenths of our mind is submerged. What person can claim to know the contents of that submerged part of his or her mind? How do you tell when you are being truthful?

If Satya means "non-lying," then are you practicing Satya when you refuse to tell the white lie that saves someone from hurt? It is obvious that a simple interpretation of what constitutes the truth is not Satya. For that inner spiritual truth has to do with the most difficult thing that any of us can come to—that is the truth to the Self, acknowledging the flaws, looking within and seeing what is there, facing it without fear, and going within, even if it tears one apart.

In the West we have a particular type of Yoga that does this very successfully—yes, this is Yoga—called psychotherapy; it is one of the most valuable heritages that Western civilization has produced. In fact, I do not believe that for Western people who are serious about Yoga there can be any Yoga in their life without—at some time—psychotherapy. That going within and facing the truth about the self and the acceptance of the self, this is Satya.

Asteya: Non-stealing

The third Yama, Asteya, literally means "non-stealing." At a general level we say that stealing is taking that which one has not earned. I accept that each of us must earn what we possess, that if we take something that we have not earned then we are breaking Asteya, or the rule of non-stealing.

However, Asteya goes much deeper than that. Each person in life, in his or her personal existence, is a vital cog in the wheel of life. Each person fulfills a potential. Each person, in being part of that cog of this whole thing that we call life, fulfills Dharma, or obligation to life. Esoterically, one who steals, one who breaks the law of Asteya or non-stealing, is one who steals the time of the spirit, the time of the higher consciousness, that is meant to be devoted to the unfoldment of the higher being.

That stealing that takes place in our life is the stealing of time. From birth to death, from womb to tomb, and each moment of life that we fail to struggle with ourselves, we are stealing the time of the spirit, that time of Dharma that has been given to us. This is the true essence of that rule of Asteya. Killing time isn't murder—it's spiritual suicide!

Brahmacharya: Divine Action

Fourth, there is the Yama of Brahmacharya. Perhaps of all the Yamas that have been written about in popular Hindu books, this has been the most misunderstood—yet it deals with the most potent essence of being. Fools have said that Brahmacharya is celibacy; that it has something to do with the banking up of sexual forces. Yet one who has any knowledge of Indian philosophy, who examines Buddhist and Tantric tradition, knows that there are other traditions in Indian philosophy, besides the simplistic Bhakti Vedantist tradition, that belie the whole concept of Brahmacharya as mere celibacy.

In the Upanishads it is clearly indicated that the sexual potential lying within each human is communion, a divine force. The Upanishads say that the vulva is an altar and that the hairs upon the vulva are the flames upon the altar. The body is a temple and the sexual act is an act of divine worship.

And yet fools have said that Brahmacharya means celibacy. Consequently, whole hordes of people in India and the West are knotting themselves up sexually trying to follow this rule, thinking it means celibacy. Well, it doesn't mean that. What does it mean?

Brahma means God, *charya* means action. And the word itself means "God-action" or "Divine action." What it says is that the celibacy of sex is not in the act, but in the attitude that is held in consciousness. Brahmacharya is an attitude of divine worship. It has nothing to do with the physical action itself. In the scriptures the body is spoken of as the castle of Brahma, and in this castle we worship an inner instinct as an aspect of the Divine self.

Charya is even more accurately translated as "to wander," and the Brahmachari wanders for eternity, in the consciousness of GOD, his or her mental body rapt in contemplation of the infinite varieties of Cosmic G-eneration, O-rder, D-ecay—a kaleidoscope of shifting aspects of Brahma, Vishnu, and Shiva.

Freud's Discovery

Freud discovered for the Western world what the Tantrist of India, the early Dravidians, and certain schools of Buddhism had known for thousands of years. He found that the primal force of power within each of us is the sexual mainspring, that the foundation of being lies in sexual forces. People have badly misunderstood Freud when they interpreted him to mean that everything has to do with sex.

What Freud said was not that the sexual energies were the most important thing in life, but that they provided the power for the basis of behavior.

Just as the wiring in a factory provides the power for the making of its products, and if that wiring is faulty nothing will be properly made, so if the sexual energies that run in us through the nervous system are faulty or twisted, then the rest of the activity of the person is going to be influenced.

This is what the whole concept of Brahmacharya is about. It means something very special. What it means in each person's life, I cannot tell you. At a theoretical level, it means that this worship of the body should be for everyone. But at a personal level, in practice, this is something that each person has to struggle to work out for him or herself.

In theory we say that this divine act of expression of love should be free, provided that no hurt accrues and provided no uncared-for children result. That is simple common sense. But each person has to work out the inner significance of this on a deeply personal level.

Aparigraha: Non-possession

Finally, we come to the last Yama—Aparigraha, which means non-possession. In the classical Vedantist tradition it should mean that when a person becomes a Sannyasin he or she abandons all worldly goods. Now, what is important about this idea of Aparigraha? It is obvious that if you are a Westerner living in a materialistic, commercial world, you cannot survive without goods. What is meant by non-possession?

Only fools take the Yamas and Niyamas literally. This Yama has nothing to do with the acquisition of goods. What it has to do with is the attitude or the attachment to these goods. All things, all material goods, are here for our use or for our misuse. All goods, all fruits of the earth, all fruits of the brain in the sense of manufacture of material goods, are here for enjoyment and pleasure, provided our consciousness does not center around acquisition. Again, Aparigraha is not an act, it is an attitude of mind. It is not a question of possessing goods—rather, do the goods possess us?

Saucha: Purity

Now we move to the Niyamas. They represent the positive element in the sense of things to be done, acts to be worked at, concrete realities. The first of these is Saucha, which means purity. Fools have thought that it means purity of mind. Who can say that one has purity of mind? Only an infant—and even that can be argued from a certain psycho-analytic viewpoint—has the possibility of a pure mind, if it means the mind.

Saucha does not mean the mind; it refers to the body. It means purity of the body in a physiological sense. For the purity of the body, which is the vehicle for the expression of consciousness, is the removal of toxic wastes, the malas, the phlegms, that alter the nervous system of humanity, that clog up the consciousness, the brain. The maintenance of that purity of the body temple has to do with the ways that each one of us starts to die. There are four ways in which each person begins to die. I will talk about three of them now and the fourth one later.

Beginning to Die

The first way in which each of us begins to die physically and mentally we can call the psychosomatic act. We begin to kill ourselves by misuse of the mind/body relationship. How? By misunderstanding and abusing the Yamas, by committing mental acts of violence, by killing our higher consciousness, by refusing to acknowledge the truth of the self, by stealing the time that has been given to us from birth to death, by misusing the nervous system in its sexual function, and by becoming attracted to physical goods and suffering the tension of their loss.

Perhaps sixty to seventy percent of people who come to doctors are suffering from psychosomatic diseases, a disease process that started from emotion tensions.

The second way we start to die has to do with the fundamental care of our being, the nucleus of the cell. It is currently thought in Western biology that individual cell death is programmed in the chromosomes. We suspect that the practice of Yoga may be able to alter the programming in the nucleus of the cell and thus prolong the physical act of life.

The third way that we start to die has particularly to do with Saucha, or purity. It is simply this: we begin to die at a cellular level by drowning in our own excretion. The semipermeable membrane of the cell wall becomes clogged with wastes and loses its ability to take in nutrients and throw out waste products.

The practices of Hatha Yoga—the internal cleansings, the internal massage of the postures, diet and fasting—maintain the health of the cell wall and prevent its deterioration. Saucha (purity) means consistent removal of internal wastes from the physical body to prolong life and cleanse the nervous system for higher states.

Santosha: Contentment

The second Niyama, Santosha, means contentment—the practice of being contented. How? By living in present time, forgetting the past, leaving the day-dreams of the future, keeping the energies of the mind/body complex for the present moment. We can cultivate contentment by using the twilight period between waking and sleep and between sleep and full waking to seed our unconscious mind with positive suggestions of happiness.

What is this Thing Called Yoga?

The oldest definition of Yoga is the cessation of the fluctuations of the mind, those wanderings, those tensions, those emotional jumps. One who practices Yoga is one who can pull the mind together to stop those fluctuations; one who can reach inside to bring out the energies, regardless of what has happened; one who can, in his or her mind, be chased by the hounds of hell and torn to pieces, and can stop these fluctuations of mind when necessary—this one has Yoga.

Tapas: Indifference

The third of the Niyamas is called Tapas, roughly translated as "indifference." Tapas is the practice of indifference to discomfort when no useful purpose is served by taking notice of that discomfort. Tapas is a cultivated attitude of nonchalance to extremes.

Swadhyaya: Self-study

The fourth Niyama is Swadhyaya—self-study. Its inner essence deals with the fourth way we begin to die. This self-study means that the act of living is a continuous process of learning. Stop learning, and you begin to die in a very special way. Psychologists know that at least fifty percent of senility is psychological—loss of interest in life, loss of willingness to learn by life's experience. In this context, Yoga is a form of reeducation.

The Final Process

The final process, Ishwarapranidhana—crudely interpreted—means devotion to God. In Samkhyan terms, it means devotion to the Self as the essence of God. For what is God? It is that on-going life process. It is no being, no person, it is this whole process of life and life awareness. One who practices Ishwarapranidhana is devoted to the on-going process of life and evolution in the self.

For Yoga to survive in an intelligent way for thoughtful people in the West, a new recasting must come about. The classical texts of Yoga are the testimonies of Indian civilization at its greatest peak. India is a badly decayed civilization at present, but it has left us a heritage in the classical scriptures which are short, succinct statements for the minds of future ages to expand, expound, and enlarge upon.

Some schools have created morals and dogmas from the classical scriptures. Let them. Those who want simplistic Yoga, let them have it. But those who want to find out what it is really about are involved in becoming builders and recasters of this thing called Yoga.

★★

Chapter Thirteen

Advanced Techniques

Ajna is directly connected with Muladhara Chakra. If any awakening takes places in Ajna Chakra, it first takes place in Muladhara Chakra. And anything taking place in Muladhara has to go to Ajna Chakra.

— Paramahansa Satyananda Saraswati

We have dealt with the Panch Chakra system (i.e., the five chakras below the head). Now we can begin to meditate upon Ajna (pronounced "ag-nyah"—G as in "agate"), the so-called "Third Eye," and in doing so we enter the realm of the shat-chakra or six center system. (The classical Tantric text is *Shat-Chakra Nirupana*).

Ajna, between the eyes, is usually compared with the pineal gland, on the functional basis that:

1. The pineal gland is light-sensitive.
2. The pineal has a braking or accelerating effect on puberty (this is a direct connection to the Swadhisthana-Muladhara complex).
3. In terms of the phylogenetic scale, the pineal is considered related to a vestigial eye, which a particular type of Australian lizard actually has at the top of its skull.
4. Some of the pineal secretions trigger sleep-wakefulness cycles and are implicated in producing altered states of consciousness.

On the other hand, the pituitary gland:

1. Anatomically sits at the root of the nose, in the sella turcica ("Turkish saddle" of the sphenoid bone), between and behind the eyes.
2. Has been referred to as the "master" gland or "gland old master," exhibiting control over most of the gland/chakras below it.
3. Functionally influences gonadal maturation and continuing cyclic activity.
4. Anatomically, with its two lobes, anterior and posterior, resembles the two "wings" or petals *(dalas)* of the mandala (full diagram) of Ajna.

Since a chakra is but a concept for attention-focusing it does not really matter, and I suggest both glands are involved and anyone that wants to argue about this is going to have to deal with messy pieces of brain anatomy, including the hypothalamus and the thalamus.

A full mandala diagram of a chakra—i.e., containing a God, Goddess, Element God (hidden or present by implication; e.g., Agni, the fire god, is present in Manipura), animal vehicle, Yantra, Bija mantra, and Sanskrit letters of petals *(dala mantra)*— is an information storage and retrieval system, which the initiated can read for hours. (Classical color mandalas of the shat chakras, with an esoteric Tantric commentary, may be found in my book *Ecstasy Through Tantra*, Llewellyn Publications.)

Focusing upon Ajna is a royal road to the unconscious, especially when the prior chakras have been meditated upon. The meditation will be divided into two stages:

1. Internal Chakra Dharana utilizing Trataka
2. Copper Chakra Breathing

> *The map is not the place.*
> — *Korzybski*

When meditating upon Ajna, I must emphasize that the way to find out what will happen is a case, like death, in which experience is the best (only?) teacher!

INTRODUCTORY INFORMATION

The Sanskrit word "Ajna" means "command center," that place where we worship with our consciousness the Guru-Atman, or highest self, and receive instruction.

The element associated with Ajna is Manas, or "mind-stuff," the very energy of consciousness.

The Bija mantra is the "lost word" OM, and the yantra symbolizing Ajna is a winged globe, an emblem of the imagination which can "fly" anywhere, beyond limitations of space and time. Other more traditional yantras include the triangle, apex down (as also found in the Chakra mandalas of Muladhara and Manipura), and the unconscious symbol of OM embossed upon a gold disc.

Note in the sketch outline of Ajna, that the two Dalas or petals (to become the wings) have the Sanskrit letters upon them of *Ha* and *K'sha*, representing the Sun and Moon, mind and body, Ida and Pingala, all subsuming at Ajna or the root of the nose.

Our symbol upon which we will perform Tratak will be a black winged globe (like Hermes' caduceus), so that with our eyes closed the complementary image will be a white winged globe.

Internal Chakra Dharana Technique for Ajna

1. Place yourself comfortably in either a sitting meditation pose or on a chair; in either case, have the control of a bright desk lamp within reach.
2. Place the Ajna Internal Chakra Dharana Yantra at eye level or upon your lap.
3. Gaze, inhibiting your blink reflex (i.e. Tratak), at the white Bindu or spot in the center of the black winged globe (it may take one or two minutes) until a white rim aura starts to appear around the black margins and the black itself probably begins to turn whitish or pale.
4. At the same time as you are performing Tratak, silently recite the Bija mantra OM, aligning it with the natural inspiration (Oh) through the forehead, and the natural expiration (Mmmmm)—the "Oh" flows into the Ajna with the inspiration, and "Mmmm" flows out through the Ajna point with the expiration. (See the illustration on the facing page.)
5. When the rim aura is well manifested, simultaneously switch the light off and close your eyes. Continue the silent repetition of the Bija OM, as in Step 4, while gently looking through your forehead and closed eyes. With relaxation a white winged globe will gradually emerge, floating in the dark space in front of you. Watch the winged globe, constantly adjusting the focus of your attention, in order to perceive the afterimage as long as possible.
6. When the afterimage has totally faded, recreate it with your imagination and hold it between your two physical eyes while continuing with the Bija mantra meditation. This can be continued for up to twenty minutes.

After one or two weeks, concentration upon the Ajna External Dharana Tattwa may be dispensed with and you may proceed with the Internal Chakra Dharana phase only,

AJNA BIJA MANTRA AND BREATH CHART

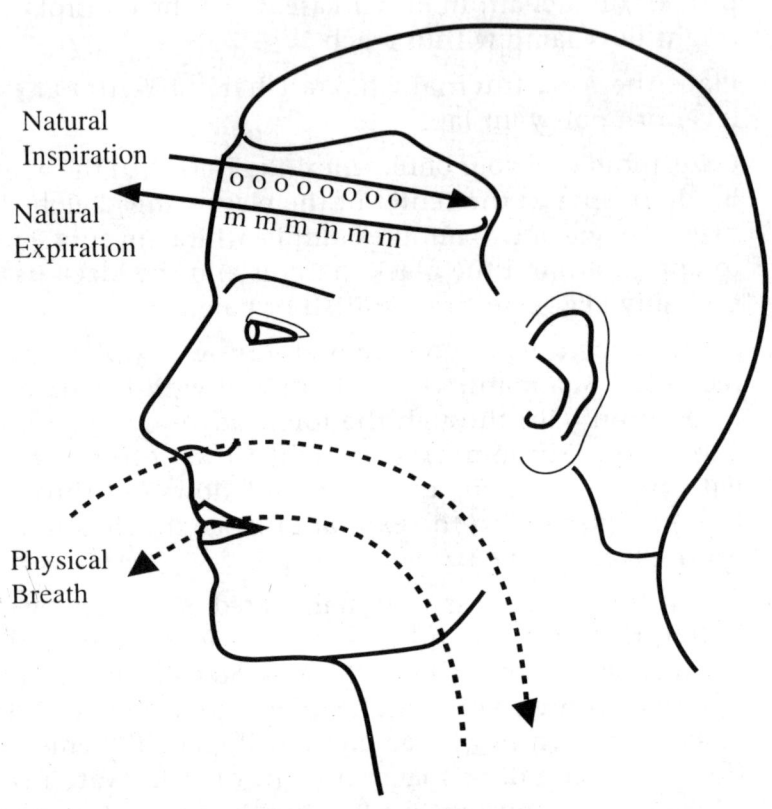

visualizing the winged globe behind the forehead and focusing on the Bija mantra OM synchronized with the breath.

External Chakra Dharana produces the afterimage, which serves as what I call a psychophysiological attention fixer. Swami Satyananda used to teach us to smear the Ajna point, about where the Tilak of Hindu women is, with saliva—which has just the right viscosity for producing a slow evaporation sensation that makes concentration on the Marma easier. Of course, the creation of these Tattwa afterimages accelerates contact with unconscious archetypes.

Advantages of Internal Ajna Chakra Dharana

By the time External Tratak has been completed a conditioning procedure is established, which amounts to a mobile "de-stression" through the meditation technique. Almost anywhere, anytime, the eyes may be closed, and an altered state of consciousness rapidly induced through focusing attention on the Yantra of a winged globe and coordinating the Bija mantra OM with the uninhibited, spontaneous breath rhythm: in, "o;" out, "m."

This ASC (altered state of consciousness) is marked by physical signs accompanying each level:

1. **Relaxed wakefulness:** Subjective contentment with warming of hands and feet, slowing of respiration, raising of GSR (galvanic skin response) threshold, and lowering of blood pressure.
2. **Dreaming:** REM (rapid eye movement) and sudden flaccidity of the neck muscles, producing head nodding, with subjective images, dream scenarios, and psychedelic color patterns.
3. **Deep dreamless sleep:** Often accompanied by snoring. It is possible to retain consciousness in this state—Yoga refers to it as "Turiya."

Some take Ajna as a literal "Third Eye" which can be opened to produce clairvoyance. Certainly something unusual can occur by meditating upon this point, and I may suggest that any psychic effects take place in two stages:

1. This is always to spontaneously see the Third Eye, which traditionally may appear as an eye, blue pearl, or an intense point of light.
2. This is the phenomenon of actually seeing through the Third Eye.

Clairvoyance, from the French, means "clear seeing," and so this is a magical change of perspective, in which things just *are!*

This sixth sense is intuition (inner tutor), the consequence of a Yoga between the right and left hemispheres of the brain. The feminine, receptive, right hemisphere processes information and flashes the conclusion across to the masculine, logical left hemisphere, producing an altered state of consciousness experienced as a sudden gestalt or "Eureka!" grasp of reality.

— Ecstasy Through Tantra
(page 80)

THE THIRD EYE

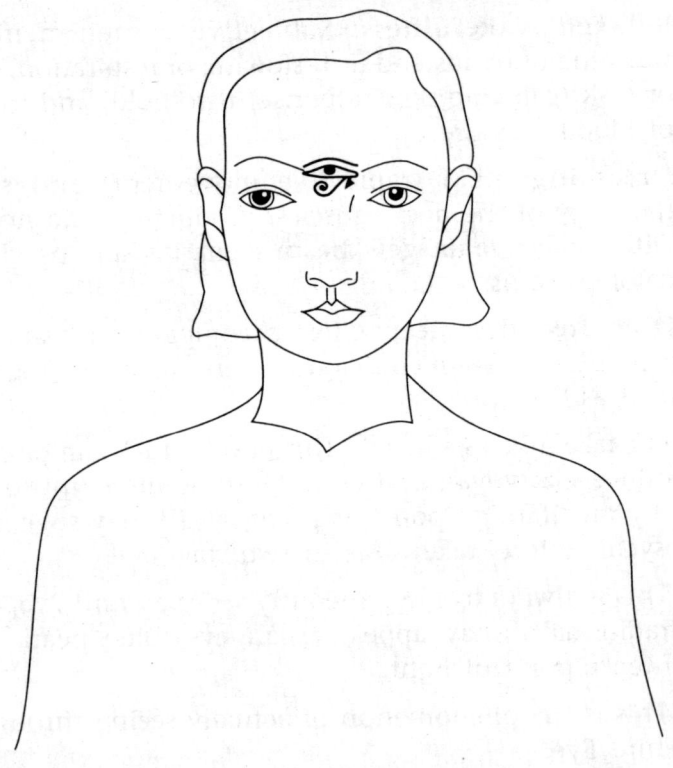

As an interesting experiment, do Tratak on another person's eyes from a distance of about twelve inches. A Third Eye will appear between the other two so long as your partner doesn't look away.

Paramhansa Swami Satyananda Saraswati's Yoga Chakra Breathing for Brain Hemisphere Integration

By 1966 Swami Satyananda had commenced releasing hitherto unknown Tantric meditation techniques to the Western world. One of the most powerful of his methods involved uniting breath and energy (PRANA) through PURELY MENTAL concentration upon unilateral and alternate nostril breathing. This practice was a concrete example of the classical yoga injunction of "UNION OF MANAS (MIND) and PRANA (BREATH)" The outstanding psycho-physiological implications of his methodology was vindicated by a plethora of Western laboratory research in the 1980's.

"Researchers have reported a left-to-right Hemisphere shift as breathing changes from the right nostril to the left. The nasal cycle may prove to be the Rosetta stone of research. It is a window of cerebral hemisphere dominance and can be brought under voluntary control." Ernest Rossi: Brain Mind Bulletin, 1986.

"Breathing out of only one nostril stimulates activity in the brain hemisphere on the opposite (contralateral) side. This finding suggests a possible noninvasive treatment for mental and mood disorders". Werntz: Neurosciences Department, UCLA, 1988. (Reported in Brain Mind Bulletin)

To fully appreciate the genius of Swami Paramhansa Satyananda consider the work in the late 1970's of two Harvard psychologists, Richard Davidson and Gary Schwartz. They researched "counting sheep" as a classic way of dealing with insomnia.

"Visualizing sheep prevents the brain's right hemisphere from processing anxiety provoking imagery, while the counting itself keeps the left hemisphere from straying into problematic auditory and verbal thought." Harvard University papers 1979.

Their conclusion was that the time-honored practice of counting sheep tied both sides of the brain up simultaneously and therefore prevented the type of disturbing brain activity often responsible for insomnia.

With this introduction we are now ready to explore the utilization of Swami Satyananda's method in a dynamic technique I have dubbed "Copper Meditation."

COPPER MEDITATION: AN AJNA CHAKRA PSYCHIC BREATHING TECHNIQUE

This meditation employs an unusual attention fixer for Ajna, coupled with a process of breath visualization and backward counting. The method is extremely effective for smoothing out the brain wave patterns, synchronizing the hemispheres, and allowing the parasympathetic branch of the autonomic nervous system to quickly gain ascendancy.

Remember, concentration upon an image, idea, sensation, or sound is not meditation but only the method *(yukti)* to achieve the state of integration (Yoga). In other words the brain is, in the Hindu view, only the vehicle through which the consciousness has to filter itself on a material plane. As we alter our brain state so we experience pristine consciousness or "supra-consciousness."

Inherent in all practices of this book is an underlying recognition that for true meditation to take place, integration of both cerebral hemispheres is necessary. Each technique has built-in methods for occupying the brain holistically.

The left hemisphere may be said to represent Pingala, Shiva, the Sun, rational, verbal processes; while the right hemisphere is the polar opposite, relating to Ida, Shakti, Moon, intuitive, non-verbal processes.

With this meditation we take care of the left hemisphere by silently counting backward, in synchronicity with the respiratory cycle, from 10 to 1. Since we tend to count forward automatically, by counting backward the "gears" of the left brain tend to become more "engaged."

The right brain is occupied by visualizing a stream of white light (or blue or yellow light, if preferred) going into Ajna, also in synchronicity with the breath.

Finally, both hemispheres have their respective sensory cortex strips (tactile-touch areas) simultaneously bombarded by pressure over the Ajna region with a common United States copper penny, or one-cent coin.

The "magic" of the penny, is, of course, copper, and the association of copper with Venus or Aphrodite (remember the IUD "Copper 7"?) is traditional, as well as the fact that copper is an analgesic and anti-inflammatory substance (copper bracelets for arthritis have long been in vogue) now made into a cream for joint pain. These are just a few of the interesting relationships. Copper is also a fine conductor of heat and electricity; its magical properties, according to folklore, are comparable with those of quartz crystal.

At a serious level, the penny becomes a superb and inexpensive biofeedback device, monitoring the tension of the forehead frontalis muscle, contractions of which trigger tension headaches (in which the head feels squeezed as if in a vice), where pain is constant and non-throbbing.

Using a Copper Penny as an Ajna "Attention Fixer"

The frontal bone of the forehead is the only area in the body where a vacuum suction effect can be created. The anatomical indentation is about the middle of the forehead, at a subsection of Ajna chakra, called Rudhra chakra. A clean one-cent piece should be used: i.e., wipe off any grease with tissue. (Sometimes before classes I soak a dozen pennies in vinegar for an hour and then polish them dry.)

Technique

(Refer to the chart on the following page.)

1. Place the penny flat between the eyebrows, just at the root of the nose, or nasion, holding the penny with a forefinger.
2. Slide it up to roughly the center of the forehead.

3. Push the penny firmly into the forehead with the forefinger and take the forefinger away.

4. The penny will now stay in position as long as you keep the frontalis muscle relaxed; it will continue to stay there for the duration of the meditation. Note that if you contract the muscles of the forehead, voluntarily or involuntarily, the penny will drop off.

Using the Penny as a Biofeedback Device for Tension Headaches

If you gently relax and focus on keeping the penny in position, you will train yourself to relax the muscles in that area. Headaches tend to be either vascular throbbing (including migraine) or constant vice-like pain, as a band around the head. The latter type, tension headaches, respond well to using the penny as a biofeedback method. The penny is the world's least expensive biofeedback device.

PLACING THE PENNY

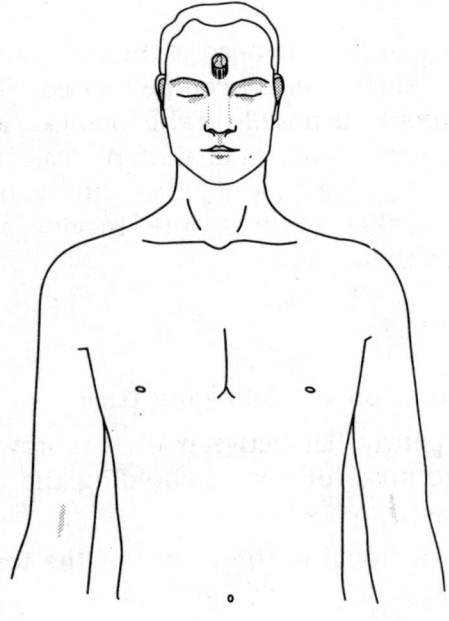

We are now ready to consider "Vertical Breathing" (refer to the chart below). With the penny in place, become aware of the natural breath flowing in and out of your nostrils. As the inhalation takes place, visualize energy (white, blue, or gold) flowing up your right nostril to the Third Eye, which you will now be able to feel by the sensation of the penny. As you exhale, imagine the colored energy flowing from the Ajna point down and out your left nostril. You then reverse this so the incoming breath flows up the left nostril to the penny, and on the subsequent exhalation, from Ajna out the right nostril. Say to yourself "Ten." You have now completed one round. Continue the procedure, and on completion of the round mentally say "Nine," and so on until you reach "One," at which point you start again with "Ten."

In the right nostril to Ajna, from Ajna out the left nostril.
In the left nostril to Ajna, from Ajna out the right nostril.
Say "Ten."

In the right nostril to Ajna, from Ajna out the left nostril.
In the left nostril to Ajna, from Ajna out the right nostril.
Say "Nine."

In the right nostril to Ajna, from Ajna out the left nostril.
In the left nostril to Ajna, from Ajna out the right nostril.
Say "Eight."

In the right nostril to Ajna, from Ajna out the left nostril.
In the left nostril to Ajna, from Ajna out the right nostril.
Say "Seven."

In the right nostril to Ajna, from Ajna out the left nostril.
In the left nostril to Ajna, from Ajna out the right nostril.
Say "Six."

In the right nostril to Ajna, from Ajna out the left nostril.
In the left nostril to Ajna, from Ajna out the right nostril.
Say "Five."

In the right nostril to Ajna, from Ajna out the left nostril.
In the left nostril to Ajna, from Ajna out the right nostril.
Say "Four."

In the right nostril to Ajna, from Ajna out the left nostril.
In the left nostril to Ajna, from Ajna out the right nostril.
Say "Three."

In the right nostril to Ajna, from Ajna out the left nostril.
In the left nostril to Ajna, from Ajna out the right nostril.
Say "Two."

In the right nostril to Ajna, from Ajna out the left nostril.
In the left nostril to Ajna, from Ajna out the right nostril.
Say "One."

Now repeat the sequence. This countdown is done for the duration of the meditation (twenty to thirty minutes) and it should be expected that you will lose count. This is a sign of dropping into dreaming or dreamless sleep. When you do lose count and become aware of coming out of the state you are in, simply pick anywhere you thought you left off, or start at the beginning. The counting is a device intended to "cut out" the left brain.

VERTICAL BREATHING

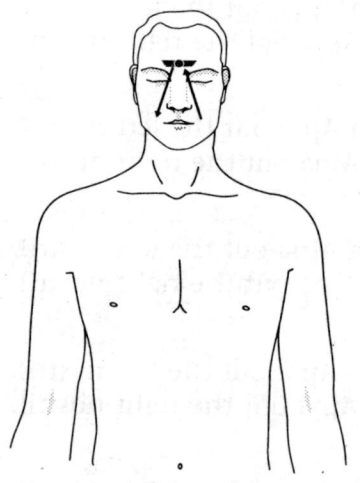
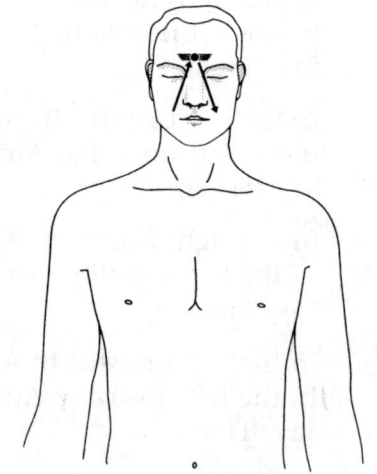

Breathe in the right nostril to Ajna, from Ajna out the left nostril.

Breathe in the left nostril to Ajna, from Ajna out the right nostril.

Summary

1. Prepare yourself in a sitting meditation posture, on a chair or the floor.
2. Place the copper penny on the Ajna spot. (Note: if the penny should drop during meditation, do not try to retrieve it but continue with the counting in rhythm with the breath.)
3. While sensing the tactile pressure of the penny against your skin at Ajna, become also aware of your breath flowing through the nostrils.
4. Begin to exclusively focus on breath movement in the right nostril, then exclusively out the left nostril, tracking the movement of air with a psychic imagined color leading up to Ajna on inspiration and down from Ajna on exhalation. Count down one round each time you return to Ajna. Count from ten to one and repeat.

Simultaneously, you imagine the colored breath reaching and receding from Ajna, you sense the penny at Ajna, and you count the rounds down and repeat for the duration of the technique.

Advantages of Copper Meditation

After several weeks you will be able to dispense with the penny; as a consequence, you will then be able to induce an altered state on consciousness anywhere; on the bus or train, in the office, etc.

YOGA NIDRA

The particular form of Yoga Nidra ("Yoga Sleep") we are going to discuss was first released to the Western world by Paramahansa Satyananda Saraswati around 1965. Swami Satyananda was a brilliant Yoga Mind-Body technologist (he is now in retirement) and this method, as with so much in

Tantra and Yoga, contains very clever mechanisms not approached in Western psychology.

Many epithets have been used to attempt to convey in English the meaning of Yoga Nidra. Descriptions include:

Psychic sleep

Sleepless sleep

Sleep in a state of awareness

Yogic tranquilizer

The prefix "Ni" is the Sanskrit root of our English word "nether," or down, as in "nether world" (underworld), while the suffix "dra" may be cognate with the English "drowsy:" "to be half asleep, to be inactive or present an appearance of peaceful inactivity or isolation" *(Webster's Third International Dictionary).*

Therefore I will define Yoga Nidra, in essence, as a practice producing an altered state of consciousness, marked by some physical "drowsiness" with accompanying mental access to "worlds under" the perception of normal waking consciousness.

Upanishadic doctrine, and at least three classical schools of Indian philosophy, teaches the existence of four levels of consciousness; these are:

1. Waking consciousness
2. Dreaming consciousness
3. Dreamless sleep
4. Turiya (Conscious dreamless sleep?)

I cannot help equating these levels (without wishing to go into details) with the four basic brain wave patterns of Western psychophysiology—keeping in mind the messy alacrity with which Westerners allocated the endocrine glands to the chakras.

> *Swamiji often expressed it as*
> *"The body sleeps, but the mind does not."*

Notwithstanding the inherent weakness of analogy (similarities are highlighted, but not dissimilarities), I suggest that EEG patterns can be useful in understanding aspects of Yoga and Yoga Nidra.

Consider the oldest written definition of Yoga (300 BC to AD 200 is the estimated time range):

Yogas Cittavritti Nirodhyah: "Yoga is the (intentional) stopping of the spontaneous activities of the mind-stuff."

— Patanjali, *Yoga Sutras* I.1-2

Or a looser translation:

"Yoga is the cessation of the fluctuations (modifications) of the mind."

This fundamental axiom of Yoga, to me, always seemed strikingly parallel with the psychophysiology of the cerebral cortex electrical activity.

> **Yoga is autonomic nervous system gymnastics.**

Then I suggest, as a viewpoint, a theoretical construct only:

> ***Yoga is a volitional modification and/or reduction of the electrical discharge rate of cerebral cortex (brain) neurons.***

Given that this may be a vast simplification and rationalization; nonetheless, such a hypothesis has pragmatical mapping value. Consider:

THE FOUR BRAIN WAVE PATTERNS

Name	State	Cycles per second*
Beta	Awake; cognitive processes, RAS alerting responses, Reason, logic, rationalization, Anxiety affective states.	14/28
Alpha	Relaxed wakefulness; Awareness not dominated by thought content, Nothing or "no-thing," Consciousness without content.	8/13
Theta	Dreaming (REM); Creative thought processes, Spontaneous images, Inspiration, Kinesthetic distortions of body images.	7/4
Delta	Dreamless Sleep; "Unconsciousness."	3/1

The correlations between Alpha and Theta EEG (electroencephalograph) studies, demonstrating dominance of these patterns in meditating Yogis and Zen monks, is now voluminous.**

A short comment regarding hypnosis and meditation states: They are not the same, although they share some common features; the psychophysiological, particularly EEG, correlations of meditation are much more specific. One common feature

---

*Cycles per second vary slightly depending on measuring parameters.

**See *Altered States of Consciousness*, edited by Charles T. Tart (John Wiley and Sons, 1969). This is a classic, over twenty years old; extensive research in the interval has only refined and substantiated the data.

is the starting point. Both phenomena involve concentration producing monoideism or single-pointedness of attention. In Sanskrit, Ekagrata (one-pointedness).

Returning to my original conjecture regarding Patanjali's basic aphorism, meditation reduces the rate of brain wave frequency—for example, we could postulate an individual starting to meditate from a Beta wave, high alertness state, maximum 28 CPS, dropping him or herself down to a Theta minimum of 4 cycles per second, for a period of recuperation and rejuvenation, or as the TM people would say, "the *rest* of your life."

> **Yoga is the modification of the fluctuations of the mind stuff.**

The practice of Yoga Nidra tends to alter your level of consciousness, so that you experience "floating in and out" of levels.

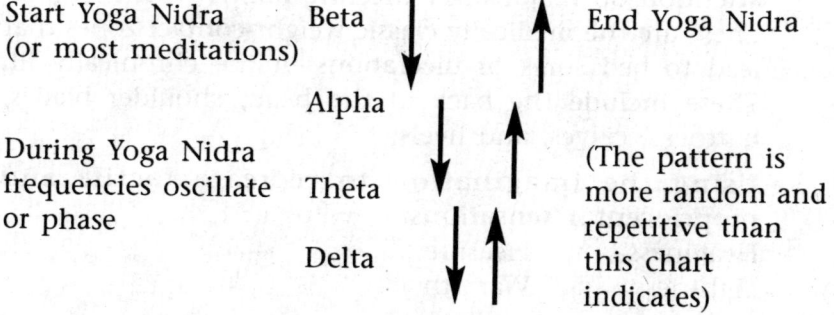

Start Yoga Nidra   Beta   End Yoga Nidra
(or most meditations)

                        Alpha

During Yoga Nidra   (The pattern is
frequencies oscillate   Theta   more random and
or phase   repetitive than
                        Delta   this chart
                                            indicates)

The topology I suggest is equally applicable to the majority of techniques in this book.

CHARACTERISTIC FEATURES OF SWAMI SATYANANDA'S YOGA NIDRA

1. **Rapid rotation of consciousness through the multiple Marmasthananis:** Restlessness of the Beta wave state is brought under control by rapid one-pointed (Ekagrata) kinesthetic rotation of attention throughout multiple areas or segmentations of the body. There is, literally, no time to get bored, provided you do what you are asked to do.

   > *Sense it!*
   > *See it!*
   > *Say it!*

   Note the accompanying chart with an example of segmentation of the right hand. More advanced forms include even finer, incremental segmentation: e.g. individual joints-phalanges of the fingers and mounds of the palm.*

2. **Pressure point awareness:** The script focuses your attention on major body meeting points with the floor. These are the medically classic weight-contact zones that lead to bed sores or ulcerations in the chronically ill. These include the back of the head, shoulder blades, buttocks, calves, and heels.

3. **Using the imagination to recreate tactile and proprioceptor sensations:**
   Heaviness   Pleasure
   Lightness   Warmth

4. **Chakra symbols visualized in ascending and descending scales:** In this Yoga Nidra script, a modified version of many such scripts developed by the Swamis of the Bihar School of Yoga, Monghyr, Bihar, and based on

---

*Jasmine Riddle, M.A. and I collaborated in 1977 to produce an advanced Yoga Nidra tape. She recorded this with a musical background. This tape is available through Llewellyn Publications.

Satyananda's work, we are using the five Tattwa three-dimensional elements for visual stimulation of the chakras. Ajna (Third Eye) is seen as a white, winged sphere (or globe), while Sahasrara uses a Tantric unconscious symbol, the red lotus, occupying the space of the brain. This powerfully reviews actualizes, and integrates the psychic centers.

5. **Flashing of random images to stimulate the unconscious:** A selection of images are presented which you quickly flash through your imagination, using color, size, and movement to vivify them. This stimulates the flow of unconscious material and probably enhances creativity.

There remain other features of Yoga Nidra, as taught by Swami Satyananda, but they are best assimilated by personal contact with those who have trained with him.

Yoga Nidra Tape Preparation Notes

The script on the following pages is to be recorded—usually it is best to use your own voice to make a personal audio tape. A quiet time should be selected to do the tape recording; you need to allow thirty to forty-five minutes. The script should be in front of you, illuminated, and you should have easy access to the pause button on the tape recorder. Movement is rapid; however, allow a few extra seconds for images and feelings.

Once you have made the tape, you have a very powerful instrument for personal evolution.

When getting ready to play the Yoga Nidra tape, prepare yourself as for Shavasana*, and establish a peaceful, dark, and undisturbed environment. If you fall asleep (Delta dreamless sleep), you will awaken spontaneously. Satyananda always encouraged students to attempt to maintain some awareness or consciousness throughout. The most likely scenario is that you will drift in and out of awareness, finishing the exercise rejuvenated.

YOGA NIDRA SAMPLE MARMASTHANANI CHART (SENSE ... SEE ... SAY ...)

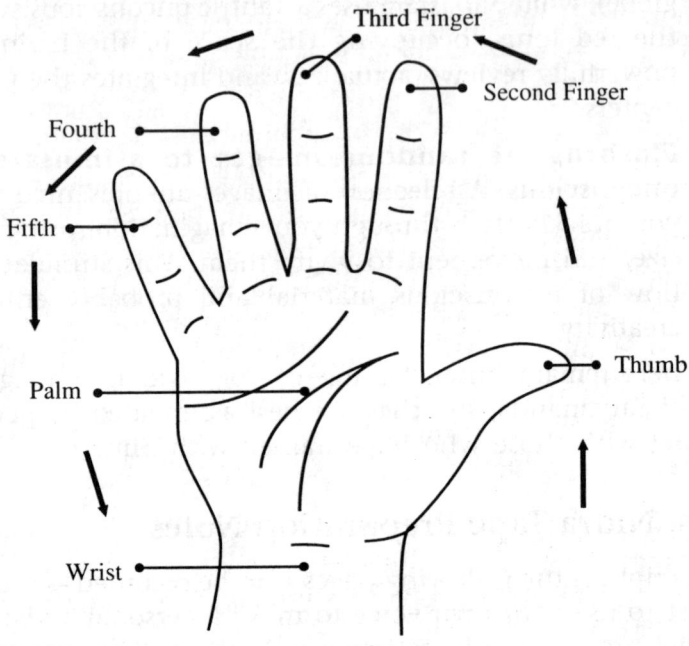

SCRIPT FOR YOGA NIDRA RECORDING

Preparation

Lie down in Shavasana*, your body stretched out, feet apart, the palms of your hands turned upward. Close your eyes. *(pause)* Make all the necessary adjustments so that you are as comfortable as possible—there must be no movement, conscious nor unconscious. *(pause)* Remember that you are about to practice Yoga Nidra, psychic sleep, and that you have only to maintain awareness of hearing and feeling. *(pause)*

---

*(Alternate script for use with sitting position) Seat yourself comfortably, as in the Egyptian God Posture: your back is erect, your feet are flat on the floor, and your hands are relaxed and on your knees with your palms turned upward.

The body sleeps but the mind remains awake ... you remain alert so that you do not sleep. *(pause)* Take a deep breath; as you breathe in, feel calmness spreading throughout your body ... as you breathe out, feel your cares and concerns flowing out of you.

Relaxation

Become aware of your body and relax yourself completely; make yourself physically calm and steady. *(pause)* Feel that your legs are relaxed, your trunk, your head, your arms and bones. *(pause)* Develop the awareness of your physical body right from the top of your head to the tip of the toes, and say in your mind: *O-o-o-m-m-m*. *(pause)* Have complete awareness of the whole body ... say to yourself again, *O-o-o-m-m-m;* and again, mentally: *O-o-o-m-m-m*. *(pause)* Relax your whole body, relax yourself mentally, relax yourself by breathing normally and becoming aware of the breath as it moves between the navel and throat. *(pause)* Have awareness of your natural breathing; do not force it. *(pause)* Breathing from the navel to the throat, please go on with this awareness and slowly feel yourself becoming more relaxed. *(long pause)* Now leave your breathing and become aware that you are going to practice Yoga Nidra.

Yoga Nidra begins now.

Let your mind jump freely from one part to the next. *(pause)*

Right side: Right-hand thumb, second finger, third, fourth, fifth, palm, wrist, elbow, shoulder, armpit, waist, hip, right thigh, kneecap, calf muscle, ankle, heel, sole, right toes: one, two, three, four, five ...

Left side: Left-hand thumb, second finger, third, fourth, fifth, palm, wrist, elbow, shoulder, armpit, waist, hip, left thigh, kneecap, calf muscle, ankle, heel, sole, left toes: one, two, three, four, five ...

Right side reverse: Go to the right toes and start from the bottom. Right big toe, second toe, third, fourth, fifth, sole, heel, ankle, calf muscle, kneecap, thigh, hip, waist, armpit, shoulder, elbow, wrist, palm, right thumb, second finger, third, fourth, fifth ...

Left side reverse: Go to the left toes and start from the bottom. Left big toe, second toe, third, fourth, fifth, sole, heel, ankle, calf muscle, kneecap, thigh, hip, waist, armpits, shoulder, elbow, wrist, palm, left thumb, second finger, third, fourth, fifth ...

Whole back down: Go to the back of the body; go to the back of the head, where it touches the floor. Back of the head, right shoulder blade, left shoulder blade, whole spine, right hip, left hip, right buttock, left buttock, back of the right thigh, back of the left thigh, back of the right knee, back of the left knee, right calf muscle, left calf muscle, right ankle, left ankle, right heel, left heel ...

Whole back up: Right ankle, left ankle, right calf muscle, left calf muscle, right back of the knee, left back of the knee, right back of thigh, left back of thigh, right buttock, left buttock, right hip, left hip, whole spine, right shoulder blade, left shoulder blade, back of the head ...

Whole front down: Go to the front of the body; go to the top of the head. Top of the head, forehead, right eyebrow, left eyebrow, the space between the eyebrows, right eye, left eye, right ear, left ear, right nostril, left nostril, right cheek, left cheek, upper lip, lower lip, chin, throat, right collarbone, left collarbone, right chest, left chest, middle of the chest, navel, upper abdomen, lower abdomen, right groin, left groin, right thigh, left thigh, right knee, left knee, right toes, left toes ...

Whole front up: Right toes, left toes, right knee, left knee, right thigh, left thigh, right groin, left groin, lower abdomen, upper abdomen, navel, right chest, left chest, middle of the chest, right collarbone, left collarbone, throat, chin, lower lip, upper lip, right cheek, left cheek, right nostril, left nostril, right ear, left ear, right eye, left eye, right eyebrow, left eyebrow, space between the eyebrows, forehead, top of the head ...

Major parts: Now the major parts of the body. The whole of the right leg, whole of the left leg, both legs together. Whole of the right arm, whole of the left arm, both arms together;

whole of the back; whole of the front; whole of the head; the whole body, whole body, whole body. Visualize the whole body ... say "whole body" and visualize the whole body. *(pause)* Intensify your awareness ... the whole body, the whole body, the whole body. *(long pause)*

Body Awareness

Become aware of the meeting points between your body and the floor. *(pause)* Feel the meeting points between body and floor ...sharp meeting points ... body and floor. *(pause)* Feel the floor holding you, like a baby in arms. *(pause)* Now concentrate on your body as if seeing it from the outside; look on your body as an object. *(pause)* See your head, your clothes, your whole body from top to bottom, lying in Shavasana on the floor of this room. *(pause)* See your body as an object, a reflection in an imaginary mirror. *(pause)* You are looking at your own reflection in the mirror and you see yourself lying on the floor ... your feet, legs, belly, chest, arms, hands, clothing, nose, closed eyes, forehead, hair ... everything reflected in that mirror. *(pause)* Have awareness of your body as an object. *(pause)* Make sure you are not sleeping. *(long pause)*

Breathing

Bring your attention to the natural breath, the quiet breath; become aware of the breath through the nostrils. *(pause)* The natural breath flows through both nostrils and meets at the top of the nose to form a triangle. *(pause)* The spontaneous breath enters through the nostril openings, moves upward and draws together to form a triangle with its apex in the eyebrow center. *(pause)* Be aware of the breath passing through both nostrils ... become aware of both breaths, separately ... and simultaneously. (pause) Think of the breaths as starting separately from a distance, drawing near and uniting in the eyebrow center. *(pause)* Now concentrate on each breath and try to determine its temperature ... move back and forth and compare the temperatures. *(pause)* In Yoga we say the left nostril breath is Ida, moon, and the right is Pingala, sun. *(pause)* Ida, the left breath, is cooler; Pingala, the right breath, is warmer. *(pause)* Continue your awareness of breathing, but imagine you are now breathing through alternate nostrils ... in through one nostril, and out through the other; up and down the sides of the triangle and back again. *(pause)* Maintain your awareness and start counting each breath with full attention: inhale left ... 54, exhale right ... 54, inhale right ... 53, exhale left ... 53, inhale left ... 52, exhale right ... 52, inhale right ... 51, exhale left ... 51, and so on ... continue counting to zero. *(long pause)* Keep total awareness of counting and breathing; if you make a mistake or reach zero, start again at 54. *(long pause)* Stop your counting and remain aware of the breath only ... inhaling evenly through both nostrils, exhaling evenly through both nostrils; you have total awareness, no sleeping ... no sleeping. *(1–2 minute pause)*

Feelings

Heaviness: Heaviness; waken the experience in the whole body of the feeling of heaviness. *(pause)* Become aware of heaviness in each part of the body as it is named: toes, heels, ankles, calves, knees, thighs, buttocks, back, belly, chest, shoulders, arms, palms, head, eyelids, the whole body ... heavy, the whole body ... heavy. *(pause)* Experience this feeling of heaviness in the whole body. *(pause)*

Lightness: Lightness; manifest the experience of lightness in the body. *(pause)* Manifest the feeling of lightness from the top ... from the top of the head, then the whole head; then shoulders, palms, back, chest, abdomen, thighs, knees, calves, heels, soles, toes ... manifest the experience of lightness in the whole body from top to toe. *(pause)* The lightness of the body can be developed by feeling the meeting points between the body and the floor ... point by point, or as a whole; a whole surface of meeting of body and floor. *(pause)* Concentrate on this area of meeting and gradually experience lightness. *(pause)* Feel yourself floating up from the floor ... you are so light that you are floating to the ceiling, drifting back and forth. *(pause)*

Continue this experience until lightness is manifest, then go on. *(pause)*

Pleasure: Pleasure; try to experience the feeling of pleasure, any pleasure. *(pause)* Concentrate and remember the feeling of pleasure ... it may be according to your senses of touch, smell, taste, hearing, sight or any kind of mental pleasure. *(pause)* Recall that pleasure and try to develop it into an intense ecstatic experience ... go deep into the enjoyment of pleasure, relive it, make it vivid. *(long pause)*

We are now going to rotate the consciousness by ascending the chakra chain and descending, sensing, seeing, saying. (Don't pause overly at each center, but keep the consciousness moving.)

Ascending

Muladhara: Yellow cube in the lower pelvis
Swadhisthana: Silver crescent moon melon below navel
Manipura: Ruby red inverted pyramid

Anahata: Blue sapphire six-pointed star behind the breast bone on a level with the nipples

Vishuddha: Black oval egg nestled in the throat

Ag-n-ya (Ajna): White winged globe behind the forehead and between the eyes

Sahasrara: Red lotus occupying the brain or cranial cavity

Descending

Sahasrara: Red lotus filling the brain

Ag-n-ya (Ajna): White winged globe behind the forehead and between the eyes

Vishuddha: Black oval egg occupying the throat

Anahata: Dark blue sapphire six-pointed star behind the breast bone

Manipura: Deep red inverted pyramid inside the abdomen between the navel and the bottom of the breast bone

Swadhisthana: Silver crescent melon moon below the navel and above the pubic bone

Muladhara: Yellow-gold cube within the pelvic floor

Ascending Again

Muladhara: Yellow solid cube in the pelvis *(See it ... sense it ...)*

Swadhisthana: Silver crescent melon moon in the lower abdomen

Manipura: Deep ruby red inverted pyramid ("fire in the middle") above the navel

Anahata: Dark blue star sapphire occupying the heart cavity

Vishuddha: Black egg within the throat

Ag-n-ya (Ajna): Winged white globe between the eyes

Sahasrara: Red rose filling the skull

Rapid images

Bring your awareness to the present and make sure you are not sleeping; no sleeping, please. I am going to name a few objects and you should try to visualize them on the levels of feeling, awareness, emotion, and imagination as best you can. *(pause)* As fast as I go, so fast should you move ... jumping your mind from image to image; do not waste your time concentrating on one image, but keep moving.

Shiva Lingam ... standing Christ ... flickering candle ... weeping willow tree ... tall palm tree ... car moving on a road ... colored clouds gathering ... yellow clouds ... blue clouds ... starlit night ... moonlit night ... full moon ... dog standing ... cat resting ... elephant moving ... horse racing ... rising sun ... setting sun ... ocean with waves ... Shiva Lingam ... standing Christ ... a big pond with clear water ... blue lotus ... white lotus ... pink lotus ... golden spider's web ... sandy bank of a wide river ... boat sailing on the water ... ripples ... yourself lying down without clothes, a golden cord extending from your navel into the sky ... cross over a church ... within the church a priest praying ... worshipper kneeling ... chimney smoke rising from an old house ... a cold winter ... a fire burning in the fireplace ... dawn of the day ... temple bell ringing ... a monk with shaven head ... a Yogi sitting in deep meditation ... Buddha in repose ... Christ showing compassion. *(pause)*

Ocean/Jungle

Intensify your awareness ... intensify your awareness ... go to an infinite ocean, calm and quiet ... try to discover a sound there. *(pause)* There is a sound, an infinite ocean, dark green jungles on the shore, snakes, lions, and goats living in friendliness. *(pause)* From the shore a path leads to a lonely cottage in the jungle, and a Yogi sitting in the lotus position. *(pause)* There is a small fire and a smell of incense, the fragrance of flowers, and an atmosphere of tranquillity. *(pause)* All around can be heard the sound of OM, the chanting of OM over the infinite ocean. *(long pause)*

Golden Egg

Become a witness of your awareness ... not the body, not the senses, not the mind, nothing but the different awareness. *(pause)* Become aware that you are aware of yourself. *(pause)* Look within and try to be aware of one who is looking, who is aware of what you have been doing so far. *(pause)* Go into *chidakash* ... go into the cave you find there. *(pause)* Within the cave, within the cave, very dark, very dark ... within that cave there is a flaming light ... find that light. *(pause)* Find that light and find a small golden egg in the center of the light ... a small golden egg, very bright, with light all around. *(long pause)*

Finish

The whole body ... the whole body ... the whole body. *(long pause)* Relax all efforts and bring your attention to the natural breath, the natural breath flowing in and out of the nostrils.

(long pause) Maintain your awareness of breath and at the same time develop your awareness of physical relaxation. *(pause)* Develop awareness of relaxation ... and awareness of your physical existence; become aware of the physical existence of your body. *(long pause)* Develop awareness of your body and visualize your body lying on the floor. *(pause)* Take your mind out and visualize the surrounding room; let your mind become completely external ... do not open your eyes. *(pause)* You are practicing Yoga Nidra; become aware of this fact. *(pause)* Lie quietly until your attention is completely externalized. Start moving, moving your body and stretching yourself ... please take your time, there is no hurry. *(pause)* When you are sure that you are wide awake, sit up slowly and open your eyes. The practice of Yoga Nidra is now complete. *Hari om tat sat.*

★★

Part Six

Tangible Transcendental Yoga for the Higher Life

Kundalini (Cinderella: of the sleeping embers) is quiescent in the pelvic palace of homo sapiens. She is bride, virgin, wife, divorcee, and widow.

This is the celestial dance of lovers, and upon "nowhere" will be inscribed the templar temple foundation, and in the center will the thorn wed the rose "now-here," secreting the dew of vicarious immortality.

Tantra, like love, promotes neither the rational nor the irrational, but rather the para-rational.

— Swami Anandakapila Saraswati
Indonesia 1989

Prologue

Magical Sexuality

Our culture has divorced mind and body (Cartesian dualism), brain and spinal cord, cerebral cortex and limbic system; slain intuition ("inner tutor") for logic, and castrated emotion for thinking. This ritual is the coupling Yoga of left and right hemispheres: intellect and feeling; Adam (mind) and Eve (body). This is the Yoga of sex: The "sex" comes from the Latin root *secare,* meaning "divided," and yet through magical sexuality may this schism be "re-paired."

Let the Man-God and Woman-Goddess *be a-ware* of absolute purity necessary for the magical implements before proceeding to "square the circle." Shiva will enter with wand and Shakti with rose, the "squared circle," and each with "wise serpent" and "gentle dove," for it is written:

Be ye therefore wise as serpents and gentle as doves ...

— Matthew 10:16

During communion of serpent and dove, wand and rose, let the heart containing the blood of red wine soften and the skull chalice become empty and void, for only the empty vessel can receive.

The heart has reasons that reason knows not of.
Do you love by reason?

— Blaise Pascal

Chapter Fourteen

Tantra Yoga for the Shared Life

The material I have presented herein is delicately balanced. I do not wish the instructions to be misconstrued as either a sexual manual or a sex therapy book. Excellent volumes on both these topics abound.

Tantra is to be approached from a sensitive experiential viewpoint. Sexual Tantra cannot be vulgarized, nor entirely excised from its traditional Indian heritage. Realize also, that what I share represents but a fragment of the Tantric teachings.

Individual differences dictate unique and myriad responses to the exercises. Each student will discover his/her favorite exercise, but all the methods require practice and patience to be fully appreciated.

The heightened sensations ensuing may result in extended orgasm and certainly a profound altered state of consciousness.

TANTRA: WHAT IS IT?

Tantra is a Sanskrit word associated with an ancient Indian philosophy sometimes called "the doctrine of celestial sex."

Tantra has given us two English derivatives: tender and tendon. "Tender" reminds us that the essence of love—sexual relations—is dependent upon softness, gentleness, and caring caresses. Touching without feeling is mechanical, producing no depth of experience. "Tender" implies emotional involvement: attention to the partner and submission to the relationship.

"Tendon," a muscle attachment, implies "stretch out" or "attenuate." The practical value of Tantra is that the excitement phase is prolonged as long as possible, thereby ensuring the deepest or orgasms.

What can be Achieved with Tantra?

Tantric methods pre-date, by thousands of years, Western sexual techniques such as "Sensate Focus" (Masters and Johnson) and "Kegel Exercises" (pelvic contractions of urethra, vagina, and anus).

The original Tantric approach produces a depth of climax far exceeding our Western standards of mere ejaculations and convulsive muscle contractions.

> *If orgasm is a "pelvic sneeze"*
> *and a sneeze is a "cranial orgasm,"*
> *then Tantra produces both simultaneously.*

The statement "a sneeze is a cranial orgasm" is not a capricious comment. The nose is lined with the same erectile tissue as the genitals. "Honeymoon" rhinitis (nasal congestion from sexual excitement) is a reality, and the result of a sneeze is physiological nasal decongestion, exactly equivalent to pelvic-penile decongestion resulting from an orgasm.

What is Required to Begin?

R–4C Formula:
Relaxation
Cooperation
Caring
Caressing
Concentration

The above formula may be applied to auto-erotic mysticism or magical sexuality between sexual partners.

Each evening w(rite) out the following statement three times on three separate pieces of paper by candlelight:

Tantra* is the Yoga** of Lingam and Yoni,
Wand and Cup, Spine and Skull, Arrow and Heart,
Wafer and Wine, Candle and Bell, Sword and Blood,
Taper and Flame.

Place the three pieces of paper under the candleholder and retire. As you fall asleep, visualize as many of the above image pairs as you can. It is not necessary that the statement is consciously understood, as the evocative images speak to the subconscious.

Repeat the above on the second and third evenings adding each night's papers to those already under the candle holder.

On the night of the Full Moon, burn each of the nine papers in the candle flame while chanting the incantation given above.

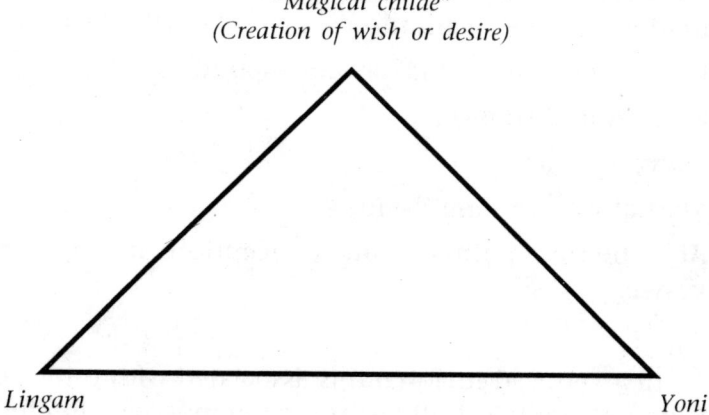

"Magical childe"
(Creation of wish or desire)

Lingam   Yoni

---

*Sanskrit: "Loom," prefix "tan"—meaning "weave" or "extend." English derivative "tender."

**Sanskrit root "yug" means "yoke." "Yoga" means "union." The French derivative "jugum" moves into English as "jugular"—i.e., veins uniting the head and the heart.

The number three stands for the three points of an equilateral triangle with its base on the earth plane. It signifies action, reaction, and result, or lingam, yoni, and "magical childe."

The number nine is "thrice times thrice" (Shakespeare's *Macbeth*) or "triple triplicity," meaning absolute completion.

The Purpose

This ceremony affiliates the student with the *egregore* or mental plane of Tantric tradition through the centuries.

EXERCISE ONE

Visualization And Concentration Upon Primary Erogenic Zones Related To Psychic Centers

A psychic center (Sanskrit "chakra") is defined as whirling vortex of psychic energy at the conjunction point of the mind and the body, i.e., psychosomatic point, or transducer, where imagination—image in mind—creates physical effects.

These seven primal chakras correspond to:

1. Endocrine glands
2. Nerve ganglia
3. Martial arts striking points
4. Acupuncture points along conception and governing vessels.

The first center (Muladhara) is associated with tumescence or swelling of genitals, nipples, and nasal mucosa. The thumbs reflex to this chakra.

The second center (Swadhisthana) controls all sexual secretions including vaginal lubrication, semen, prostatic fluid, urine, sexual blood flush, and combined ejaculate in men and some women. The forefinger reflexes to Swadhisthana chakra.

PSYCHOSOMATIC CENTERS

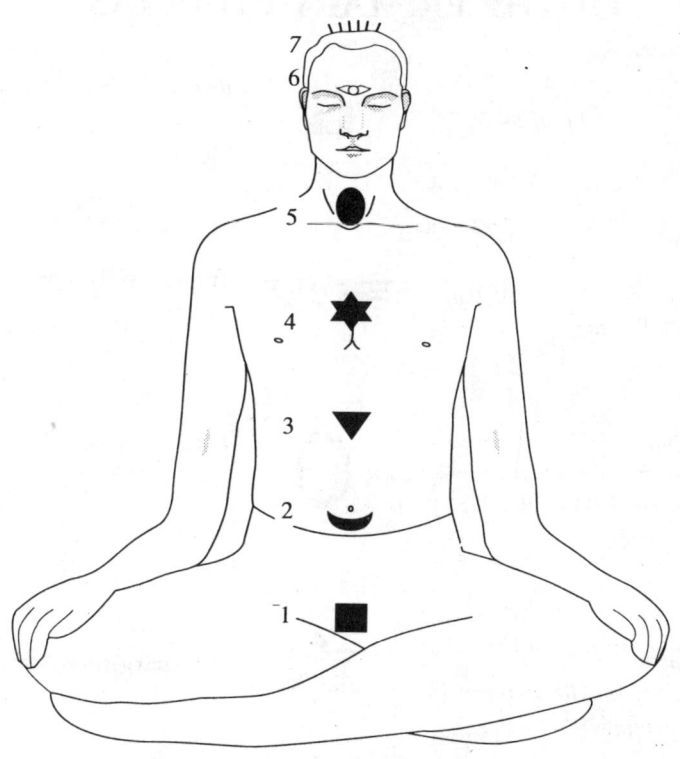

Number	Glands	Organs	Acupuncture	Martial arts
7	Pineal	Brain	Gov. V. 21	Bregma
6	Pituitary	Optic chiasma	Gov. V. 24.5	Nasion
5	Thyroid Parathyroids	Larynx	Con. V. 22	Thyroid cartilage
4	Thymus	Heart	Con. V. 17	Cardio-pulmonary plexus
3	Pancreas	Liver	Con. V. 8	Solar plexus
2	Adrenals	Kidneys	Con. V. 4	Hypogastric plexus
1	Testes/Ovaries	Genitals	Con. V. 1	Gonads

THE LOCATIONS AND ASSOCIATIONS OF THE PRIMARY CHAKRAS

Sahasrara
(anterior fontanelle of skull)

Red rose—blissful union

Ajna
(nasion juncture of nasal bones and frontal bone)

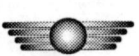

Winged globe (eye)—mind

Vishuddha
(little finger, supra-sternal notch below Adam's apple)

Black oval—ether

Anahata
(ring finger, middle sternum in line with nipples)

Blue hexagram—air

Manipura
(middle finger, navel to tip of breast bone)

Red triangle—fire

Swadhisthana
(forefinger, halfway between navel and pubic bone)

Silver crescent—water

Muladhara
(thumb, anus, vulva, urethra)

Yellow square—earth

TANTRIC EROTIC ROSE MEDITATION

This is the original form of a secret kriya practice called Chakra Nu Sadhana. This will powerfully stimulate the chakras from below to above, raising the psycho-sexual energy.

It may be performed by couples or individuals and may be likened to a psychic acupuncture with an imagined rose bud. When done with attention, this is very sensual and will also relieve tension in any dis-eased body area.

Male: Visualize a red rose bud on a stem.
Female: Visualize a white rose bud on a stem.

Now imagine using the rose to psychically penetrate each of the secret, intimate parts of your body and then rotating the rose half a dozen times clockwise and half a dozen times counterclockwise.

Stimulation Order for Men
Muladhara: anus, urethra from head of penis inward.
Swadhisthana: halfway between pubic bone and navel.
Manipura: navel.
Anahata: breastbone in line with nipples.
Vishuddha: below Adam's apple.
Ajna: between eyebrows, Bregma.
Sahasrara: top of skull.

Stimulation Order for Women
Muladhara: anus, vulva, vagina (deep), clitoris.
Then as for men from Swadhisthana.

Note: Women and men may also wish to psychically penetrate each breast through the nipple.

> See it... sense it...

Feel the velvet bud sensually and slowly penetrate, while simultaneously imagining it merging deep into recesses and melting through skin and bone. Savor the rotations and sense the slow psychic withdrawal, allowing erotic shivers to go through you as you get ready for the next penetration point.

Male visualization: Perform Tratak on the above rose drawing, close your eyes, and see it float before you as a *red* rose. Use it in the exercise as described.

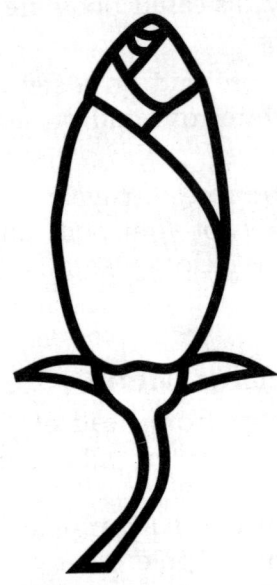

Female visualization: Perform Tratak on the above rose drawing, close your eyes, and see it float before you as a *white* rose. Use it in the exercise as described.

EXERCISE TWO

Tantric Sensate Focus

May be done alone or with a partner.
1. Partners bathe, sit cross-legged, wearing only robes, on a bed or cushioned carpet opposite each other.

2. Male lubricates his right thumb with saliva and anoints female's clitoris. The female now anoints the head of her partner's lingam with her lubricated left thumb.
3. With closed eyes, concentrate your attention on sensations from the saliva evaporating over the genital centers. Visualize and feel this area as a gold glowing ring which shrinks in diameter until not even a dot, or Bindu, remains by the time the saliva has evaporated.
4. Each partner now visualizes erotic contact with the other until the man's lingam is erect and the woman's yoni is moist. Continue sensing and feeling each other's presence, and look at each other through closed eyelids as if perforations in the lids permitted you to gaze upon your partner until you feel as if you are one. Avoid any contact with each other.

Advanced Phase

Continue this exercise until both partners climax. This may be accelerated by:

1. Rapid anal contractions alternating with rapid contraction of bladder sphincter (as if repeatedly cutting off midstream urine).
2. Intense erotic fantasy involving mental consummation with partner.

The Purpose of Tantric Sensate Focus Exercise Two

1. To prolong excitement phase as long as possible thus ensuring peak orgasm or U3 experience. U3 represents the moment of total Universal Ultimate Unity, with absolute loss of ego and mergence with the other.
2. To train the concentration faculty by using a psycho-physiological attention fixer, in this case, saliva, which has the correct viscosity to ensure slow evaporation.

3. Awaken the primal libido centers or chakras and exercise mental control over the sexual energy.
4. Allow sexual excitement to heighten so that the electromagnetic, or " auric," fields of the Tantric pair can merge and "re-pair."
5. Develop a mental synchronization amounting to "telepathy." The brain wave patterns of the two lovers will combine or harmonize in synchrony.

How do I Judge Success in Tantra?

You make no judgment whatsoever. Consider each technique as an emotional experiential experiment—some will find the technique difficult, others easy. Consider the 5P Formula: "Perfect Practice Prevents Poor Performance."

Practice without Theory is Blind

Tantra describes psycho-sexual energy as running down psychic tubes on the left and right of the spine. The consummate intercourse occurs when the energies of these two tubes coalesce and run up the central canal (spinal cord). Another way of saying this is that the fire of passion is ignited in the pelvic basin and flares up "the middle pillar" to burn away thought within the Chalice of the Skull.

Yoga teaches that Ida and Pingala unite at the Third Eye—"Insight."

Sexual Tantra reveals that the contact points for activation of Ida and Pingala are the left and right ear lobe respectively.

> *Yoga (union) is the cessation of the fluctuations of the mind stuff.*
> —Patanjali (200 BC)

PSYCHIC PATHWAYS

Ida	Sushumna	Pingala
Left bladder meridan (acupuncture)		Right bladder meridian (acupuncture)
Left sympathetic ganglion (autonomic nervous system)		Right sympathetic ganglion (autonomic nervous system)
"Pharoah's Crook" (Egyptian)		"Pharoah's Flail" (Egyptian)
"Pillar of Mercy" (Qabalah)		"Pillar of Severity" (Qabalah)
The Moon		The Sun
Feminine		Masculine
Receptive		Projective
Sensory neurons		Motor neurons
Reflex contact: left ear lobe (left nipple—women only)		Reflex contact: right ear lobe (right nipple—women only)

The spinal cord
"The Middle Pillar"
Conjunction of
Venus and Mars

FLOW OF IDA AND PINGALA

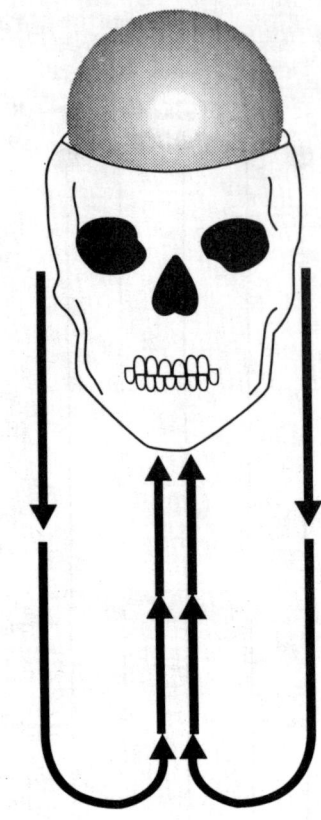

Ida and Pingala flow downward to join the base, then flow upward through Sushumna to form a glowing ball of light cupped in the skull.

> **Theory without practice is sterile.**

Shiva = Male partner = Consciousness = Adam = Phallus = Lingam
Shakti = Female partner = Body = Eve = Vulva = Yoni

EXERCISE THREE

Physical Stimulation of a Secondary Erogenic Zone to Arrive at the very Edge of the Ecstatic "U3" Moment

1. Let Shiva and Shakti bathe with perfumed bath oil, by candlelight, occasionally caressing each other.
2. Let them dry each other and slip into robes while constantly anticipating the joy of union.
3. Let them retire to a bedroom—temple—enlightened by one candle (candle equates to lingam; flame equates to yoni).
4. Let them sit cross-legged on the bed, knees touching; gently loosen each other's robes, sensing mutual excitement and focusing on anticipated Yoga (union) of lingam and yoni.
5. Let Shiva take Shakti upon his lap and begin worshipping her left ear by sucking gently on the ear lobe, interspersed with deep, darting penetration of her ear canal with the lingam of his tongue. The process may be accelerated, in the beginning, by the man stroking lightly over her shoulder and down the left side of her spine to the sacred sacrum region at the base of her spine.
6. This process is continued until unbearable sensations experienced by the Shakti produce involuntary or near involuntary climax. At approaching climax, or to push herself totally over the precipice, she inserts Shiva's lingam within her yoni and manipulates the lingam to please herself. With practice they will orgasm simultaneously. Involuntary ejaculations may be expected, and should not be considered failures or a loss of energy (an outdated idea still often espoused).

VARIATION

The technique may be done with the partners lying side by side. The man lies on his left side, cradling the woman's head in his left arm, leaving his right hand free to stroke down the left side of her spine to her buttocks, while stimulating her ear lobe. She lies on her right side facing him.

This position also has an added advantage: Once the Shakti lubricates, Shiva may manipulate his right hand so that his thumb seals her anus (Muladhara), his forefinger inserts into her yoni (Swadhisthana), and middle finger gently lies alongside her clitoris (Manipura chakra), providing additional stimulation.

Role Reversal

The partners should alternate roles so that the woman stimulates the man's right ear lobe (Pingala) bringing him to erection and inserting the lingam into her yoni for climax.

Considerations

1. Most humans are sensitive to ear lobe stimulation as this is an established reflex pathway in many mammals—remember scratching behind a dog's ear and watching its hind leg involuntarily shake? Because of individual differences, ear lobe stimulation may have to be cultivated with some sensitivity, as much as nipple responsiveness is latent in most males but can be consciously developed.

2. Many women may experience multiple orgasms with this technique (focused ear lobe stimulation) although this should not become a goal, anymore than simultaneous orgasms or female ejaculation should become a goal. Such experience are bonuses, not success indicators!

3. The method may be equally applied to the nipple if the woman is breast sensitive.

4. Prolonged excitement phase that does not end in orgasmic release may produce uncomfortable venous congestion in the female pelvis. When this happens, any method (oral sex, manual stroking, vibrator, etc.) should be used to provide release.

5. The male partner is required to sustain erection and prolong excitement phase as long as possible before

ejaculation. As mentioned previously, involuntary ejaculations may be expected and should not to be considered failures or loss of energy. This is an outdated idea still often espoused, not only by Yogis and western practitioners of sex magic, but by physicians, athletic coaches, and others that indeed should know better.

SHAKTI POWER FLOWS

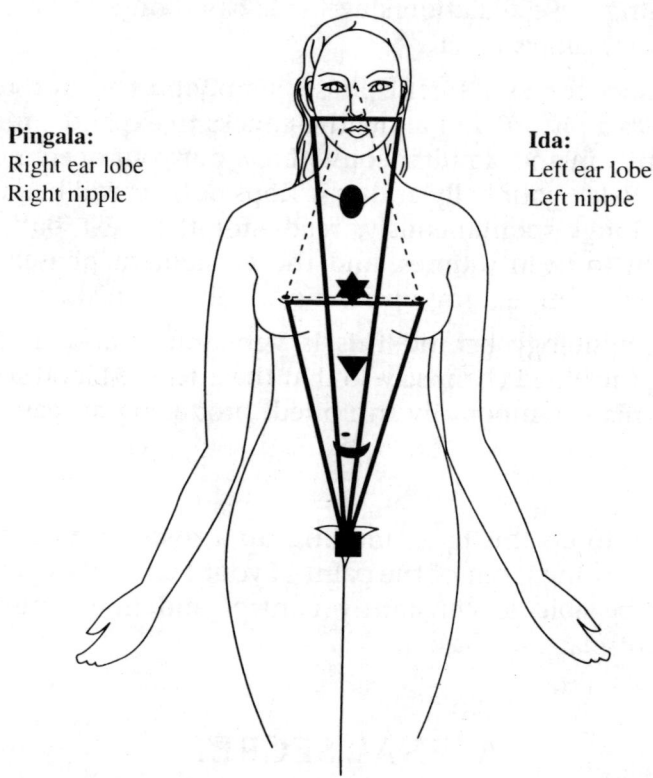

Pingala:
Right ear lobe
Right nipple

Ida:
Left ear lobe
Left nipple

The two Shakti-yoni triangles point down to awaken Muladhara (genital center) while one Shiva triangle points up to the Third Eye. This is a neuro-psychological tract from a woman's nipple to the pituitary gland that then releases a hormone stimulating uterine contractions. Thus the visionary world opens for her with mounting excitement.

RETARDING EJACULATION BY TANTRIC BREATH POWER

Western sexologists have developed several techniques to retard ejaculation, including the Masters and Johnson "squeeze technique" and a testicle traction method. By Tantric standards these are relatively cumbersome.

The key (never before revealed in print, to my knowledge) is gentle hyperventilation when the excitement phase is approaching the ejaculation stage. It is based on a variation of Bhastrika ("bellows breath").

To reduce the excitement phase, simply puff air out, using the belly as a piston, and allow the cheeks to expand. Pull the belly slightly in and simultaneously blow out your open mouth in a puff. Relax your belly and as it flops out, air will be pulled into the lungs spontaneously, ready for the next puff out. Repeat ten to twenty times, and the excitement phase, with the feeling of impending ejaculation, will diminish.

The physiology behind this is very sound and involves changing the blood chemistry so that the arteriole blood supply to the penis is temporarily inhibited, producing an easing of tension.

Tip: Learn to do this by crumpling up a tissue in your hand and puff-blowing it out of the palm of your hand. With practice you will be able to constantly control and fine tune your excitement-plateau phase.

A FINAL SECRET

At the moment of climax, Shiva and Shakti may intensify their mutual experience by holding their breath for as long as the orgasmic reverberations continue.

This Pranayama conjoins life (Prana) and death (Yama), and floods the psychic bodies with bio-energy (Prana) while controlling (Yama) the mind-body complex.

Her lap is a sacrificial altar;
her hairs, the sacrificial grass;
her skin, the soma-press.
The two lips of the vulva
are the fire in the middle of the yoni ...
So great is the world of him
who practices sexual intercourse,
knowing this.

— Brhadaranyaka Upanisad, Vi, 4,3.

CHAKRAS

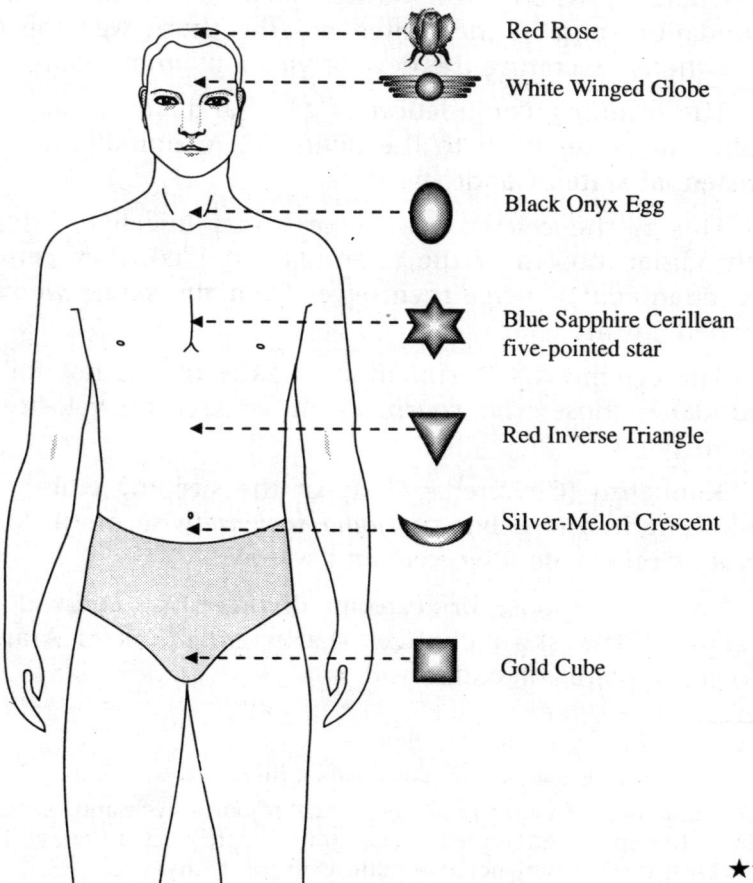

Red Rose

White Winged Globe

Black Onyx Egg

Blue Sapphire Cerillean five-pointed star

Red Inverse Triangle

Silver-Melon Crescent

Gold Cube

★★

Epilogue

The Ultimate Ritual

Kissing awakens the sleeping princess of beauty, and there begins the ultimate ritual* of Tantra leading to the Yoga of lingam and yoni, wand and cup, spine and skull, arrow and heart, wafer and wine, bell and candle, sword and blood, taper and flame, thorn and rose.

Upon "nowhere" will be inscribed the Templar temple foundation, and in the center will the thorn wed the rose "now-here," secreting the dew of vicarious immortality.

The resulting conjunction of Mars and Venus, Ares and Aphrodite, gives birth to the divine hermaphrodite and the existential state of androgyny.

This is the celestial dance of lovers injected with the aphrodisiac venom of the tarantula. Coupled, they perform the tarantella** to free themselves from the spider woman's tangled Tantric web.

The ceremony—"karma-mony" (Sanskrit)—is not for the mundane, those who spurn sperm, or sacrifice velocity for intensity.†

Kundalini (Cinderella: "lady of the sleeping embers") is quiescent in the pelvis of *Homo sapiens* (wise ones). She is bride, virgin, wife, divorcee, and widow.

Shiva, her spouse, bridegroom, divorced one, and widower, sleeps in the skull chalice. (Latin *calvarium* is Aramaic Golgotha—"hill of skulls.")

---

*Sanskrit "rita," meaning "to flow."
**A wild and vivacious folk dance of southern Italy.
†To ignore necessity for a prolonged sexual response cycle and excitement phase, hasten the attempted orgasm (often mere ejaculation), and miss the Tantric U3 experience (Ultimate Universal Unity).

Lord Shiva, prince of serpentine charmers, awaits the moment to enter through the bramble-guarded (pubic pubescence) castle gate; his goddess, kundalini, flares with fire divine, bestowing bountiful beatitude.

The emergence of the full Muladhara chakra (libido center in humans), as a mandala which contains animal and divine beings plus letters of the Sanskrit alphabet, evolves from the primal Tantric yantra. A yantra is characterized by pure geometric lines and curves only.

(From Ecstasy Through Tantra*)*

The essence of the classical Hindu temple foundation square is oriented East and West, from the primal Tantric yantra. This is drawn on holy ground by two men using rope and pegs to scrape the outline in earth. The square is formed last, by connecting intersection lines of *vesica pisces,* and it is within the square that bricks are laid to provide the base for the three-dimensional structure to be built by Hindu architects. This method has been used for thousands of years in India and follows the dictates of classical *shipla* texts.

PRELIMINARY PURIFICATION

Let the couple preparing for Tantric coupling ascertain the directions of N(orth), E(ast), W(est), and S(outh) in a clean room of their choice.

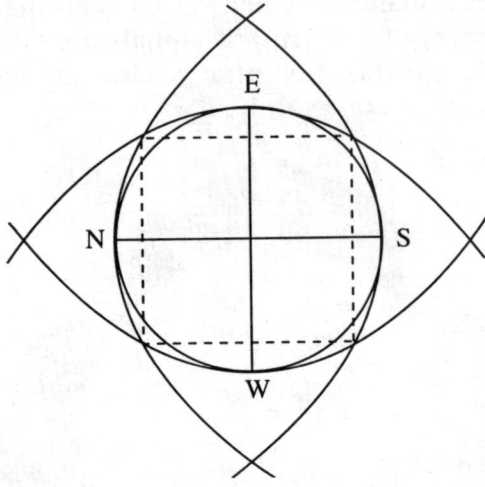

Rose incense may be burned in the East (feminine) and sandalwood in the West (masculine) while the psychic circuit (yantra) is being drawn upon the floor.

Construction

At the center of the chosen space, let the man hold a cord that is equal to the woman's height (or, if space is limited, equal to the distance from her navel to the soles of her feet); the radius of the circle described using half this length. The woman, holding the other end of the rope, traces a circle with white chalk as she walks.

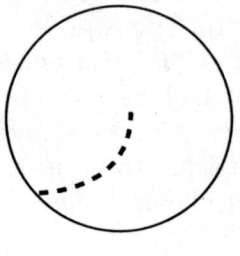

Construction Method as Used by Indian Surveyors to Outline for a Hindu Temple

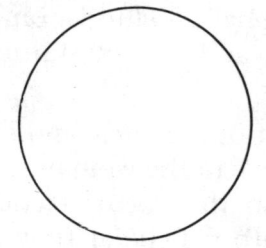

(Student does exercises with ruler and compass.)

Draw a circle, using a compass.

Mark the circle diameters within, at right angles, oriented East, West, North, and South.

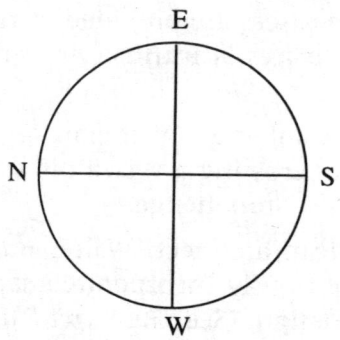

Extend compass from radius to diameter of the circle.

Place the compass point at East and mark the first arc on the West side. (This is half of vesica pisces.) Move the compass point to the West and make a second arc, completing the first vesica pisces, or "yoni." Repeat the procedure North-South and South-North, creating the second yoni.

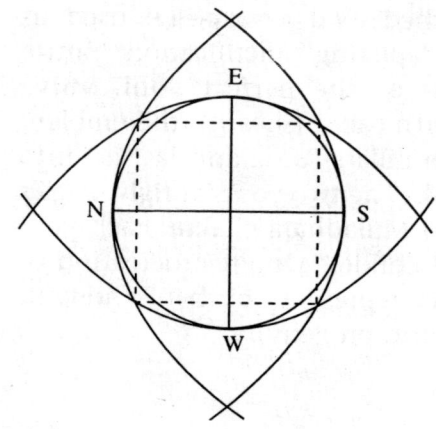

Connect the intersections of the two yonis to form a square.

The erected house divine will rest on the square.

Symbology

The circle is a cross-section both of lingam and breast, the white chalk is both semen and milk—they respectively represent the nutrients for the unconceived and nourishment for the newborn, as well as cosmic elixir ("Milky Way"). The circle center is the nipple, lingam-phallus, clitoris, omphalos (center of the microcosmic world), and axis mundi (axle of macrocosm or universe).

The man now moves to the East of the circle and extends the cord the full diameter of the circle to the woman standing at the opposite (Western) point on the circumference. She inscribes a half arc North-South, with red chalk. They reverse positions and repeat the procedure by walking clockwise around the circumference. The same construction is used from North and South positions so two vesica pisces are provided at right angles to each other. The vesica pisces is intrinsic to sacred architecture around the world.

The capital city of Australia, Canberra (Australian capital territory), was centred on ley lines crossing a vesica pisces, in the tradition of Ancient Rome and Stonehenge.

The eccentric, brilliant American architect, Walter Burley Griffin, early this century surreptitiously incorporated sacred geometry into Canberra's urban design. (See *The Secret Plan of Canberra*, Professor Peter Proudfoot, Published 1993 by the University of N.S.W.)

A vesica pisces is the arched oval (ovary-egg) used in medieval painting as an aura depicting sanctification. Tantra and Hinduism recognize this as the perfect yoni, vulva (enfolded petals), vagina, or birth canal (sheath), the emblem of initiation between the thigh pillars (Boaz and Jachin) into the journey from womb to tomb. The two yonis at right angles form the four dalas or petals of Muladhara chakra. Each yoni represents a different "magical childe." One is procreation or physical birth, while the other represents birth of thought, i.e., mental children (true Tantric progeny).

The red chalk outline is the sign of each woman as lunar goddess, the "rose flower" or "flow-er" weeping blood between conceptions and at births

The magical geometry is completed by pulling the cord taut between the points where the two vesica pisces intersect and drawing straight lines with yellow chalk to form a square.

Symbology

The yellow square is the element earth, signifying solidarity, stability, grounding, and material existence. The square may be filled in with a yellow woolen blanket, preferably overlaid with yellow silk.

This becomes consecrated ground wherein a psychic bridge may be created between the mundane and the arcane, the physical and the spiritual realms.

The tantric linkage occurring within this sacred area transforms the participants into divine *(deva)* beings possessed of wisdom *(veda)*. Therein mutual desires will crystallize, actualize, and materialize when implosive sex magic occurs within this "squared circle."

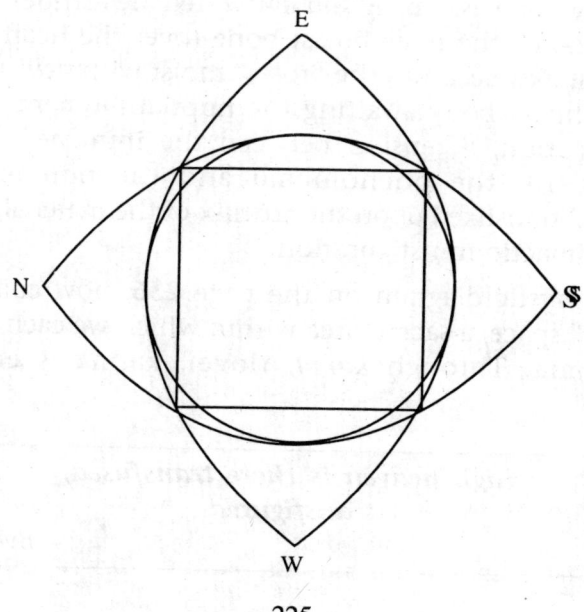

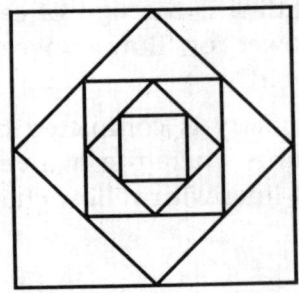

The constrained, contained power of the square is demonstrated in terms of sacred geometry by noting that perfect squares can be constructed within the primal square, each with ever-decreasing area, to infinity.

This design is found on the roof of the "womb house" or sanctum sanctorum in all Hindu temples.

Note also that the two-dimensional outline of the square extends into the astral as a three-dimensional cube or "perfect Ashlar." The cube with six sides unfolds to become the Latin or "rosy" cross, consisting of six equal squares.

When, within the central square, a cross is formed by the supine male body (head East, arms extended North and South) with the woman assuming *kali asana* (female astride), her yoni pressed against the male breast bone (over the heart chakra), then the shakti becomes the "rose," moist with dew, upon the cross of Shiva's body awaiting the nuptial moment. Theirs is an anticipation, a tension between the immanent and the transcendent, the phenomenal and the noumenal, the immaterial transfixed upon the crucifix of the material, resolved by the climactic transfiguration.

The mystic diagram on the page 236, now complete, is "ga-lactic" space, a sacred area within which we each work out our ka(r)ma. Through *kama*, (love), karma is eradicated

> High heaven is there transfused,
> transfigured.
> —Byron

ESOTERIC "NET" OF PLATONIC HEXAHEDRON

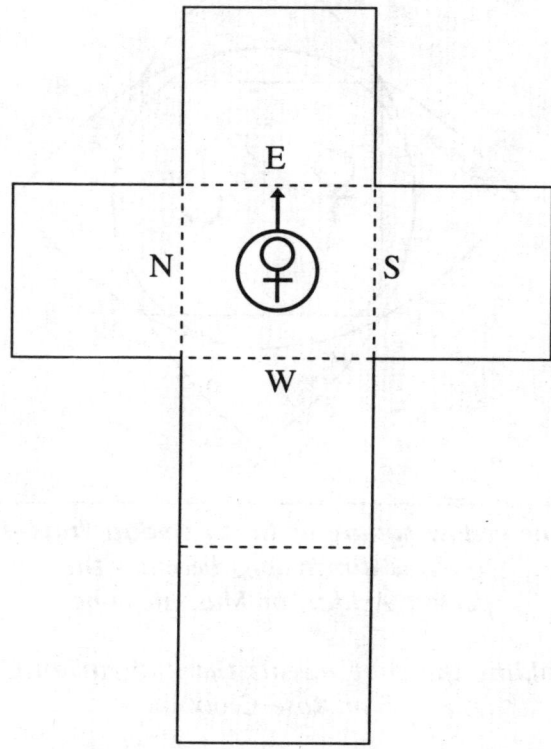

according to the purity of each male and female candidate (*candida* = "whiteness;" i.e., the blending of the whole solar spectrum).

The square is the earthy, material bodies of the two participants in sexual communion. The circle is the eternal rebirth of the species and birth after birth of thought patterns. The two vesica pisces (forming four dalas or petals of the Muladhara chakra) become the doors to initiatory birth—physical and spiritual.

Square: Earth—material, physical body, manifest creation, matter; the space within which Adam and Eve incarnate to enact coital conjunction

"What is Matter?" ... "Never Mind!"

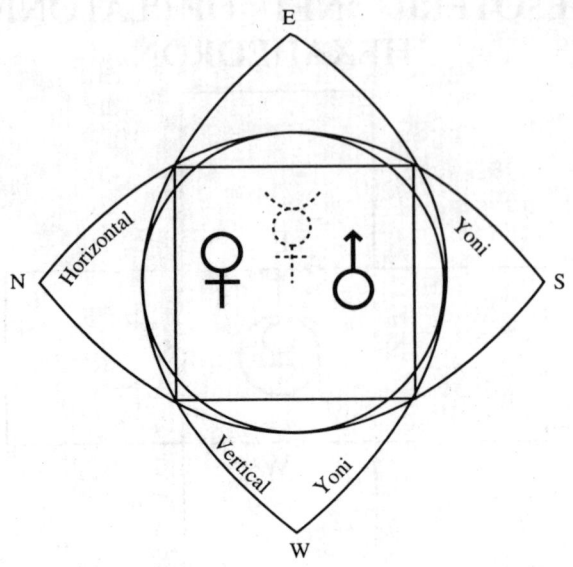

> The yellow square of Earth chakra "raised" to three dimensions becomes the perfect Ashlar, or Masonic cube.
>
> Unfolding the cube reveals the Rosicrucian Cross or Rose Croix.
>
> Think about the underlying concept of such phrases as "bed of roses" ... "rose-colored glasses" ... "om mani padme hum" ... "the jewel in the lotus" ... "the dew within the rose."
>
> Rosa Crux (Latin): "rose cross."
> Ros Crux (Latin): "dew cross."
> Ras (Arabic): "wisdom."
> Rus (Arabic): "concealment."
>
> Tantric rose (lotus) cross is the "hidden knowing of the feminine transudate upon the lingam."
>
> — Brewer Dictionary of Phrase and Fable

Circle: Eternity—recurrence, consciousness, mind
"What is Mind?" ... "Never Matter!"

Horizontal yoni (North and South): Creative conception—inspiration, insight

Vertical yoni (East and West): Physical conception—expiration, expulsion

Ritual Accoutrement

THE VESTMENTS

After a mutual hot bath with oils (amber or rose), Shiva should don a white (*shukra* = semen) cotton or silk robe, and Shakti a red (*rajas* = menses) cotton or silk robe. Other than these vestments, they are skyclad.

RITUAL PLACEMENT OF TANTRIC LITURGICAL INSTRUMENTS

The following are to be placed at compass points in clockwise order:

1. **The central square area:** Cover with a yellow blanket and the censor or thurible to be placed at the Eastern extreme of the square. Use amber incense or a rose and sandalwood combination.
2. **The Eastern petal/dala:** Chalice containing a mixture of two parts champagne, one part white rum, one part gin, and sweet lime juice to taste, ice cold. (The total amount to equal one bottle of champagne.) Paten with cardamom seeds.
3. **The Southern petal/dala:** A large dripless candle, one white rose (*sukhra*—male), and one red rose (*rajas*—female) or one hibiscus (a lingam within a yoni).
4. **The Western petal/dala:** Two pieces of dark blue silk cloth, cut in the shape of equilateral triangles and arranged as a hexagram (*shatkona*) or six-pointed star.
5. **The Northern petal/dala:** Large bell with handle and clapper. (The handle and clapper represent the lingam;

the bell cup is the yoni. Note: *Fuck,* Germanic root *ficken,* means "to strike." By assonance, "clang" associations; by shape, the receptive yoni. Also *belladonna,* meaning "beautiful lady.")

Let the couple now enter the sacred space, a realm of self-created sacred geometry, with knowledge of TAN-gible TRA-nscendence.

Theirs is to become a unique, unrepeatable journey, as is existence itself unique and unrepeatable.

A penultimate ritual has structure; an ultimate ritual is an individual labyrinth—beyond words!

RITUAL ARRANGEMENT AT COMMENCEMENT OF CEREMONY

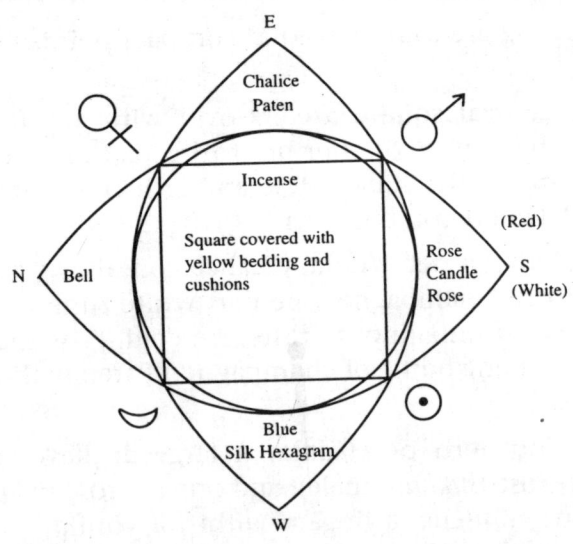

> From a certain point onward there is no longer any turning back. That is the point that must be reached.
> — Franz Kafka

> *Das ewig weibliche zieht uns hinan.*
> *(The Eternal Feminine draws us upward.)*
> — Faust (Goethe)

Upon commencing Maithuna, ever concentrate upon the flame, and so persevering in Dharana, avoid the ashes, and the end.
— Sutra 43 Malini Vajaya Tantra (c. 2000 BC)
(Translation by Swami Anandakapila)

The male and female construct a microcosmic circle, from a circle a square, then mutually evolve a triangle around which emerges a macrocosmic circle, and they shall possess the Philosopher's Stone. For a philosopher is not a lover of wisdom but one who knows the wisdom of love.

SYMBOL OF HEART CHAKRA (ANAHATA)

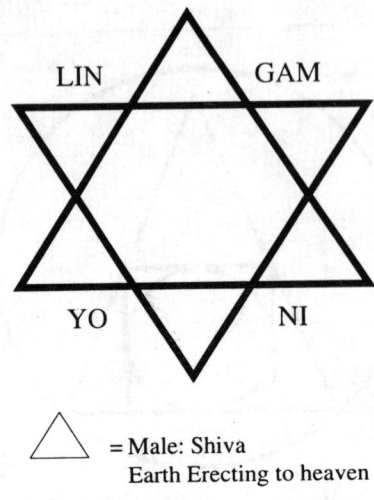

△ = Male: Shiva
Earth Erecting to heaven

▽ = Female: Shakti
Heaven Descending
to Earth

Memorial

*Yogarishi Dr. Swami Gitananda Giri
Yoga Samadhi 2:20 am, December 29, 1993*

Guruji, where would I be if you had not been? You once told me that "I have hitched my wagon to a star," and now you are with the stars.

*Ram Nam Satya Hai
Om Shiva*

— Jonn Mumford (January 4, 1994)

Appendix One

Twelve-Week Practice Schedule

This is a program designed to insure mastery of the core techniques in the first nine chapters of this book.

First Week (Chapter 1)
Sukhasana: Twenty minutes each morning and evening.

Second Week (Chapter 2)
Sukhasana: Twenty minutes each morning.
Shavasana, Elementary: Twenty minutes each evening.

Third Week
Sukhasana: Twenty minutes each morning.
Shavasana, Advanced: Thirty minutes each evening.

Fourth Week (Chapter 3)
Sukhasana: Ten minutes each morning.
Yoni Mudra, Elementary: Fifteen minutes each morning.
Shavasana, Advanced: Thirty minutes each evening.

Fifth Week
Sukhasana: Ten minutes each morning.
Yoni Mudra, Advanced: Fifteen minutes each morning.
Shavasana, Advanced: Thirty minutes each evening.

Sixth Week (Chapter 4)
Yoni Mudra, Advanced: Fifteen minutes each morning.
Polarization: Fifteen minutes each evening, *or*
Shavasana, Psychic: Thirty minutes each evening.

Seventh Week (Chapter 5)
Yoni Mudra, Advanced: Fifteen minutes each morning.
Polarization: Fifteen minutes each evening.
External Dharana: Fifteen minutes each evening.
Shavasana, Psychic: Thirty minutes each evening.

Eighth Week
Yoni Mudra, Advanced: Fifteen minutes each morning.
Polarization: Fifteen minutes each evening.
Internal Dharana: Fifteen minutes each evening.
Shavasana, Psychic: Thirty minutes each evening.

Ninth Week (Chapter 6)
Yoni Mudra, Advanced: Fifteen minutes each morning.
Revitalization: Fifteen minutes each evening.
Internal Dharana: Fifteen minutes each evening.
Shavasana, Psychic: Thirty minutes each evening.

Tenth Week (Chapter 7)
Yoni Mudra, Advanced: Fifteen minutes each morning.
Revitalization: Fifteen minutes each evening.
Internal Dharana: Fifteen minutes each evening.
Shavasana, Psychic: Thirty minutes each evening.

Eleventh Week (Chapter 8)
Yoni Mudra, Advanced: Fifteen minutes each morning.
Revitalization: Fifteen minutes each evening.
External Chakra Dharana: Twenty minutes each evening.
Shavasana, Psychic: Thirty minutes each evening.

Twelfth Week (Chapter 9)
Yoni Mudra, Advanced: Fifteen minutes each morning.
Revitalization: Fifteen minutes each evening.
Internal Chakra Dharana: Twenty minutes each evening.
Solar Plexus Charging: Twenty minutes each evening.

★★

Appendix Two

Loss of Consciousness During the Yoga Class: A Guide for Yoga Teachers

(This article was written in 1973 while I was studying with Paramahamsa Satyananda Saraswati at Monghyr, Bihar State, India.)

HANDLING EMERGENCY SITUATIONS

Your maturity as a yoga teacher may be judged by how efficiently you handle emergency situations in the class. The moment an incident arises, if possible, isolate the student requiring attention and keep the others occupied under the supervision of a senior student.

A faint: When a person falls or sags unconscious to the ground and rapidly recovers.

A seizure: The collapse of a person who falls unconscious and then jerks or twitches. (Most commonly epileptic.)

A fall: A student slips or trips and lands on the floor, often in balance exercises. When this occurs, consider the possibility that the student may have struck his or her head when landing, particularly if the student seems dull after the incident and fails to get up. Although you may think that the student overbalanced, always ask if the fall was because he or she felt strange, weak, giddy, or sick.

Students attending Yoga classes on an empty stomach or after a working day may be predisposed to giddiness and fainting. Any healthy person can, under the right circumstances, faint. All that is necessary is sufficient retardation of blood flow to the brain (a student with low blood pressure comes suddenly upright after an inverted posture), lack of adequate oxygen (an anemic student in a crowded class who breathes in a shallow fashion), or lack of adequate blood-sugar level for energy metabolism (a diabetic student or exhausted student who has not eaten faints after Surya Namaskar, having suddenly lowered the blood sugar level through muscular exertion).

FAINTING UNDER VARIOUS CIRCUMSTANCES

Fainting occurs in a variety of circumstances—high temperature (air condition or ventilate studio, if possible), crowding (ideally, never have more than twelve to a class), or emotional shocks such as a fright or the sight of an accident or blood.

Susceptibility to fainting varies; some people having a high threshold requiring very strong stimulus, but given the right circumstances, anyone—fit or not—will faint. In sickness, fainting will be precipitated by the same factors as in health. However, the stimulus required will be much less, thus Yoga students should stay away from classes when ill.

Since fainting is a reduction of blood flow to the brain, nature's method of causing unconsciousness and falling to the ground is, in fact, self-correcting. Blood flow to the brain rapidly returns in the prone position and the victim recovers.

If consciousness does not return shortly, something more serious than a simple faint has occurred. Concussion (or actual damage to the brain in the cranial cavity) may be indicated by a continuing stuporous or comatose condition, vomiting shortly after, and unequal eye pupil size. All those fainting and/or striking their heads on the floor should be recommended for examination by a medical doctor Other students should witness the recommendation.

A stupor: A semi-conscious state in which the individual is prone, appears unconscious, but responds to strong pain stimulus or auditory stimulus such as pinching the skin or shouting the student's name. (In Varami we alter the psychic and emotional state by blowing sharply in the student's ear, particularly to bring him or her out of trance or deep meditation).

A coma: A profound unconsciousness, usually due to a drug overdose, poison, or severe organic brain damage. A quick and safe trick used by the Japanese police to differentiate between a stupor and a coma is to press a thin coin, key, or other thin, blunt object strongly under the thumbnail. If the condition is a stupor, arousal will be almost instantaneous, as the nerve fibers conducting pain impulses are exquisitely sensitive under the fingernails, inducing cortical alertness. (Ever heard of bamboo splinters inserted under the nails? The Chinese have found them marvelous for facilitating memory when people seem to be having difficulty answering questions.)

Frequently the student has warning signs of an impending faint; these include a feeling that things are receding far away, or the world is becoming strangely quiet. He or she may go pale, yawn, or begin to perspire (particularly if hypoglycemic or suffering from lowered blood sugar), with beads of sweat or droplets bursting out on the forehead. (Treat by getting sugar, candy, honey, etc., into the person immediately.) Fellow students may notice the above signs.

Let the student assume the hare posture, prone with the head low and hips or buttocks high to restore normal circulation to the brain; or place him or her supine with feet propped up at a right angle against a wall.

In the case of a full faint, quickly observe the following points:

1. See that there is no obstruction to the neck from tight clothes.

2. Check that false teeth are not loose in the mouth or have not fallen back into the throat.

3. See that the student is not in a position that is harmful or dangerous to him or herself—for example, with one arm bent at an unusual angle under the body.

VARMA KALAI SOUTH INDIAN RESUSCITATION METHOD (SIDDHA TRADITION)

Place the student supine and—quickly grasping his or her heels—firmly raise his or her legs abruptly and sharply to a right angle with the floor, then quickly smack the soles of his or her feet with the fingers of one hand, while holding both feet upright with the other hand. You are stimulating a point we call "Kidney I" (a sub-chakra related to Muladhara), which is very popular with Indian and Chinese healers for reviving victims of drowning and initiating the cardio-respiratory cycle in cases of syncope.

In Western medical practice, obstetricians have now abandoned the routine of slapping the buttocks of the newborn to stimulate breathing. They have discovered that if this is done carelessly, spinal damage can sometimes result. The preferred method is to grasp the infant upside-down by the ankles with one hand and slap the soles of his or her feet with the other. Raising the legs suddenly at right angles reverses venous stasis in lower limbs and rushes blood out of the limbs, through the abdominal cavity, into the chest, and then to the brain.

As the person recovers, persuade him or her not to get up for a while, as a faint may occur if there is too rapid a return to the normal upright posture. (Note: Placing a person upright who is still in a dead faint will induce an epileptic seizure, as the motor cells of the cortex will then be so severely oxygen-deprived that they will discharge erratically, causing tonic and clonic contractions of the muscular-skeletal system).

There are no after-effects of a simple faint, unless the patient is held upright while he or she is unconscious. This has occasionally happened when a person in a crowd cannot fall or a person sitting upright in a dental chair faints.

Bhastrika (the bellows), Bhujangasana (the cobra), and Simhasana (the lion pose) may all induce fainting in students with organic abnormalities or low blood pressure.

In cases of an epileptic seizure, use a cushion to protect the patient's head from banging on the floor, and otherwise make no attempt to restrain the person. Recovery is usually spontaneous and followed by the desire to sleep. A post-incident medical check should be advised.

In Yoga, we have a special secret science of "fainting" called Murcha. This induces ecstasy and a state beyond Nama-rupa (name-form), which is egoless. There are forty-four such Murchas, which alter the blood chemistry and the blood flow to the brain, as well as affecting the activity of the autonomic nervous system. My own master of this hidden science was Swami Shantananda, who initiated me at Birla Mandir Temple, New Delhi, in 1960.

★★

Appendix Three

A Note Regarding Indian Yoga Schools

India abounds with ashrams and Yoga schools. I am personally acquainted with the following institutions, having studied with three of the four respective founders.

The Bihar School of Yoga
Monghyr, Bihar State
North East India

Paramhamsa Swami Satyananda Saraswati established the Bihar School of Yoga in 1964. It is now a very modern and large complex with research facilities and excellent accommodations for six-month live-in courses.

An amazing amount of books are available from the ashram printing presses on the subject of Yoga, medical topics, and Swami Satyananda's unique North Indian Yoga—Tantric technology.

The Bihar school of Yoga is also the central training base for Swamis of the Saraswati order. A particular bonus for Western students is a good grounding in Hindi, taught in residence as part of the general course.

Paramahamsa Satyananda is now retired and the head of the order and the new director is Paramahamsa Swami Niranjanananda Saraswati, a truly worthy successor. Under his leadership the world's first truly Yoga University has been established, affiliated with the University of New Delhi, and offering undergraduate and postgraduate degrees in various aspects of Yoga. Information can be obtained by writing to:

The Registrar
Bihar Yoga Bharati; Institute for Advanced Studies in Yogic Sciences
Ganga Darshan, Munger, Bihar 811201, India

International Centre for Yoga Education and Research (ICYER).
16/a 16/b Mettu Street
Chinnamudaliarchavady
Kottakuppam 605104 (via Pondicherry) Tamil Nadu
South India
(Write: The director, Meenakshi Devi Bhavanani)

Yogarishi Dr. Swami Gitananda Giri founded the school in 1969. Excellent residence facilities for live-in three-month and six-month teacher training courses. Correspondence study is a prerequisite for entrance.

Swamijii founded Ananda Ashram upon a firm foundation of Ashtanga Yoga plus a unique Kriya and Yoga therapy (Yoga Chikitsa).

Dr. Swami Gitananda had his Mahasamadhi (transition) December 29th, 1993 and his successor is his son, Dr. Ananda, now completing his medical residency.

South Indian culture is totally different, and an extra feature for Western students is an opportunity to study Bharat-Natyam and Carnatic vocal music within an integrated Yoga course.

Swami Gitananda was the most creative mind I have ever encountered; they didn't call him "The Lion of Pondicherry" for nothing. The result of his work with Indian village children is spectacular.

Kaivalyadhama Yoga Research Institution
Lonavala: 410403
India

Established 1924 by Swami Kuvalayananda.
Resident Yoga teacher training courses.

I have not studied at Kaivalyadhama, but I possess a complete set of their Yoga journals "Yoga Mimamsa" (Yoga Enquiry), from 1928–1982.

The amount of applied scientific research into Yoga that they have done since 1924 is overwhelming. Subscriptions to "Yoga Mimamsa" are still available upon written request. Copies are often at university libraries. A quick overview can be obtained by reading *Abstracts and Bibliography of Articles on Yoga from Kaivalyadhama up to December 1982*, published in 1983 by Kuvalayananda Birth Centenary Publication.

The Yoga Institute
Santa Cruz
Bombay 25
India

Founded in 1918 by Shri Yogendra.

This school can proudly be acknowledged as the oldest International Yoga Foundation in India "which pioneered the scientific Yoga renaissance."

Swami Gitananda sent me to study at the Yoga Institute in 1961 (rather like being passed from one lion's mouth to another!). Shri Yogendra turned out to be "The Lion of Bombay," and taught me methodology and common sense.

The Yoga Institute is now headed by Shri Yogendra's eldest son, Dr. Jayadeva. Dr. Jayadeva's Ph.D. thesis on Samkhya was the longest ever submitted to Bombay University and won a special prize.

Facilities for live-in teacher training were fabulous in 1961 and can only have improved since then. If you are in Bombay (now 'Mumbai' also known as 'Bollywood') look them up in the phone book—they prefer visitors on Sundays!

Spiral Concepts
P.O. Box K474
Haymarket NSW 1240, Australia

The president, Mr. Geoff Whitefield, offers interesting resources through the mail.

Sanskrit Glossary

Ahimsa: "Non-killing." Hindu doctrine of non-violence and non-injury. The Yama (control) of the first stage of Ashtanga Yoga. "Himsa" means "hurting, injuring, harming, slaughtering." The prefix "A" (negations) = A-Himsa—that is, doing no hurt, being harmless, and avoiding injury. Philosophically, the application incorporates not only action (conation), but speech (affect) and thought (cognition). Ahimsa represents a 3,000-year-old ideal of transcending the inherent biology of humankind.

Ajna: "Command Center." The sixth psychic center (Third Eye) anatomically indicted by the pituitary gland, and in terms of psycho-physiology, the pineal gland. Ajna is described as a two-petaled lotus between the eyebrows (nasion)—the two petals corresponding to the anterior and posterior pituitary lobes. Conversely, the mandala of Ajna represents the "winged" (of imagination) Hermes Caduceus with the coloured iris (globe), framed by the two white pennants of the sclerotic coat of the eyeball.

Akasa: The fifth element, Ether (compare with the European alchemists' "Quintessence"), is symbolized by a black oval or a spiral. Akasa is the Tattwa (quality) associated with Vishuddha chakra; its manifestation is sound vibration (shabda), yet it is not sound. Neither Ether nor Quintessence are exactly equivalents to Akasa. Akasa is a form of reality described as dimensionless, all-pervading space. The root of Akasa is "kas," meaning "to shine" or "to appear." Vyasa Bhasyam mentions infinitude and indivisibility as properties of Akasa. The Hindu philosophical implication of Akasa predates Greek Epicurean atomistic physics and is a cogent concept equitable with current astronomical cosmology. Lucretius (c. 94-55 BC), the greatest Roman apologists of the Epicureans, in his hexameter poem "On the Nature of Things," makes two statements which approach the Indian concept of Akasa:

1. "Whenever I step I am at the Center of the Universe" (implied infinitude)
2. Nothing comes out of Nothing" (implied eternity).

Anahata: "Unstruck Sound." The fourth psychic center, indicated physically by the heart, thymus gland, and the cardiopulmonary plexus. The spiritual essence of this chakra may be best expressed by "Where the heart lies, let the brain lie also" (Robert Browning, 1865).

Antar-Anga: "Inner limbs." The four higher phases of Ashtanga Yoga, comprising Pratyahara, Dharana, Dhyana, and Samadhi.

Apas: The second element, Water, symbolized by a silver crescent. The Tattwa of Swadhisthana. In the body, Apas rules from the knees to the hips. The root "ap" means "water," which is to be understood as the principle of liquid; that is, fluid manifestation of matter. Contraction (evaporation) and taste (Rasa) are inseparable qualities of ap. Consider the tongue, which cannot have its gustatory receptors fire without saliva or fluid present in the mouth.

Asana: "Seat." Also taken to mean the eighty-four classical body posture or exercises taught in Hatha Yoga. Unfortunately no one knows which are the eighty-four classical Asanas, as the Hatha texts enumerate them into the hundreds. The literal meanings of Asana is "sitting, sitting down, sitting position, halting, encamping, abiding, seat, throne, or office." Asana is the third stage of Ashtanga Yoga, and Patanjali mentions four sitting postures only. Within this context, Asana is any position in which the body has a stable base of gravity, the proprioceptors (joint movement indicators giving the sensation of "one's own property" or body boundaries) and touch receptors are inhibited from impinging into the central nervous system; e.g., body sensations do not disturb concentration.

Ashtanga Yoga: "Eight-limbed" Yoga. A term applied to the system outlined in Patanjali's Yoga Sutras wherein Yoga is divided into eight steps or stages: Yama (control), Niyama (observances), Asana (posture), Pranayama (breath control), Pratyahara (sense withdrawal), Dharana (concentration), Dhyana (sustained concentration), and Samadhi (universal consciousness or the apparent experience of total psychological and physical integration). Note: Yoga emphasizes "experience" rather than "explanation."

Audgita: The silent or mental chanting of a mantra. The mantra becomes an attention-fixing, cognitive device, leading to the absence of perturbation. A subtle question arises: is it possible to "think" a mantra without subvocalization? (i.e., psychosomatic involuntary movements of the lips, tongue, and larynx as a result of concentration upon a sound.) To my knowledge this has not been researched with EMG (electromyograph) tracings. I suggest that it is possible, as such meditation starts with vocalization (chanting) of the mantra, followed by whispering, leading to inaudible movements of the lips and tongue and finally pure cerebration.

Bahira-Anga: "Outer limbs." The four lower phases of Ashtanga Yoga comprising Yama, Niyama, Asana, and Pranayama.

Bhakti: That path of Yoga which seeks realization through the practice of devotion and love in both a religious (Bhakti) and a philosophical (Para-bhakti) sense. Sanskrit root is "bhaj," meaning "to serve, honor, love, trust." Bhakti is a difficult concept for Westerners as they associate it with deification of the Guru; Ramakrishna stated that your Guru could be a tree, a criminal, or a god, which is reminiscent of our saying "Beauty is in the eye of the beholder." I will transpose this proverb to "Love is in the heart of the lover." We may also remind ourselves of Edward III's comment, upon rescuing the fallen garter of the Countess of Salisbury: "Honisoit Qui Mal Y Pense" (Evil be to him who thinks evil of this).

Bija: "Seed." The root sound of each chakra which, when intoned as a mantra, will release its potential. The Bija sounds of the first five chakras are Lng, Vng, Rng, Yng, and Hng.

> *In a full heart there is room for everything, and in an empty heart there is room for nothing*
> —Antonio Forchio

Bramacharya: In Yoga, the fourth Yama or discipline of the first stage (Yama) of Ashtanga Yoga. The first of the four Hindu Ashramas (life stages), that phase of education and studentship. Compound of the roots "brahm" (divinity) and "char" (to study, to perform). Bramacharya is popularly interpreted as sexual celibacy, but is better interpreted as moderation and control of passion. Considering that both celibacy and monogamy are biologically unnatural, Bramacharya, taken as literal "continence," is another attempt to oppose the dictum "Biology is Destiny" (Freud). Bramacharya (as indeed all the Yamas and Niyamas) may be considered akin to the statement "Civilization is the intelligent monitor of emotions."

Chakra: "Wheel, disc, whirlpool." The term is applied to the basic seven psychic centers outlined in Yoga and Tantra. Chakra implies a vortex, and thus we may define a psychic center as a "whirling vortex of psychic energy at the conjunction points of the mind and the body." I must emphasize that just as the Cartesian division of "Mind" and "Body" is arbitrary, so a "chakra" may well be an imaginary, albeit useful, artifact for purposes of attention-fixing. I perceive a chakra as outside the space-time continuum and equivalent to the Euclidean "Point"—i.e., without magnitude, possessed of location but not dimension.

Dharana: "Concentration." The sixth stage of Ashtanga Yoga.

Dhyana: "Sustained concentration." The seventh stage of Ashtanga Yoga and an advanced state of Dharana. Some have applied the English words "contemplation" and "meditation" to Dhyana, but the classical Yoga texts state that so many Dharanas (measured in a specific time unit) equal one Dhyana, and in turn so many Dhyanas equal one Samadhi. The essential difference between Dharana and Dhyana is of degree (quantitative) rather than kind (qualitative).

Gnana: That path of Yoga which seeks realization through the pursuit of philosophical knowledge. The Sanskrit root means "knowing," and is cognate with the Greek "Gnosis" (direct appreciation of universal truth). Unswerving centering of the mind of the highest awareness of oneness.

Ham Sa: A mantra affirming "I am He" or "I am Brahman." When used in meditation, becomes "So" (on the inhalation) "Hum" (on the exhalation). Ham Sa, translated by nineteenth century indologists as the "Divine Swan," a symbol of purity. Actually, Ham Sa is the Indian goose *(Indicus anser)*, a most elegant bird, but called swan because of the English tradition of denigrating geese. This mantra is one of the most potent methods for releasing positive emotional attitudes, of omniscience and omnipresence, from the conscious.

Hatha: "Violence; obstinacy; absolute necessity (as the cause of all existence); forced meditation, inevitably, compulsorily." (*A Practical Sanskrit Dictionary*, Arthur Anthony MacDonell.) One of the four Yogas mentioned in the Upanisads (the remaining being Mantra, Raja, and Laya); and misunderstood in modern parlance as being a set of physical postures. The *Yogasikhopanisad* defines Hatha as the union ("Yoga") of the sun ("Ha") and the moon ("Tha"); the dissolvement of all polar opposites experienced through the mind-body interface. Hatha, from the root "Hath" ("to strike"), esoterically implies a "blow" against the inertia of the total human organism.

Ida: One of the three major psychic nerves or nadis. Ida is visualized as running up the left side of the spinal column conveying feminine, cooling, intuitive energy. Exits in the left nostril and is a trigger for right-hemisphere functions.

Japa: The practice of driving mantric affirmations deep into the subconscious through constant repetition, either silently or audibly.

Karma Yoga: The path of Yoga seeking realization through detachment from the fruits of all action and dedicating all activity to Ishvara (anthropomorphic aspect of God), or—in a more Western mode of expression—as exemplified by Ralph Waldo Emerson's dictum (1844), "The reward of a thing well done is to have done it!" The Karma Yogi seeks conscious, aware action—"See the need, do the deed!" Karma, as a doctrine, is the recognition of the fundamental laws of action and reaction in the human nervous system. It is a sophisticated overview of Western psychology's "Stimulus-Black Box-

Response arc" with ramifications into the past (lives) and the future (lives).

Kundalini: Hypothesis of latent nerve energy within the central nervous system. Symbolically and allegorically represented by a snake coiled three-and-a-half times. Although a cobra may seem a little sluggish, anyone who has seen the Indian krait (Hindi "karait") attack by throwing itself three feet through the air will understand how graphic the coiled snake metaphor is. Traditionally, kundalini can move from static to kinetic activation in a split second. The profusion of anecdotal and apocryphal stories concerning superhuman strength released under stress gives credence to the concept of kundalini, as does the acceleration of mental activity experienced in the manic phase of a bipolar affective incidence. Kundalini means "coiled, spiral," and stems from an earlier root: "kunda," meaning "fire pit."

Laya Yoga: "Rhythm, absorption." That branch of Yoga dealing with the arousal, release, and control of latent nerve energy (kundalini) hidden (absorbed) within a human's nervous system.

Linga: "Mark, totem, sign, emblem, characteristic, proof, evidence, sign of sex, sexual organ, Shiva's phallus (as an object of worship); image of a god, subtle body (indestructible original of the gross, visible body in Vedanta philosophy)." (From *MacDonell's Sanskrit Dictionary*). In Hindu temples displaying a Shiva Lingam as the central object of veneration, it should be noted that the base of the Lingam is set in a Yonic base; it does not represent penetration of the Yoni but rather is emerging from the Yoni as matrix; Yoni gives birth to the Lingam.

Maithuna: "Paired; coupled, being a male and female; connected by marriage; related to or worn during copulation; having copulation in view (adjective); neuter form means sexual union." (From *MacDonell's Sanskrit Dictionary*.)

Manipura: "Gem city." The third psychic center; physically represented by the pancreas and the solar plexus. Also known as Nabhi (navel) chakra, Agni (God of Fire) chakra, and Surya

(Sun God) chakra. The latter two epithets reinforce the metabolic, heat producing activities associated with the epigastric area.

Mantra Yoga: The systematic use of sound vibrations (usually monosyllables) to bring about physical, psychic, and psychological changes. Composed of the prefix "man" ("mind, to think") and the suffix "tra" (a tool or instrument), so literally, a "mind tool" for manipulating consciousness.

Marmasthanani: The sixteen vital body areas that are concentrated upon in certain exercises of Raja and Hatha Yoga. The location varies in different traditions.

Mritasana: "Dead pose." Another name for the relaxation posture commonly known as Shavasana.

Muladhara: "Root base." The first psychic center physically represented by the testes or ovaries and the sacral, or pelvic, plexus. The Earth center; also called Adhi chakra (base center), suggesting grounding and the fecund matter (Latin "Mater," meaning "Mother") from which our being evolves as a seed sprouts.

Nadi: "Motion." A psychic or astral nerve tube, with the Sanskrit root suggesting the polarization and depolarization waves of activity in the nervous system. Yoga teaches that 72,000 such nadis exist in the psychic counterpart of the gross body.

Nadisuddhi: The purification of the nadis through conjoined breathing and mental exercises.

Padma: "Lotus." Another term for the psychic centers. Padma refers to the potential growth and development of our psychic centers, just as a lotus bulb is capable of development into a lotus in full bloom. The lotus root is embedded in mud (darkness, unconsciousness, inertia, blind instinct, ignorance), with the stem immersed in water (emotions, activity, sea of sorrow, consciousness of sentience through feeling), and the bloom floating above water in the full sunlight of "self-realization."

Padmasana: "Lotus pose." An advanced foot lock suitable for meditation. The symmetrical arrangement of the legs produced by placing the right foot on the left thigh and the left foot on the right thigh (Buddhists reverse the position with the right foot on top) is said to resemble a lotus flower. The pose produces a total solid base with a low center of gravity, while conserving blood for the torso and head.

Parang Mukhi: "Turning away." Another term for Yoni Mudra used in the text *Hathayogapradipika*. The Sanskrit "parang" has found its way into Malaysia as a type of machete for cutting undergrowth away.

Patanjali: The author of *Yoga Sutras* who lived sometime between 200 BC and AD 200 (the earlier date is now more plausible). He is responsible for the division of Yoga into eight distinct branches, or stages, and as a result his outline of Yoga is known as Ashtanga.

Pingala: One of the three major nadis. Pingala is visualized as running up the right side of the spinal column conveying masculine, heating, rational energy. It exits in the right nostril and is a trigger for left-hemisphere functions.

Pranayama: The control of life force (prana) through the regulation of the respiratory process, coupled with visualization. "Pra" means "first or before," and "ana" means "breath"—literally, the first essence underlying the breath. Prana is comparable to Chi (Chinese), Ki (Japanese), vitality globules (Theosophical), Nous (Rosicrucian), Orgone (Wilhelm Reich), animal magnetism (Mesmer), Quintessence (Alchemical), and Mana (Hawaii priests).

Prithivi: The first element, Earth, symbolized by a yellow square or a cube. The Tattwa of Muladhara with cohesion and solidity as principle characteristics.

Raja Yoga: "Kingly or Royal Yoga." The science of creating a merger or union (Yoga) between the conscious and subconscious mind, thus producing a third state which becomes superconsciousness. Sanskrit "Rajan" becomes the Hindi "Raj" ("rule or reign"), and Hindi "Raja" ("King") is cognate with Latin "Rex," while Hindi "Rani" ("Queen") is cognate with

Latin "Regina." The implication of Raja Yoga is a rulership over the many facets of our being.

Saguna: "With form." Concentration upon a definite form or that which is of a very concrete nature.

Sahasrara: "Thousand-petaled." The seventh psychic center; physically indicated by the pineal gland and the cerebral cortex (containing billions of cells or "petals"—"Sahasrar," in Sanskrit, is often used to indicate a number beyond enumeration). Sahasrara is said to be the dwelling-place of Shiva, the destroyer of ignorance (Maya). This is an esoteric statement concerning the ability of humans to destroy ignorance (Maya) by the use of enlightened consciousness (Shiva) which results from the awakening of Sahasrara chakra. The brain is currently coming to be viewed as the largest endocrine (ductless) gland in the body. Given that mood alterations are primarily triggered by brain chemistry, then Sahasrara chakra is a Hindu conception of "The Seventh Heaven" and releasing ecstasy may, like Sheherazade, involve "a thousand-and-one nights" of meditation.

Samadhi: "With God." The state of consciousness resulting from the merging of the individual consciousness with universal consciousness. In terms of Jung's psychology, Samadhi would be the eruption of the "Collective Unconscious." Samadhi is the final stage of Ashtanga Yoga and the goal of all Yoga. Samadhi, in Samkhya, is the connective "at-one-ment" of the meditator with the universe as a process of eternal G-eneration (Brahma), O-rder (Vishnu), and D-ecay (Shiva).

Samyama: "With control." The three higher phases of Ashtanga Yoga. These are Dharana, Dhyana, and Samadhi.

San Mukhi: "Six orifices." An alternative term for Yoni Mudra found in the *Yogasopana*. "Mukhi" means "mouth," as well as an opening or orifice; the implication is that we feed upon sensory impressions from outside our bodies and therefore are distracted from subtle inner impulses.

Shavasana: "Corpse Pose." The technique of consciously relaxing the body, section by section. An exercise of immense value for fatigue, exhaustion, auto-immune diseases, insomnia, and certain types of high blood pressure. It is particularly efficacious if combined with certain mental exercises. Only Occidentals could be upset by the name "Corpse Pose," for the Hindu mind has accepted that each night we die into dreamless, Delta wave sleep, and are reborn each morning upon awakening.

Shakti: Divine energy in its manifested form; considered feminine. Christians speak of the "Fatherhood of God" and Hindus speak of the "Motherhood of God." The bridge between these two concepts is the bridge between materialism and spirituality, passion and compassion.

Siddhis: From "sidh," meaning "to succeed, accomplish." Extra-sensory, extra-sensual, and extra-sensational "psychic" powers and experiences that develop as the student advances along the path of Yoga. Undeveloped abilities which most people are unaware of possessing.

Sukhasana: "Easy pose." Simple cross-legged position for meditation and neuromuscular training. European tailors sat cross-legged (i.e., "Tailor's Pose") and Sukhasana stretches the "tailor's" muscle, the sartorius; hence, "sartorial elegance."

Sushumna: The major central nadi corresponding to the spinal cord. The channel through which spiritual fire (kundalini) ascends to unite with Sahasrara. The physical correlates of Sushumna with the spinal column and spinal cord are amazing; consider the following quotation from the Yoga Shikopanisad, Chapter One, Verse 119: "There are twenty one round bony structures forming the vertebral column (Brahmadandu—God's Staff), which are situated just around the Sushumna, like many beads (forming a chain) inter-woven with a thread." In 1968, Dr. K.S. Joshi, Ph.D., Head of the Department of Yogic Studies, University of Sagar, Sage (M.P.), India, commented, in an unpublished manuscript:

> *The number twenty-one in this description is very important, because it confirms completely with modern findings in human anatomy. It leaves hardly any doubt that the ancient masters of Yoga indicated by "Sushumna Nadi" nothing else but the spinal cord as we understand it today.*

Anatomists tell us that the spinal cord is a tube formed of nervous tissue, between the first and second lumbar vertebrae. The first lumbar vertebra is twenty, if counted from the beginning of the vertebral column in the neck, and the second lumbar vertebra is the twenty-first. Assuming this, what our ancients called Kanda (Kunda) is above the bone called sacrum and what they called Sushumna is the spinal cord, it all falls into place.

Swadhisthana: "One's own place." The second psychic center above Muladhara; the way water is cradled by earth. Physically indicated by the adrenal glands and the hypogastric plexus. Sometimes called Chandra (Moon) chakra, as Swadhisthana is the control center for the fluid tides of the body.

Tantra: "System, ritual, doctrine, loom." Traditionally the original philosophy of the Dravidian inhabitants of India, but historical proof of this is sparse. Probably developed by the Aryan warrior class as a reaction to Brahmanical control and now considered the revealed teaching for this age (Kali Yuga). Tantra possibly contains the deepest doctrines and the most potent techniques of Indian philosophy. Three distinct types of Tantra exist: Hindu Tantra, Buddhist Tantra, and Jain Tantra. Hindu Tantra also subdivides into North Indian and South Indian.

Tattwa: "Quality." The essence or quality of any given substance. Reality, category; "Tattwa" means "Thatness."

Tejas: "'Sharp." The third element, Fire, symbolized by a red triangle or a tetrahedron. In Western alchemy, the symbol for fire is always a triangle with the apex up; in Yoga, it often appears with the apex down; e.g., the Trikona (triangle) in Manipura chakra. The Tattwa of Manipura. Heat, incandescence, and transformation are Tejas characteristics. Its highest function is transmutation.

Udgita: Verbal intonation of a mantra.

Vayu: Sanskrit root "to blow." The fourth element, Air, symbolized by a blue hexagram. The Tattwa of Anahata (heart center). Vayu represents motion (unceasing beat of heart), principle of vapor, and gaseous manifestations (oxygenation of red blood cells).

Vishuddha: "With purity." The fifth chakra; physically represented by the thyroid gland, the parathyroid glands, and the pharyngeal plexus. Also termed Kantha (throat) chakra, Vishuddha is considered a main alchemical transmutation point in Kriya Yoga. It is said to secrete a fluid of immortality ("Amrit," meaning "against death") which is usually burned by Manipura chakra. When this process is reversed, decay is slowed.

Yantra: "Conception instrument." A geometric design used for concentration, ritual, or as an amulet. A mandala ("mind petal") tends to be circular and always contains the figure of a deity or animal as distinct from the purely abstract lines and curves of the yantra. The prefix "yan" means "to conceive, perceive, imagine, visualize," and the suffix "tra" equals an "instrument, implement or tool"—hence a yantra is a tool for focusing the mind and encouraging clarity of conception.

Yoga: "Union." The science of mental, physical, and universal integration. From the Sanskrit root of Yoga we derive the English "yoke," which not only implies a linking with cosmic forces but also suggests the harnessing (a yoke is a harness) and control of our own energies. The Sanskrit root "yug" gives rise to the following meanings:

1. Yoking, team; vehicle; equipment (of an army).
2. Performance, employment; occupation.
3. Use, application, method.
4. Remedy, cure, wholeness.
5. Means, device, instrument producing a result.
6. Spell, magic dextrous feat.
7. Opportunity, undertaking, task performed perfectly.
8. Union, contact with, relationship.
9. Combination, mixture, bringing together of polarities or complementaries (e.g., arrow with target, key with lock).
10. Aquisition of, gain, profit (alchemy).
11. Order, succession, correctness.

12. Aggregate, sum, conjuction (of stars); constellation.
13. Fitness, propriety, strenuousness, extertion, endeavor, zeal, assiduity.
14. Mental concentration, systematic abstraction, system of philosophy.
15. Unity of soul (Purusha) and Nature (Prakrit) (alchemical marriage).
16. Connection of a word with its root, etymological meaning of a word, deriving one word from another.

— *Macdonell's Sanskrit Dictionary*

Swami Gitananda always insisted on the following differentations in terms. Yoga is the state of cosmic union or oneness. Yogi is an individual who has obtained that state of Yoga while living (Jivan-mukta). Yogin is a male engaged in practiced which may lead to Yoga. A Yogini is a female engaged in practices that may lead to Yoga. When these definitions are understood it is evident that most of us are certainly not Yogis but Sadhakas (practitioners of spiritual exercises). You cannot be part of, nor conduct, a "Yoga class" but rather are engaged in Sadhanas (a collection of disciplines leading to the state of Yoga or self-realization). The perspective these definitions give allows one to grasp Yoga as a total art and science of living. We may sum up by quoting a psychology lecturer of mine, who defined neurosis as "inefficient behavior" and couple this concept with Krishna's definition of Yoga as "skill in action."

Yoga-Nidra: A mental exercise peculiar to Yoga which encourages Turiya (conscious dreamless sleep), sometimes defined as "meditation-sleep," which is particularly useful if you define meditation as "the moment of postponing sleep."

Yoni: "Lap, vulva, womb, birthplace, home abode, nest, lair, place of production, origin, source, repository, receptacle, seat, place, birth, produced or sprung from." (From *MacDonnell's Sanskrit Dictionary*.)

Yoni Mudra: "Womb gesture." So named by the Gerandsamhita (c. tenth century). A profound technique of neuro-muscular coordination designed to induce profound sensory withdrawal

(Pratyahara) leading to the oceanic oneness with the "unconscious," or Brahman. Western psychophysiology has determined that constant bombardment through sensory input is necessary for activation of the reticular system (that area of the brain responsible for alerting and awake responses). In the 1950s, numerous experiments were done with the effects of sensory deprivation and isolation stress. Sensory isolation tanks were used and most experimental subjects demonstrated emotional disintegration, anxiety, and frightening hallucinations. Yoni Mudra produces the opposite spectrum of calmness, positive hallucinations, and integration of mental processes. The difference has to do with "goal orientation" (the Yogi actively seeks Ultimate Universal Unity) and the method is sensory withdrawal (freedom from environmental disturbance). The experimental subject is goaless (prey to random eruption of unconscious material) and is involved in a method called sensory deprivation (implied attitude that environmental stimulus is a prerequisite for reality anchoring).

Laboratory for Profound Sensory Isolation

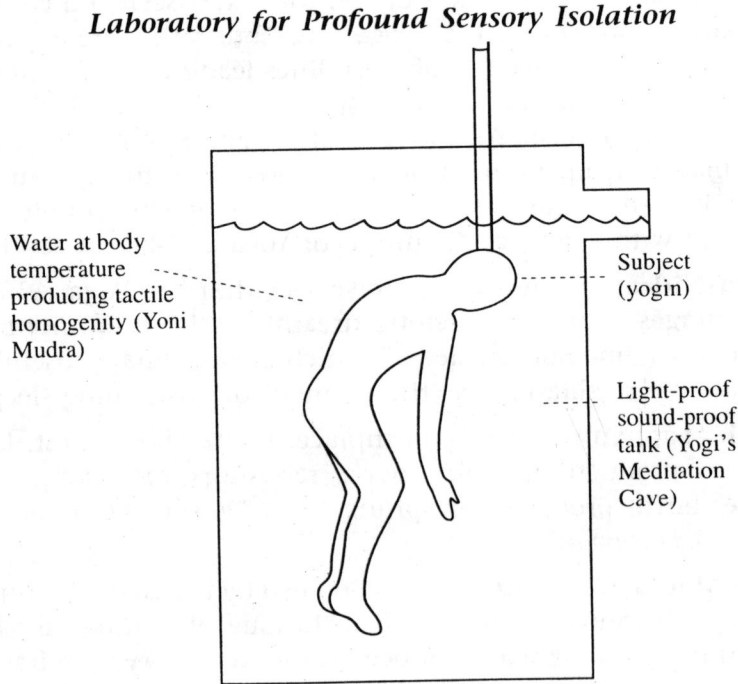

Water at body temperature producing tactile homogenity (Yoni Mudra)

Subject (yogin)

Light-proof sound-proof tank (Yogi's Meditation Cave)

Bibliography

This bibliography is an annotated specialized list rather than a makeshift conglomeration of titles. The selection has been made on the basis of topics germane to this book and I am personally familiar with every reference. The choice offers insight into contemporary Indian Yoga, as well as the classical matrix.

Hindu Medicine and Martial Arts

P. Kutumbiah MBBS. *Ancient Indian Medicine*. New Delhi, India: Orient Longmans Limited, 1969.

> Probably out-of-print but worth finding. An excellent section on the 108 Marmas.

Lok Swasthya Parampara Samvardhan Samith; c/o Center for Indian Knowledge Systems, No. 2, 25th East Street, Thiruvanmiyur, Madras 600-041, India.

> They produce a stunning series of monographs which may be ordered by writing them; the following list is current and current as of 1993. Marma Chikitsa is particularly useful in relationship to Indian martial arts and I acknowledge kind permission from them to use the Elephant Marma Chart.

LSPSS Monograph Series:
Monograph 1 Local Health Traditions: An Introduction
Monograph 2 Ayurvedic Principles of Food and Nutrition, Part 1
Monograph 3 Mother and Child Care in Traditional Medicine, Part 1
Monograph 4 Mother and Child Care in Traditional Medicine, Part 2
Monograph 5 Marma Chikitsa in Traditional Medicine
Monograph 6 Ayurvedic Principles of Food and Nutrition, Part 2
Monograph 7 Nidaana Diagnosis in Traditional Medicine
Monograph 8 Bheshaja Kalpana Pharmacology in Traditional Medicine

Heinrich Zimmer, Ph.D. *Hindu Medicine*. Baltimore: The John Hopkins Press, 1948.

Out-of-print and rare. A series of lectures he gave at Columbia University in 1943 collected and published after his death. Well worth accessing at university libraries.

Hindu Philosophy

B. Bhattacharya. *Saivism and the Phallic World,* Vols. I and II. India: Oxford and IBH Publishing Co., 1975.

A definitive, monumental work.

Mircea Eliade. *Yoga, Immortality and Freedom.* New York: Bollingen Series, LVI Pantheon Books, 1958.

Not to be missed; due for reprinting.

S. Radhakrishnan. *The Bhagavadgita.* Bombay, India: Blackie and Son Publishers, 1982.

In my opinion, the best translation of the *Gita* and the preferred edition placed in Indian hotel rooms.

Margaret and James Stutley. *A Dictionary of Hinduism.* San Francisco: Harper and Row, 1977.

Reliable.

Benjamin Walker. *The Hindu World,* Vols. I and II. New York: Fredericka Praeger, 1968.

Mostly available in reference libraries. Despite the author's prejudice against Hindu culture (he was educated in Calcutta), a brilliant resource work.

Heinrich Zimmer, Ph.D. *Philosophies of India.* New York: Meridian Books, 1956.

The classic textbook from my student days.

Kundalini

Arthur Avalon. *The Serpent Power (Shat-Chakra-Nirupana and Paduka-Panchaka).* Madras: Ganesh and Co., 1953.

A total foundation must for the serious student. *The Serpent Power* was the last book Sir John Woodroffe wrote under the pen name "Arthur Avalon" and the first edition was 1918. Sir John Woodroffe was a great jurist and Sanskrit scholar. The anecdote of how he became interested in translating Sanskrit Tantric texts bears repeating. He was an English judge in the early 1900s in India and found great difficulty focusing on a case he was hearing. One of his servants told him a Tantric Sadhu had been employed to sit outside the courthouse chanting mantras that would jam his mind. Upon investigation, he discovered the said vagrant squatting on the courthouse steps engaged in an endless Sanskrit litany. The Indian police promptly threw the "Fakir" down the steps and chased him out of the city. Sir John's head immediately cleared and he passed judgment on the case. The result of this experience was the first translation of Tantric texts into English and a tireless lifetime devotion to the task by Woodroffe.

Itzhak Bentov. *Stalking the Wild Pendulum.* Great Britain: Wildwood House Ltd., 1978.

> Bentov was closely associated with Dr. Lee Sanella. *Stalking the Wild Pendulum* was one of the first bridges between scientific (quantum physics) and the mystical model of existence.

Shyam Sundar Goswami. *Laya Yoga.* Routledge and Kegan Paul, 1980.

> Wonderful chakra diagrams and the most comprehensive comparative analysis of Sanskrit kundalini texts to appear in English.

Lee Sannella, M.D. *Kundalini: Psychosis or Transcendence?* San Francisco: Privately published, 1976.

> Updated reprinted edition now available. Dr. Sannella is a medical doctor who is also a psychiatrist and an opthamologist. When I was with him he researched the relationship between glaucoma and depth relaxation in an effort to see if intra-ocular pressure could be reduced. He presents full details of his and Bentov's kundalini theory, delineating the signs and symptoms of sensory and motor strip stimulation.

John White, editor. *Kundalini, Evolution and Enlightment.* Garden City, NY: Anchor Books, 1978.

> Scintillating anthology of everybody who is anybody and their kundalini theories.

Psychosomatics and Psychophysiology

Michael S. Gazzaniga, Ph.D. *Mind Matters.* Boston: Houghton Mifflin Co., 1988.

> Very readable account of biochemical reductionism in terms of brain function and neurotransmitters.

Onslow H. Wilson, Ph.D., F.R.C. *Glands: The Mirror of Self,* Rosicrucian Library Volume XVIII. San Jose, CA: AMORC, 1983.

> Hopefully to be reprinted as just out of stock October 1993. Dr. Wilson gives the best summary of endocrine glands available. He was former

president of Rose-Croix University. Many do not realize that AMORC is America's pre-eminent twentieth century esoteric co-fraternity. Rosicrucian Park with its Egyptian Museum, Planetarium, research library and gardens remain as a tribute to H. Spencer Lewis and Ralph M. Lewis—a special type of "American Dream" objectively crystallized. The order has historical European origins and a traditional relationship to the Egyptian mysteries, and the work goes on!

A. T. W. Simeons, M.D. *Man's Presumptuous Brain.* New York: Dutton Paperback, 1962.

> Probably out of print. The best book I have ever read on psychosomatics. An exciting evolutionary interpretation with hints about practical clinical issues.

Charles T. Tart, Ph.D. *Altered States of Consciousness.* John Wiley and Sons, 1969.

> Edited by Dr. Tart and an A-Z of A.S.C.s.

Charles T. Tart, Ph.D. *Transpersonal Psychologies.* Harper & Row, 1975.

> All of Dr. Tart's books are either reprinted or widely available in university libraries.

Shri Vijayadev Yogendra, editor. *Mind-Made Disease—Is Your Sickness Real?* Melbourne, Australia: The Helen Vale Foundation, 1977.

> Privately printed; outside Australian Universities God only knows where to find it. One would find a copy very worth reading for timeless essays on Eastern and Western views of psychosomatics. It may be that the Yoga Institute in Santa Cruz, Bombay, has reprinted it. Shri Vijayadev, the youngest son of Shri Yogendra, has a special place in my heart, as he was one of my tutors in Bombay in 1960. Later Vijayadev moved to Melbourne, Australia, and set up a branch of the Yoga Institute.

Note: I have avoided referencing the new bridging discipline of psychoneuroimmunology. Psychoneuroimmunology in fact is a multidisciplinary approach, utilizing endocrinologists, immunologists, hematologists, and psychologists in an attempt to definitively sort the potpourri of mind-body interface. I assume anyone interested in PNI has read the historical antecedent *Stress Without Distress* (Hans Selve, M.D.).

Do not accept anyone's "pop" psychosomatic theories, including any inadvertent statements I may have made, let alone such Aquarian nonsense as "AIDS is the result of guilt"! I am diametrically opposed to unsubstantiated New Age claims that cancer, for example, is a product of negative thinking and can be cleared by ferocity of positive thinking.

Such attitudes destroy compassion by placing blame and guilt upon the patient and allowing society to distance itself from human suffering, conveniently ignoring genetics and other independent variables.

By the same token I do not deny the possibility (with some evidence, although the jury will still be out for a long time) that meditation, optimism, and rational emotive thinking can increase the quality of life and sometimes the quantity.

Tantra

The English-speaking world is afloat with a profusion of Tantric books, most —including mine—emphasizing the minuscule portion of Tantric doctrine concerning sexuality as religious ritual. This is quite a fascinating injection into the contemporary literary stew of American anti-sex sectarian feminism, fundamentalism, puritanism, victim consciousness (never take self-responsibility; always find someone or something to litigate!), all blended with body piercing, sex therapy, gay and lesbian lobbies, Wicca and Goddess worship and a libertine underground press.

Do not take my comments as a criticism—these are precisely the things I love about America—my only fear is that one of the more totalitarian groups will gain ascendancy to the detriment of the others. Better to have a boiling cauldron than a stagnant pond!

Although the Indians do not all agree upon what constitutes Tantra, I didactically state that only the Hindus are capable of fully appreciating Tantric philosophy. I have hand-picked six references, which in my opinion, offer Westerners the best approach to the sea of Tantricism and its inherent depth and beauty.

Professor Agehananda Bharati. *The Tantric Tradition*. London: Rider and Company, 1965.

> If not reprinted, freely available in libraries. Scholarly, heavily academic—not for tyros to cut their teeth on. Professor Bharati is a first class Indologist and Sankritist and generally would not speak to lesser mortals—although he and my father spent hours drinking and talking at the University of Washington staff club in Seattle. You may think they were engaged in STDs ("Serious Theoretical Dialectics") about the universe and everything—no! They were World War II ex-army officers and enjoyed replaying the battle lines with knives, forks, glasses, and napkins.

B. Bhattacharya, M.A. *The World of Tantra*. New Delhi, India: Munshiram Manoharlal Publishers PVT. Ltd.

Still in print as of 1993. The only autobiography I know, in English, of a Hindu raised in the Tantric tradition. Indescribably sensitive and beautifully evocative. B. Bhattacharya, M.A. was born in 1910 and wrote his autobiography at age 76. I also recommend his two volumes *Savism* and *The Phallic World*.

Swami Satyananda Saraswati. *Kundalini Tantra*. Bihar School of Yoga, Monghyr, Bihar, India, 1985.

Privately printed and still in print. Available at some bookstores and Satyananda Ashrams in India and around the world. A compilation of Swami Satyananda's teachings on Kriya Yoga and full of research articles by many of our Australian medically trained Swamis who lived for several years in the central Bihar Ashram. Excellent, with the reservation that the Kriya should only be practiced under the direct guidance of an initiated Swami of our order.

Miguel Serrano. *El/Ella Book of Magic Love*. (Translated from the Spanish) Great Britain: Routledge and Kegan Paul Ltd., 1973.

Miguel Serrano is one of my favorite authors. He was the Chilean Ambassador to India for nine years and displays a delicacy and transcendence in El/Ella that is unparalleled. Wonderful to read before bed as Tantric archetypes will be conjured up during sleep.

A.K. Sinha, Ph.D. *Science and Tantra Yoga*. Kurukshetra, India: Vishal Publications, 1981.

Still available in India. Good analysis by a Hindu scholar of Western science and Tantric cosmology, cosmogeny, and mysticism.

Sir John Woodroffe. *The Great Liberation* ("Mahanirvana Tantra"), Sixth Edition. Madras, India: Ganesh and Company, 1985.

Always in print. Direct translation, with footnotes, of one of the most important classical Tantric texts.

Yoga

Kovoor T. Behanan, Ph.D. *Yoga: A Scientific Evaluation*. New York: Dover Publications, 1994.

Good introduction with special reference to Samkhya.

Theos Bernard, Ph.D. *Hatha Yoga*. Rider and Company, 1969.

Always in print. Total classic and absolute treasure. Copious footnotes from the twelfth century. Yoga text concerned with internal cleansing of the body. Dr. Bernard was tragically murdered in 1947, in Western Tibet; his death represents probably the greatest loss of an Indologist who had experienced initiation and practical Hatha Yoga in a way no other Westerner has.

Steven F. Brena, M.D. *Yoga and Medicine.* Pelican Books, 1973.

> Probably out of print. A thoughtful and careful correlation of Yoga and allopathic philosophy.

Aleister Crowley. *Eight Lectures on Yoga.* Dallas, TX: Sangreal Foundation Inc., 1970.

> Always in print, but with varying publishers. Priceless and witty commentary by one of the most controversial geniuses of this century. In retrospect, I realize that reading this book thirty-five years ago enabled me to dismiss literal interpretations of the Yamas and Niyamas.

Dr. Swami Gitananda Giri. *Mudras.* Privately printed and available from International Centre for Yoga Education and Research; 16-A/16-b, Mettu Street, Chinnamudaliarchavady, Kottakuppam 605 104 (via Pondicherry), Tamil Nadu, India.

> Swamijii has written many books but I recommend his *Mudras* as outstanding. Details of the Hatha Mudras I allude to in Chapter 10 are fully explained.

Swami Kuvalayananda. *Asanas.* Bombay: Popular Prakashan, 1964.

Swami Kuvalayananda. *Pranayama.* Bombay: Popular Prakashan, 1966.

> Both the above texts were originally published in 1931 and are frequently updated. Always in print.

Yoga and Western Medicine

Swami Kuvalayananda and Dr. S.L. Vinekar, M.B.B.S. *Yogic Therapy.* New Delhi: printed by Ministry of Health, Government of India, 1971.

> This, and the other two books by Kuvalayananda, are the products of India's foremost Yoga Research Institutes. Kaivalyadhama S.M.Y.M. Samiti, Lonavla, 410 403 India.

New Perspectives in Stress Management. Collection of articles by Indian medical doctors and physiologists.

New Horizons in Modern Medicine. Edited by H. R. Nagendra, Ph.D.

> Both of the above books may be ordered from Vivekananda Kendra Yoga Research Foundation, No. 9, Appajappa Agrahara, Chamarajapet Bangalore, 560 018 India.

Shri Yogendra. *Yoga Physical Education.* Santa Cruz, India: The Yoga Institute, 1966.

Shri Yogendra. *Yoga Personal Hygiene,* Volumes I and II. Santa Cruz, India: The Yoga Institute, 1958.

These volumes are classics, first written in 1931 and subsequently updated over the years. I am deeply grateful that I had the privilege of studying with Shri Yogendra, as he taught me the appropriateness of scientific methodology in approaching some aspects of Yoga.

Addendum

The bibliography represents the best references with which I am familiar; however, the amount of research material available within India is staggering. If any lesson may be garnered from the bibliography it is the undeniable fact that Yoga represents an indigenous Indian philosophy and the Indians are best qualified to research the subject.

Benefits of Vaastu & Feng Shui
—Rajendar Menen

The art of attracting health, wealth and happiness

Vaastu (an ancient Indian science) and Feng Shui (an ancient Chinese science) are both concerned with aspects of harmonious living in the home. This book helps you understand Vaastu and Feng Shui better, as it delves into the origins of each science. Proper knowledge about these subjects will enable you to make effective changes in your daily life and help you fulfil your potential in every way and ensure health, wealth, peace and prosperity.

Through proper designing of homes and offices, Vaastu and Feng Shui:
- ❖ Attract good fortune.
- ❖ Enhance positive energy.
- ❖ Promote careers and business.
- ❖ Increase employee productivity.
- ❖ Ensure physical, mental and emotional well-being.
- ❖ Harness the power of *prana* or *chi* (cosmic energy).
- ❖ Utilise natural elements to promote peace, prosperity and harmony.

Demy Size • Pages: 144
Price: Rs. 80/- • Postage: Rs. 15/-

Vaastu Corrections Without Demolitions
—A.R. Hari

Ensure health, happiness and harmony in your home

This book deals with the problem of correcting defective vaastu field where conventional correction methods cannot be applied. This aspect mainly applies to those who live in rented buildings or apartments.

There can also be cases, where the strength of the building and the cost factor may not allow the use of conventional correction methods. **Vaastu Corrections without Demolitions** helps you to correct Vaastu defects with the help of:
- ❖ Feng Shui gadgets
- ❖ Installation of Pyramids, Crystals and Ionisers etc.

Demy Size • Pages: 92
Price: Rs. 72/- • Postage: Rs. 15/-

Astrology for Layman
—Dr. T.M. Rao

The most comprehensible book to learn Astrology

Astrology today is universally recognised to be a 'science', based on sound mathematical principles and calculations. But while it is easy to agree with this promise, it is difficult to find a well-researched comprehensible book to guide the general reader. Answering this need, *'Astrology for Layman'* is designed to bring home to the reader the fundamentals of the discipline along with the predictive aspect.

The book is a complete astrological guide that begins from the basic fundamentals viz. how 12 *rashis* have been formulated, the basic principles of casting a horoscope, what are the qualities ascribed to people born under different signs (for instance, people born under Aries are of independent view), what's the meaning of *Bhavas* (viz. what does a planet indicate in a specific house), what do the *Mahadashas* of different planets mean, what are *'yogas'* (for instance, *'Sakaka yoga'* makes a person stubborn and hated by relatives and *'Parvata yoga',* makes a person passionate) – besides offering special section on the subjects of matrimony, compatibility along with case studies predicting major events of a person's life like career-change, gain or loss of fortune, etc.

Demy Size • Pages: 184
Price: Rs. 80/- • Postage: Rs. 15/-

Marriage-Matching Astrologically
—T.M. Rao

- *'Marriages are made in Heaven'* — discover its true essence
- How stars influence your marriage
- Find the *'made-for-each other'* partners through horoscope matching

There have been many astrological books on marriage-matching available in the market—but most of them deal only with certain aaspects and not all the essential information are available at one place.

The aim of this book is to put in a concise form all the essential principles of 'Marriage-Matching' so that the readers can have their satisfaction of getting all the information at one place. This book tells us how to dispel the unnecessary and unknown fears that may crop up in the selection of *bride* or *groom*. It also tells us how the Divine approval and blessings of heavenly stars play the role on the search for perfect combination.

❖ Know how stars influence the marriage
❖ Find the right partner through correct horoscope matching ❖ Ensure remedial measures to pacify conflicting *Nakshatras* and *Rashis* in the event of mismatch.

Demy Size • Pages: 142
Price: Rs. 80/- • Postage: Rs. 15/-

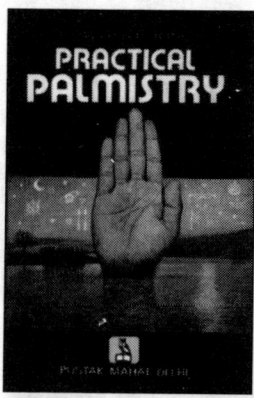

Practical Palmistry
—Dr. Narayan Dutt Shrimali
The Dawn of Self-knowledge

Palmistry is an important organ of the science of astrology, which can forecast the future of an individual authentically. Human existence confronts many hurdles and uncertainties. Hence, man suffers from indecision and is unable to concentrate on his goals.

Of all the sciences of the world, Palmistry has come to the rescue of modern man because it cannot only tell us about the past, but can also predict the future. A palm is a treasure of vitality and working power of a human being from the materialistic point of view and is the source of all activities of life from the astrological point of view. By means of our palm, we know our past and believe it, we understand the present and try to mould ourselves by acquainting ourselves with the future, so that we may remain constantly active.

This book is an endeavour to introduce the vast knowledge of Palmistry for the readers' benefit. It contains all the aspects of Palmistry with illustrations and complete information. The vast knowledge of palmistry is encapsulated, but the language is kept simple, which enhances its readability and wider acceptance.

Demy Size • Pages: 365
Price: Rs. 80/- • Postage: Rs. 15/-

Instant Handwriting Analysis
—Ruth Gardner

Do your 'Gs' divulge a sensitive nature? Does your writing slant show you to be impulsive? Find out with Ruth Gardner's **Instant Handwriting Analysis.**

Handwriting patterns signal elements of your unconscious, and reveal your desires, fears, weaknesses, strengths, attitudes and more! With this book, someone who doesn't even know you could learn all about you in just a few moments!

This work covers some of the most important and basic factors of handwriting analysis for the explorer of Graphology — a scientific study on the field.

Now you can analyse your own handwriting and that of friends and family with this easy-to-use book. In just a few moments, you will know what the slant, stroke, word-spacing, margins, size and pressure, letter formations and signature reveal about your personality. You can even learn to change certain aspects of yourself by changing the way you write! Compare your writing with the samples in this book — it's that simple! There is even a section on doodles. You may find that graphology is your next career or hobby!

Demy Size • Pages: 152
Price: Rs. 88/- • Postage: Rs. 15/-

Healing Power of Gems And Stones

—*V. Rajsushila*

In this book, readers may find the descriptions of selection of gems and stones through various easy and useful methods. Wearing appropriate gems and stones creates wonders in solving day-to-day problems and offers protection from the evil influences of planets to enhance their beneficial effects.

The author writes about gems and stones appropriate to the people born in different Zodiac signs, stars, months and dates.

Of all the methods of selecting gems and stones, the best method is the one based on the date of birth of a person and his or her name. Planets influence the destiny of a person through their distinctive numbers and their characteristic colours. The book deals with the auspicious day and time to wear a gem or a stone and about the rituals to be performed for the best benefits.

Demy Size • Pages: 136
Price: Rs. 80/- • Postage: Rs. 15/-

Richer Life Through Hypno Meditation

—*Dr. Sanjoy Mukerji*

A Journey to Prosperity, Self Development & Transformation

The indepth knowledge of human psychology, behavioural science and disorders, hypnosis, different types of meditation coupled with medical background led the author to develop 'Hypno Meditation', which is a unique amalgamation of western science and eastern wisdom. The technique of Hypno Meditation can help anyone gain access into the subconscious mind and harness the cybernetics. This practical handbook is a result of more than a decade of his intensive study, experience and research in the field of mind control.

The book tells all about:
- ❖ Mind   ❖ Subconscious Mind
- ❖ Hypno Meditation (HM)
- ❖ Prosperity   ❖ Money and Wealth
- ❖ Goal Setting and Success Principles
- ❖ Health and Stress   ❖ Pain Control
- ❖ Result Sleep Induction   ❖ Relationships
- ❖ Spiritual Growth   ❖ General Guidelines

Demy Size • Pages: 107
Price: Rs. 80/- • Postage: Rs. 15/-

Self Hypnosis
For a Better Life

—*R.K. Murthi*

Discover the Power of Your Own Voice!

Written by the world famous hypnotherapist, the book titled **Self-Hypnosis for a Better Life** presents a breakthrough technique that teaches you how to harness the power and potential of your own voice for a better life. If you've ever tried hypnosis tapes before and found yourself disappointed with the results, it's because they weren't recorded with your voice. Using this system, you become your own hypnotherapist, you design your own self-improvement program and you make it happen!

Self-Hypnosis for a Better Life comes complete with instructions so you can get started right away. Anyone can begin using this system in minutes. Simply make yourself comfortable and recite one of the 23 ready-made scripts into a tape-recorder. Then whenever you feel like it, pop in the tape, close your eyes and allow your own voice to hypnotize you as you learn to:

• Stop smoking • Control fear and phobias • Overcome health problems • Lose weight • End insomnia • Find love and much more!

Demy Size • Pages: 184
Price: Rs. 88/- • Postage: Rs. 15/-

LAL KITAB
A Rare Book On Astrology

—*Prof. U.C. Mahajan*

English version of a very famous and rare book 'Lal Kitab', originally published in Urdu

A book on Astrology – Horoscope Reading Made Easy – was published in 2000 by Pustak Mahal, authored by Prof. U.C. Mahajan. The English version of Lal Kitab is an extension of the earlier book and both complement each other. Renowned astrologer, Roop Lal wrote Lal Kitab in Urdu, during the 19th century, based on an ancient text.

The salient points of this book are:

1. Every planet has a benefic or malefic effect according to its raashi and placement in a particular house. For example, Jupiter in house no.1 can exercise good or bad effects according to its nature, whether excellent or debilitating. Consequently, the author has classified the effect of every planet – good or bad – separately. The earlier book carried a generalised interpretation. Now, readers will find it easy to comprehend every planet's effect.

2. More case studies have been added to make it broad-based.

3. New chapters on a house, the effect of auspicious and inauspicious planets, precious stones and their significance, characteristics of all planets, nakshatras and their importance, Natal Moon chart and Saturn's transit (*Saade-Saati*) i.e., 7½ years of Saturn's malefic transit through the Moon, have been added.

4. Preparation of birth chart according to south Indian traditions has also been included.

Big Size • Pages: 336 (Hardbound)
Price: Rs. 240/- • Postage: Rs. 25/-

Numerology
Know Your Lucky Numbers for every sphere of life
—*V. Rajsushila*

Numerology is the science of numbers which reveals its immense potentialities. Every human being has problems and every problem should be approached in a numerological way.

The science of numerology will have its force whether we believe it or not, just as the fire has the power to burn, things whether we know its power or not. The numbers govern us and our everyday activities.

In the book, **Numerology,** the author has successfully encapsulated the wide subject of Numerology, its origin and its various aspects for the benefit of the readers. Being a numerologist herself, V. Rajsushila has taken care that all the queries and doubts that arise in the minds of the readers are properly dealt with.

❖ Gives the characteristics of the individuals born under different numbers.
❖ Covers financial matters, health and marital life.
❖ Helps in the selection of the appropriate gem.
❖ Gives remedial measures for negative numbers.

Demy Size • Pages: 118
Price: Rs. 75/- • Postage: Rs. 15/-

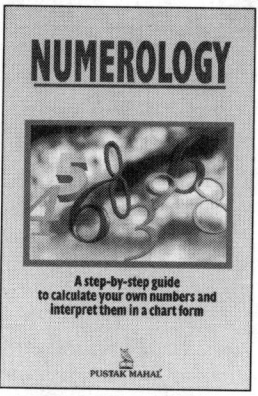

NUMEROLOGY
Key to Your Inner Self
—*Hans Decoz with Tom Monte*

Understand Your Life Better

Before the development of verbal communication, ancient man only had the most simple and basic thoughts, most of which were confined to survival. But with language, our spiritual horizon expanded, relationships became complex and the going got tougher.

This book, **Numerology: Key to Your Inner Self,** will help you to understand your life better. When one is introduced to the language of numbers, the universe seems far greater and more complex, yet easier to grasp.

World-renowned numerologist, Hans Decoz and accomplished writer, Tom Monte have teamed up together to produce an easy-to-understand guide that introduces the reader to the basic concepts and applications of numerology. The book begins with a fascinating explanation of what numerology is and gives an intriguing look at the philosophy that lies behind it. Included is a step-by-step guide to calculate your own numbers and to interpret them in a chart form.

Demy Size • Pages: 272
Price: Rs. 96/- • Postage: Rs. 15/-